Life Skills English

by
Bonnie L. Walker

AGS Publishing
Circle Pines, Minnesota 55014-1796
1-800-328-2560

About the Author

Bonnie L. Walker taught for 16 years in secondary schools and college. She holds a Ph.D. in curriculum theory and instructional design from the University of Maryland, an M.Ed. in secondary education, and a B.A. in English. She studied psycholinguistics at the University of Illinois Graduate School, and was a curriculum developer at the Model Secondary School for the Deaf at Gallaudet University. She is the author of *Basic English, Basic English Composition, Basic English Grammar,* and numerous curriculum materials in written expression, grammar, and usage. Since 1986, Dr. Walker has been president of a research and development company specializing in development of training and educational materials for special populations.

Photo credits for this textbook can be found on page 292.

The publisher wishes to thank the following educators for their helpful comments during the review process for *Life Skills English*. Their assistance has been invaluable.

Caril Baker, Librarian, Selby Public Library; Sarasota County Library System, Sarasota, FL; **Gayle Boroughs,** Special Education Teacher, Oak Ridge High School, Oak Ridge, TN; **Diane De Vito,** Supervisor of DH/SLD Programs, Warren City Schools, East Instructional, Warren, OH; **Jacqueline DeWitt,** Cooperative Consultant, Umatilla High School, Umatilla, FL; **Andy J. Dornan,** Special Education Coordinator, Didsbury High School, Didsbury, Alberta, Canada; **Geraldine Dumas,** Consultant, Bibb County School System, Macon, GA; **Joyce von Ehrenkrook,** Special Education Coordinator, Wichita Public Schools, Wichita, KS; **Melanie Eick,** Disabilities Specialist, Oklahoma Department of Vocational and Technical Education; Stillwater, OK; **Ruth Greider,** Special Education Coordinator, Wichita Public Schools, Wichita, KS; **Dr. Bessie Watson Hampton,** Coordinator of Family and Consumer Sciences, Kansas City Missouri District, Kansas City, MO; **Pamela Kinzler,** Special Education Teacher, Penn Hills High School, Pittsburgh, PA; **Ashlee Long,** Special Education Teacher, John Marshall High School, San Antonio, TX; **Bill Michel,** Manager, Research and Development, Ramsey County Library, Shoreview, MN; **Jeanette D. Pulliam,** Reading Supervisor K-12, Curriculum and Staff Development, St. Louis Public Schools, St. Louis, MO

Publisher's Project Staff

Director, Product Development: Karen Dahlen; Associate Director, Product Development: Teri Mathews; Editor: Jody Peterson; Development Assistant: Bev Johnson; Graphic Designer: Diane McCarty; Design Manager: Nancy Condon; Purchasing Agent: Mary Kaye Kuzma; Marketing Manager/Curriculum: Brian Holl

Editorial and production services provided by The Mazer Corporation, Inc.

Printed in the United States of America

ISBN 0-7854-3065-2

Product Number 93620

A 0 9 8 7 6 5 4 3 2 1

Contents

How to Use This Book: A Study Guide

Welcome to *Life Skills English*. This book includes many of the language skills you will need to use in your everyday life. Think about the things you do each day. You might prepare a meal, use the telephone, fill out a job application, read the newspaper, or shop online. In order to do these things, you need information. To get that information, you must know where to look. You also must know how to find information in different resources. In this book, you will learn where to look for the information you need. You will learn how to use many print and electronic resources.

As you read this book, notice how each lesson is organized. Information is presented and then followed by examples and activities. Read the information. Then practice what you have read. If you have trouble with a lesson, try reading it again.

It is important that you understand how to use this book before you start to read it. It is also important to know how to be successful in this course. The first section of the book can help you to achieve these things.

How to Study

These tips can help you study more effectively:

◆ Plan a regular time to study.
◆ Choose a quiet desk or table where you will not be distracted. Find a spot that has good lighting.
◆ Gather all the books, pencils, paper, and other equipment you will need to complete your assignments.
◆ Decide on a goal. For example: "I will finish reading and taking notes on Chapter 1, Lesson 1, by 8:00."
◆ Take a five- to ten-minute break every hour to keep alert.
◆ If you start to feel sleepy, take a break and get some fresh air.

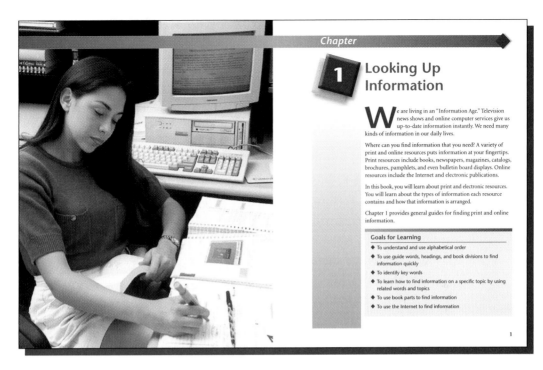

Chapter

1 Looking Up Information

We are living in an "Information Age." Television news shows and online computer services give us up-to-date information instantly. We need many kinds of information in our daily lives.

Where can you find information that you need? A variety of print and online resources puts information at your fingertips. Print resources include books, newspapers, magazines, catalogs, brochures, pamphlets, and even bulletin board displays. Online resources include the Internet and electronic publications.

In this book, you will learn about print and electronic resources. You will learn about the types of information each resource contains and how that information is arranged.

Chapter 1 provides general guides for finding print and online information.

Goals for Learning

◆ To understand and use alphabetical order
◆ To use guide words, headings, and book divisions to find information quickly
◆ To identify key words
◆ To learn how to find information on a specific topic by using related words and topics
◆ To use book parts to find information
◆ To use the Internet to find information

1

Before Beginning Each Chapter

◆ Read the chapter title and study the photograph. What does the photo tell you about the chapter title?
◆ Read the opening paragraphs.
◆ Study the Goals for Learning. The Chapter Review and tests will ask questions related to these goals.
◆ Look at the Chapter Review. The questions cover the most important information in the chapter.

Note these Features

Writing Tip

Quick tips to help improve writing skills

Note

Hints or reminders that point out important information

Writing Tip

The antecedent of each pronoun that you use must be clear to readers. Unclear antecedents confuse readers.

Look for this box for helpful tips!

Using What You've Learned
An exercise that practices
something taught
in the chapter

Using What You've Learned

Vocabulary Builder
Vocabulary practice

Vocabulary Builder

Spelling Builder
Spelling practice

Spelling Builder

Where To Find It
Information about
various reference
materials such as
dictionaries,
encyclopedias,
and more

Where To Find It

Writing On Your Own
Writing practice

Writing On Your Own

Before Beginning Each Lesson

Read the lesson title
and restate it in the form
of a question.

For example, write:
What is alphabetical order?

Look over the entire lesson,
noting the following:

◆ bold words
◆ text organization
◆ exercises
◆ notes in the margins
◆ photos
◆ lesson review

Lesson **1** Alphabetical Order

Alphabetical order
The order of letters of the alphabet

Words in **alphabetical order** appear according to the order of letters in the alphabet. Information in telephone books, indexes, and office files appears in alphabetical order. Knowing how to use alphabetical order can help you find information in these resources quickly.

Arrange words in order according to the first letter of the word.

EXAMPLE   apple   comb   egg   knee

Activity A Write each list in alphabetical order on your paper.

1. theater
concert
opera
movie
sports

2. robin
cardinal
starling
blue jay
wren

3. Maria
Juanita
Charles
Rosa
Doris

4. computer
monitor
printer
keyboard
software

5. sofa
chair
table
lamp
piano

Dictionaries list words alphabetically.

2   Chapter 1   Looking Up Information

As You Read the Lesson

◆ Read the major headings.

◆ Read the subheads and paragraphs that follow.

◆ Read the content in the Example boxes.

◆ Before moving on to the next lesson, see if you understand the concepts you read. If you do not, reread the lesson. If you are still unsure, ask for help.

◆ Practice what you have learned by doing the activities in each lesson.

Using the Bold Words

Bold type

Words seen for the first time will appear in bold type

Glossary

Words listed in this column are also found in the glossary

Knowing the meaning of all the boxed words in the left column will help you understand what you read.

These words appear in **bold type** the first time they appear in the text and are often defined in the paragraph.

Words in **alphabetical order** appear according to the order of the alphabet.

All of the words in the left column are also defined in the **glossary**.

Alphabetical order—(al fə bet´ ə kəl ôr´ dər) The order of letters of the alphabet. (p. 2)

Word Study Tips

◆ Start a vocabulary file with index cards to use for review.

◆ Write one word on the front of each card. Write the chapter number, lesson number, and definition on the back.

◆ You can use these cards as flash cards by yourself or with a study partner to test your knowledge.

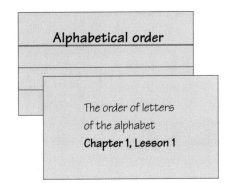

Alphabetical order

The order of letters of the alphabet
Chapter 1, Lesson 1

Using the Reviews

◆ Answer the questions in the Lesson Reviews.

◆ In the Chapter Reviews, answer the questions about vocabulary under Part A. Study the words and definitions. Say them aloud to help you remember them.

◆ Answer the questions under the other parts of the Chapter Reviews.

◆ Review the Test-Taking Tips.

Preparing for Tests

◆ Complete the activities in each lesson. Make up similar activity questions to practice what you have learned. You may want to do this with a classmate and share your questions.

◆ Review your answers to lesson activities, Lesson Reviews, and Chapter Reviews.

◆ Test yourself on vocabulary words and key ideas.

◆ Use graphic organizers as study tools.

Using Graphic Organizers

A graphic organizer is a visual representation of information. It can help you see how ideas are related to each other. A graphic organizer can help you study for a test or organize information before you write. Here are some examples.

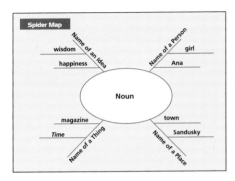

Spider Map

The Spider Map shown here can be used to connect related ideas to a central idea or concept. Write the main or central idea or concept in the circle in the center. Identify related ideas and write them on the lines that angle out from the circle. Write examples that support the ideas on the horizontal lines that are attached to the angled lines.

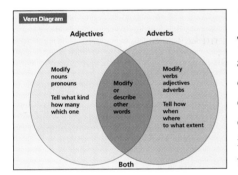

Venn Diagram

The Venn diagram shown here can be used to compare and contrast two things. For example, this diagram compares and contrasts adjectives and adverbs. List the characteristics for adjectives in the left circle. List the characteristics for adverbs in the right circle. In the intersection of the two circles, list the characteristics that both have.

1 Looking Up Information

We are living in an "Information Age." Television news shows and online computer services give us up-to-date information instantly. We need many kinds of information in our daily lives.

Where can you find information that you need? A variety of print and online resources puts information at your fingertips. Print resources include books, newspapers, magazines, catalogs, brochures, pamphlets, and even bulletin board displays. Online resources include the Internet and electronic publications.

In this book, you will learn about print and electronic resources. You will learn about the types of information each resource contains and how that information is arranged.

Chapter 1 provides general guides for finding print and online information.

Goals for Learning

◆ To understand and use alphabetical order

◆ To use guide words, headings, and book divisions to find information quickly

◆ To identify key words

◆ To learn how to find information on a specific topic by using related words and topics

◆ To use the different parts of a book to find information

◆ To use the Internet to find information

1

Alphabetical order

The order of letters of the alphabet

Words in **alphabetical order** appear according to the order of letters in the alphabet. Information in telephone books, indexes, and office files appears in alphabetical order. Knowing how to use alphabetical order can help you find information in these resources quickly.

Arrange words in order according to the first letter of the word.

EXAMPLE   apple   comb   egg   knee

Activity A Write each list in alphabetical order on your paper.

1. theater
   concert
   opera
   movie
   sports

2. robin
   cardinal
   starling
   blue jay
   wren

3. Maria
   Juanita
   Charles
   Rosa
   Doris

4. computer
   monitor
   printer
   keyboard
   software

5. sofa
   chair
   table
   lamp
   piano

Using alphabetical order can help you when writing or when using a dictionary.

When two words begin with the same letter, alphabetize by the second letter.

| EXAMPLE | Marie | Melvin | Miguel | Monroe |

Activity B Write each list in alphabetical order on your paper.

1. prune
plum
pomegranate
pineapple
peach

2. beef
biscuit
brown
blueberry
bacon

3. fur
fruit
fox
flame
farmer

4. cash
crust
companion
charge
cent

5. depth
dip
door
dust
dark

When the first two letters of words are the same, alphabetize by the third letter.

| EXAMPLE | lab | lake | lap | laws |

When the first three or more letters of words are the same, go to the next letter.

| EXAMPLE | cheek | cheer | cheese |

Activity C Write these words in alphabetical order on your paper.

kangaroo	necklace	stuff	sixty	shirt
ship	keeper	known	stump	knight
weak	shore	sixteen	neat	stuck
knife	weather	size	show	week

When all the letters of a word are the same as the beginning letters of a longer word, the shorter word comes first.

EXAMPLE   is   island

If one of the words has an apostrophe, ignore the apostrophe.

EXAMPLE   your   you're

Activity D Write each list in alphabetical order on your paper.

1. you're   **2.** they're   **3.** any
   your   their   an
   you   these   animal
   young   they   ant
   yo-yo   the   annual

Activity E Use all of the rules that you have learned. Write each of these lists in alphabetical order on your paper.

1. thirty   **3.** haven   **5.** itch
   thirteen   haven't   its
   third   heaven   item
   thirsty   heavenly   it
   thread   heart   Italy

2. record   **4.** bookmobile
   receive   book
   root   bond
   rote   bone
   rot   bookmark

Lesson 1   R E V I E W

Write each list in alphabetical order on your paper.

1.	**2.**	**3.**
tank	diamond	sweet
stage	desert	sweat
sold	difference	swam
possible	dessert	swallow
taste	direction	sweep
hall	drive	swift
fog	doctor	switch
garage	door	swimming
forty	do	swimmer
quite	doesn't	swim
jelly	dive	swing
plate	divide	swish
foggy	dime	switching
nail	dine	swept
beyond	dirt	swung

Follow the directions below. Write your lists on your paper. Use a dictionary to check your spelling.

4. Make a list of at least five sports.

5. List five states in the United States.

6. List the first names of five people you know.

7. List the last names of five people you know.

8. List five countries.

9. List five kinds of animals.

10. Now go back and rewrite each of your lists in alphabetical order.

Guide words

Words at the top of a page of information given in alphabetical order. You will find words that come in alphabetical order between the two guide words on that page

Guide words help you find information given in alphabetical order. You will find guide words at the top of the page in many reference books. Use the guide words to help you find the page that has the information you need. The first guide word is the first word on the page. The second guide word is the last word on the page. The other words on the page come in alphabetical order between these words.

These are some books that have guide words:

| atlases | dictionaries | encyclopedias | telephone books |

EXAMPLE

Sample of Telephone Book Listing

guide word   guide word

GREEN — GRIFFEN   **45**

Green Mary D	**Greenwald Howard**
45 Cannon Dr............555-8756	564 Brace Way.................555-3657
Green N E	**Greenway N A**
1000 Federal Hwy..............555-5457	311 Twig St.................555-3421
Greenberg Jr. D F	**Gregory Frank** Rt 3.........555-5645
275 Spindle Ln.................555-9001	**Gregory Maurice**
Greene Ralph W	1434 Cliffe Pl.................555-8003
456 Serena Way.............555-5464	**Grieg Frances**
Greeno Maurice Rev	4565 Oak Ave.................555-4000
3000 Maddox Ln..............555-4000	**Griffen Karen Dr**.............555-7500
GREENSTEIN JEWELRY	Meadow P tr

Activity A Which of the names listed below would appear between the guide words shown? Write your answers on your paper.

| GREEN — GRIFFEN | 45 |

A. W. Grouse

Sandra Greene

Maurice Gregory

Jack Gurney

N. A. Greenway

Michaela Ginnes

Lakeisha Gordon

N. E. Green

Activity B Three words follow each set of guide words below. Number your paper from 1 to 5. After each number, write the letter or letters to show which words would appear on the page with each set of guide words.

Example Guide words: actor—August

        A add   **B** American   **C** awful

    Answer: **A, B**

1. mad—map

    A main   **B** maze   **C** manage

2. sad—scream

    A safe   **B** sand   **C** scratch

3. raise—remember

    A rapidly   **B** remain   **C** reason

4. want ad—warp

    A wander   **B** wart   **C** ward

5. fellow—fur

    A frame   **B** Friday   **C** February

Sometimes you will see guide letters instead of guide words.

Sample Page from the Index of an Almanac

33   Ka - Le

Kansas			**Key, Francis Scott**	457
(See States, U.S.)			**Kilowatt hour**	690
Agriculture	356		**Knoxville, TN**	402
Area	356, 567		**Koran**	79
Lakes, rivers	456		**Kuwait**	
Population	563		Ambassadors	305
Wichita	400–401		Petroleum production	280
Kansas City, MO	302		— L —	
Kennedy, John F.	57–58, 457		**Labrador, Canada**	89
Kentucky			**Leap years**	102
(See States, U.S.)			**Lee, Robert E.**	458

Using What You've Learned

Guide Letters
Find a reference book in your classroom or library that uses guide letters. Read the book's title and write down three words that you would likely find in the book. Use guide letters to find the pages on which these three words appear.

Activity **C** Use the sample page above to answer the following questions. Write your answers on your paper.

1. Which pages have information about John F. Kennedy?

2. Which page has information about Labrador, Canada?

3. Which pages have information about Kuwait?

4. Which information about Kuwait will you find?

5. Which page has information about the population of Kansas?

6. Which other topic would you look up to find information about Kansas and Kentucky?

7. Would you find information about Louisiana on the page shown above?

8. Which cities in the United States can you look up from this page?

9. Which page has information about Francis Scott Key?

10. Which pages have information about Wichita?

Four words follow each set of guide words or letters. Number your paper from 1 to 5. After each number, write the letter or letters to show which words would appear on the page with each set of guide words.

1. spider—study

   A sparkle   **B** steer   **C** straw   **D** stump

2. weather—worry

   A weak   **B** welcome   **C** we're   **D** worse

3. purple—softly

   A puzzle   **B** prove   **C** softness   **D** soft

4. va—ye

   A yellow   **B** village   **C** you'll   **D** year

5. Al—Fl

   A Alaska   **B** Alabama   **C** Hawaii   **D** Arizona

Which of the names listed below would appear between the guide words shown? Write your answers on your paper.

Hidalgo—Hull

Hamaguchi	Hinton
Hill	Heche
Hoffs	O' Healihy
Harrison	Hyobanshi
Hacker	Hokusai
Holland	Hoffman

Guide Words and Headings

Some reference books have headings instead of guide words. The heading names the topic on that page.

EXAMPLE

| 32 Education–Senior Colleges | Education–Junior Colleges 33 |

Guide letters and a heading may appear on the same page.

EXAMPLE

| 22 Mi–My General Index | General Index Na–No 23 |

Guide words may appear together on one side of the page.

EXAMPLE

240   CONNECTICUT — CONNECTICUT RIVER

Activity A Study the examples below. On your paper, answer each question.

A	123	DALMATIAN—DECLARATION	
B	22	Bi—By	General Index
C	42	Boat Racing	
D	66	Sa—Sy	

1. Which example shows only a heading?

2. Which example shows guide words?

3. Which example shows only guide letters?

4. Which example shows guide letters and a heading?

5. Which pages might have information on decimals?

A Quick Way to Find the Word You Want: Dividing by Half

Here is a quick way to find words in a dictionary. Divide your dictionary into four approximately equal parts. Follow these steps.

Steps for Dividing Your Dictionary

1. Divide your dictionary in half. Open it to the middle page. You will probably find that the words begin with the letter *M*.

2. Now divide the first half by half. Open it to the middle of the first half. You will probably find that the words begin with the letter *F*.

3. Now divide the last half by half. Open it to the middle of the last half. You will probably find that the words begin with the letter *S*.

Before you look up a word, decide which part of the dictionary your word is probably in.

First Half		Last Half	
1st Quarter	2nd Quarter	3rd Quarter	4th Quarter
A B C D E F	**G H I J K L M**	**N O P Q R S**	**T U V W X Y Z**

Activity B In which quarter of the dictionary would you look to find each of the words below? On your paper, write each word. Next to it, write 1st, 2nd, 3rd, or 4th.

Use a dictionary to check your answers.

1. cheese
2. neighborhood
3. toothpaste
4. animal
5. jelly
6. Thursday
7. potato
8. birthday
9. garden
10. vacation

Activity C Follow the directions below. Write your answers on your paper. Try to do this activity in less than five minutes.

- Find the following words in a dictionary.
- Use the "divide by half" method.
- Write the time you begin.
- Write the guide words from each page.
- Write the time you finish.

1. wisdom   **6.** recognize

2. pleasant   **7.** garage

3. fierce   **8.** flashlight

4. chipmunk   **9.** machine

5. art   **10.** blueberry

Activity D Follow the directions below.

- Write the list of words below in alphabetical order on your paper.
- Find the words in a dictionary.
- Use the guide words to help.
- Use the "divide by half" method.
- Time yourself.
- Try to beat your time from Activity C.

1. usually   **6.** meadow

2. perhaps   **7.** harness

3. gnaw   **8.** resource

4. island   **9.** butcher

5. astonish   **10.** delicious

Use the "divide by half" method to find these words in a dictionary. On your paper, write the guide words from each page.

1. wrap	**6.** airplane	**11.** boat
2. scatter	**7.** pail	**12.** saxophone
3. seventy	**8.** holiday	**13.** mug
4. jewel	**9.** Friday	**14.** summer
5. eagle	**10.** quilt	**15.** joke

Study the following headings, guide words, and guide letters. Number your paper from 16 to 30. Write the headings, guide words, or guide letters where you would find the words above.

action—hourglass
Musical Instruments
island—rooster
sc—yo

Spelling Builder

Finding Words That You Can't Spell
You might have problems with words that begin with the same sound but begin with different letters. Knowing which letters make these sounds can help you—just check both places in the dictionary. Here are some letters that sound similar when they come at the beginning of a word:

Letters That Sound Similar

c and *s:*	*c* and *k:*	*g* and *j:*
cent	cage	giraffe
city	cream	gems
CD	car	giant
some	key	just
sale	kangaroo	jam
smooth	keep	jade

f and *ph:*	*n* and *kn:*
fax	name
farm	night
funny	noon
phone	knot
photo	knee
pharmacy	knapsack

1. Write another word that sounds like *s* and starts with *c*.
2. Write another that sounds like *k* and starts with *c*.
3. Write another word that sounds like *j* and starts with *g*.
4. Write another word that sounds like *f* and starts with *ph*.
5. Write another word that sounds like *n* and starts with *kn*.

Topic (subject)

What you want to find out about

Subtopic

A topic that is part of a larger topic

Key word

A word that names what you want to find out about

You can often find the answer to a question by looking it up. First, however, you must know what to look up. A **topic** or **subject** is whatever you want to know about. A **subtopic** is a topic that is part of another topic.

A **key word** is the word you look up to find information to answer a question. A key word can be a topic, a subtopic, or another word related to the question. *Animal* and *domesticated animal* are key words in the following example. They are the words you might look up to find the answer to the question.

EXAMPLE

Question	Which animals are domesticated?
Topic	animals
Subtopic	domesticated animals

Activity A Write each pair of key words on your paper. Beside each key word, write *topic* or *subtopic*.

Example   computers—topic
              software—subtopic

1. fruit   blueberries

2. oak tree   plants

3. mosquito   insect

4. table   furniture

5. game   checkers

6. mammal   cat

7. plate   dishes

8. movie   documentary

9. fish   trout

10. sailboat   ships

What to Do When You Can't Find Your Topic

Even when you know what topic to look up, you may not find it listed. When that happens, try to think of another name for your topic. A **synonym** is a word that has the same meaning or a similar meaning as another word. Try thinking of a synonym for your topic.

EXAMPLE

Key Word	Synonym
night	evening
car	auto
ship	boat

Activity B Write on your paper the word that is a synonym for the word in bold.

1. lady	person	human	woman
2. stairs	steps	elevator	building
3. dinner	meal	supper	food
4. country	nation	United States	place
5. movie	theater	cartoon	film

If you have trouble thinking of synonyms, a **thesaurus** can help you. A thesaurus is a reference book that lists words and their synonyms. Words in a thesaurus appear in alphabetical order. A thesaurus entry includes several synonyms and may include a short definition of the word, its part of speech, and a sentence using the word.

EXAMPLE

> Entry Word: **car**
> Function: *noun*
> Text: a usually private passenger-carrying automotive vehicle <drove a shabby old *car*>
> **Synonyms** auto, autocar, automobile, buggy, bus, machine, motor, motorcar

Activity C Write a synonym on your paper for each topic below. You may use a thesaurus.

1. family
2. detective
3. politics
4. genealogy
5. humorist

6. sailor
7. dinner
8. poison
9. bug
10. sad

Look for Broad and Narrow Topics

You may not find your topic listed because it is too narrow. In this case, you should look for a broader topic.

EXAMPLE	Narrow Topic	Broad Topic
	chemistry	science
	winter	seasons

Sometimes your topic may be too broad. In this case, you should look for a narrower topic.

EXAMPLE	Broad Topic	Narrow Topic
	Africa	Egypt
	music	jazz
	education	college

Activity D On your paper, write another word that you might look up for each topic listed below. Use a thesaurus to help identify synonyms as well as broader and narrower topics.

Example Topic	Synonym
nutrition	food
aerobics	exercise

1. Miami
2. farming
3. Mars
4. lawyers
5. doctors

6. presidents
7. France
8. football
9. highways
10. Thanksgiving

Use Related Words and Topics

If you cannot find information on a specific topic, look for **related topics.** A related topic is one that is connected or associated with another topic.

EXAMPLE

If you wanted to open a book store, you might not be able to find any information on book stores. In that case, you might look for information on related topics.

Specific topic   book stores

Related topics   rare books

running a small business

accounting

Vocabulary Builder

Synonyms

Synonyms are words with similar meanings.

small, little   *big, large*   *dark, dim*

You will need to use key words when using an Internet search engine. Often, synonyms for your key words allow the search engine to locate the pages of information that you need. Finding synonyms will help you make your search broader. If you do not find enough information or the type of information that you need, try a synonym for your key words.

Think of a synonym for each of the following words. Write your answers on your paper.

1. jokes
2. urban
3. car
4. England
5. writing

Activity E Write at least one related topic on your paper for each topic listed below. You may use a dictionary.

Example   Roofing a house
             Related topics: home repair, roof maintenance

1. skiing

2. vegetable gardening

3. raising poodles

4. learning word processing

5. making model cars

6. playing the guitar

7. using a computer

8. becoming a licensed practical nurse (LPN)

9. sailing

10. becoming a bus driver

Topics related to music may help you find information about playing the guitar.

Lesson 4 REVIEW

On your paper, write another word you might look up for each topic listed below. You may use a thesaurus.

Example   Olympics—sports

1. Film Awards
2. U.S. population
3. Calico cats
4. Yellowstone Park
5. European history

For each topic, write at least two key words and a related topic on your paper. You may use a dictionary for this activity.

Example   Prime minister of Canada
                     Key words: Prime Minister, Canada
                     Related topic: National Governments

6. World Series
7. Minneapolis
8. Nobel Peace Prize
9. Henry VIII
10. Mexico
11. Washington Monument
12. Harvard University

On your paper, write the answers to the questions below.

13. What is a thesaurus?
14. How would a thesaurus help you find key words?
15. How are words listed in a thesaurus?

Reference book

A book that contains facts on a specific topic or on several topics

Table of contents

A list of the chapters or sections of a book and the page numbers on which the chapters or sections begin

Chapter

A part of a book

Preface

An introduction to a book

When you look up information, you usually look in some type of **reference book.** A reference book is a book of facts. It may contain facts on a single topic or on several topics. The book may be in print or in an electronic version.

The Table of Contents

You can usually tell whether a book has the information you need by looking at the book's **table of contents.** A table of contents is a list of **chapter** titles at the beginning of a book. When you look at the table of contents, you can see at a glance what information the book contains and how it is divided. A book may contain a **preface,** which is an introduction to a book. Many books contain chapters. A chapter is a part or a section of a book. A table of contents lists the chapter titles in the order in which they appear in the book and the page numbers on which the chapters begin.

EXAMPLE

Sea Shells Contents

Preface
1. Types of mollusks 3
2. Collecting marine shells 11
3. Locations 18
    California 19
    Carolinas 20
    Hawaiian Islands 22

Car Care *Contents*

1. Buying a car 2
2. Car insurance 17
3. Financing 34
4. Cooling system 56
5. Engine oil 64
6. Tires 73
7. Emergencies 91
    Index 121

Activity A Use the sample tables of contents above to answer the questions below. Write your answers on your paper.

1. Is there a chapter in *Car Care* about brakes?

2. You want to collect sea shells in Hawaii. Will the book *Sea Shells* help?

3. On what pages does the chapter on tires begin and end?

4. Which book has an index?

5. Which book has a preface?

An Index

| **Index** |
| An alphabetical list of main topics and subtopics covered in a book |

Almost all reference books and many nonfiction books have an **index** at the back. An index lists in alphabetical order the main topics and subtopics covered in the book. Subtopics appear under some of the main topics. The subtopics also appear in alphabetical order. Page numbers appear next to each topic and subtopic.

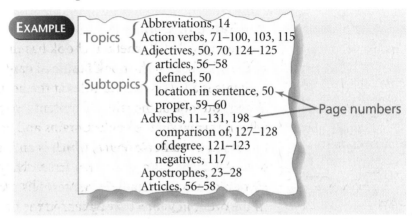

EXAMPLE

Topics {
Abbreviations, 14
Action verbs, 71–100, 103, 115
Adjectives, 50, 70, 124–125

Subtopics {
articles, 56–58
defined, 50
location in sentence, 50
proper, 59–60
Adverbs, 11–131, 198
comparison of, 127–128
of degree, 121–123
negatives, 117
Apostrophes, 23–28
Articles, 56–58

Page numbers

Activity B Use the sample index above to answer these questions. Write the answers on your paper.

1. Will page 77 tell you about action verbs?

2. Can you find facts about action verbs on page 112?

3. Which pages tell you about apostrophes?

4. Which page has a definition of an adjective?

5. Which pages tell you about articles?

6. To what other topic is "articles" related?

7. Name one subtopic under the main topic "Adverbs."

8. Which pages tell you about adverbs of degree?

9. How many pages tell you about proper adjectives?

10. How many pages tell you about abbreviations?

Indexes come in several forms— from pages in the back of a textbook to complete books. For example, the index of most encyclopedias is a separate volume. Computer software programs also have indexes.

More About Indexes

To refer means to direct someone for information.

EXAMPLE   Refer to page 87 for more information on birds.

Many indexes list **cross references.** A cross reference directs you to look for more information under a similar or related topic. Cross references often begin with the words *see* or *see also.* The page numbers after the word *see* will take you to the information you want. The words *see also* direct you to similar topics that could have helpful information.

EXAMPLE

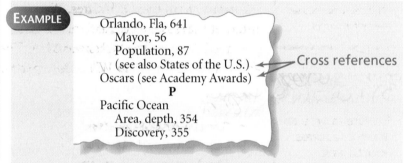

Orlando, Fla, 641
    Mayor, 56
    Population, 87
    (see also States of the U.S.) ——— Cross references
Oscars (see Academy Awards)
            P
Pacific Ocean
    Area, depth, 354
    Discovery, 355

Activity C Use the sample index above to answer these questions. Write your answers on your paper.

1. Name three pages with facts about Orlando, Florida.

2. What other subject can you look up to find facts about Orlando, Florida?

3. What topic must you look up to find out who has won an Oscar?

4. What is the difference between *see* and *see also?*

5. What pages provide information about the Pacific Ocean?

Activity D Use the table of contents and index of this textbook to write the answers to the following questions.

1. Does this book have a chapter about using a dictionary?

2. Which pages tell you about using an encyclopedia?

3. Which chapter tells you how to use the Yellow Pages?

4. Which page has a job application form?

5. Which chapter tells you about using dictionaries?

Internet

A large network of computers linked together

Web site

A source of information on the Internet; many businesses, government organizations, and individuals have Web sites that give information and provide other Web addresses for more information

Writing Tip

Be sure to type an Internet address exactly as it appears. Any mistake in spelling or punctuation will prevent access to the information source.

Not all the information on the Internet is true. Check the information you find in a reference book. Never give private information about yourself or your family to anyone online.

Internet Information

The **Internet,** a huge network of interconnected computers, can be an excellent reference tool. You can find reference books and other information, such as indexes, on a computer and on the Internet. You can get information by entering key words and phrases that describe your topic. You can also find information by entering the Internet address. The prefix *http://* usually begins an Internet address.

Government Web Sites

Federal, state, and local governments offer valuable online information on their **Web sites.** Web sites are pages on the Internet that store information. To use government Web sites, you need to know the Web site address. The letters *www* in each address stand for *World Wide Web,* a part of the Internet.

EXAMPLE

- **Government Statistics**
  http://www.fedstats.gov/
- **The Library of Congress**
  http://www.loc.gov/
- **U.S. State Department**
  http://www.state.gov/
- **The CIA World Factbook**
  http://www.odci.gov/cia/publications/factbook/
- **Environmental Protection Agency**
  http://www.epa.gov/
- **The United Nations**
  http://www.un.org/english/
- **The Government of Canada**
  http://canada.gc.ca/main_e.html
- **The European Union**
  http://europa.eu.int/index_en.htm

Have you ever seen the abbreviation *FAQs* on a Web site and wondered what it meant? FAQs means *Frequently Asked Questions*, and the answers to these questions provide all kinds of information about the site.

Activity E Study the Web site addresses on page 23 to answer the following questions. Write your answer on your paper. Some questions may have more than one answer.

1. Which Web site would offer information about international law?

2. Which would provide information about population?

3. Which would you access to get information on wildlife?

4. Which would provide you with general information?

5. Which would you access to find out how many births there were last year in Canada?

Where To Find It

Using an Index

Suppose you are reading a book about games around the world and you want to find information about coins used in games. The following example shows what a section of the index might look like this:

Clown game, 183
Coconut shell game, 150
Coin games, 177–180
Crab race, 53

As you can see, the author discusses coin games on pages 177–180. Using the index is easier than looking through the entire book for the word *coin.*

1. What topic would you find on page 150?

2. Which page would you go to for information on the crab race?

3. Find the index in the back of a book in your classroom. Name three topics in the index. Then find them, using page numbers provided in the index.

Lesson 5   R E V I E W

Study the sample table of contents and index from the two different books. Write the answers to these questions on your paper.

From *Book of Maps*:

Contents

The World 5
   Hemispheres 6
   Climate 8
   Time zones 10
North America 12
   Canada 14
   United States 16
   Hawaii 18
   Alaska 18
   Mexico 19
   Central America 20
   West Indies 21
South America 22
   Venezuela 24

From *Things to Make*:

Index

aprons, 5
boxes
   covered, 24–26
   match boxes, 20–23
decorating, 11
finding material
   (see material)
flowerpots, 13
knitting, 56
material
   finding, 94
   selecting, 10
pot holders, 80
   (see also knitting)

Book of Maps

1. On which page is there a map of South America?
2. Does the book have a map that shows only Texas?
3. Is there a map that shows only Alaska?
4. Does this book have a preface?

Things to Make

5. Which page tells you how to find material?
6. Which pages tell you about using matchboxes?
7. You can find out about pot holders on page 80. Which other page will help?
8. Which entry provides a cross reference?

Answer these questions about the Internet.

9. What are two ways to find information on the Internet?
10. What are two government agencies that offer information on the Internet?

Online

Connected to
the Internet

Data

Information

ISP

Internet Service
Provider; company that
charges a fee to give you
Internet access

The Internet is a large computer network, or interconnected system of computers, that links businesses, organizations, and individuals. Millions of people use it. This "information superhighway" links smaller networks that send information using words, sounds, and pictures. When you are using the Internet, you are **online.**

The Internet offers information about any topic you can imagine. You can use the Internet to find **data,** or information. There are also Web sites that provide entertainment. Here are some things you can do using the Internet.

- search classified ads for a job
- find help creating a resume
- find information about colleges
- check your local weather
- contact your political representatives
- reserve and renew books, films, or CDs using a library Web site

Activity A Write the word on your paper that completes each sentence correctly.

1. If you are online, you are using the _____.

2. _____ is another word for information.

3. The Internet connects businesses, organizations, and _____.

4. You can renew books by using a _____ Web site.

5. You can check your local _____ using the Internet.

Getting Connected at Home

Internet Service Providers (**ISPs**) charge a fee to connect your home computer to the Internet. If you do not have access at home, you can use a computer at most public libraries.

To find information on the Internet, you need to use a **browser.** A browser is software that allows you to search, find, view, and store information. Your ISP provides a browser. You can use the browser to reach special Web sites called **search engines.** Search engines will direct you to Web sites once you are online. To use a search engine, you type in key words. The best key words are specific. Key words will tell the search engine what to look for.

After you enter the key words, the search engine will give you a list of Web sites that may contain the information you need. Before choosing a site, read the descriptions of the top choices. Click on a site. If the first page does not have the information you need, go back to the list and try again.

Activity B Write the key words you would use in a search engine to find information on the Internet on the following topics.

1. the name of a forest in California

2. the winner of the 1978 World Series

3. the Gettysburg Address

4. books written by Charles Dickens

5. the local weather forecast

You can get information easily and quickly on the Internet.

If people or companies want to create a Web site, they need to apply for a **domain name.** A domain name is the part of a Web site address that tells you who owns the address. Anyone can apply for a domain name. There is usually a fee to get a domain name.

Domain names may contain different abbreviations. Most government sites use *gov.* Many schools and colleges use *edu.* Businesses, including many nonprofit companies, might use *org.*

EXAMPLE

gov	http://www.census.gov	Web site for the U.S. Census Bureau
edu	http://www.mit.edu	Web site for the Massachusetts Institute of Technology
org	http://www.ipl.org	Web site for the Internet Public Library

Two other abbreviations are *.net* and *.com.* These abbreviations may follow a person's or company's name.

EXAMPLE   www.person'sname.net
www.company'sname.com

Once you have access to the Internet, you can type the Web site address into the address bar on your screen. Then, press the "Enter" or the "Return" key on your keyboard. The browser will then connect your computer to the Web site.

Activity C Answer the following questions. Write your answers on your paper.

1. What is a domain name?

2. Who can apply for a domain name?

3. What are five different Web site abbreviations?

4. What type of Web site might use the abbreviation *edu?*

5. Where should you type the Web site address if you want to connect to that site?

Saving Information

The Internet can save you time, whether you are doing research for a report, looking for a distant relative, or checking the latest baseball scores. Typing out a Web site address can take time, however. One way to save time finding a Web site it to use **bookmarks.** A bookmark is a tool that allows you to store your favorite Web site addresses. Some ISPs call this feature "Favorites." Once your chosen Web site appears on the screen, click on "Favorites" or "Bookmark" and follow the simple directions. You can now easily go to a Web site without typing the address each time.

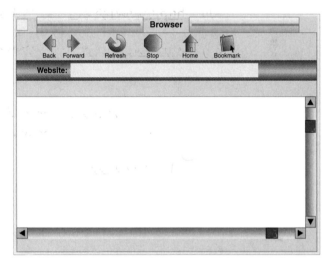

When you are online, you may find information on a Web site that you want to save. You can **download,** or transfer the data to your computer. Some Web sites charge a fee for downloading. Read downloading instructions carefully before you download anything from the Internet.

Finding Reliable Sources on the Internet

After you become familiar with the Internet, you may access information and services around the world. But, just because information is on the Internet does not mean that the information is true. For example, medical Web sites, and online newspapers and magazines may contain errors. You should check several different Web sites and print resources before you decide whether the information is reliable.

Activity D Answer the following questions. Write your answers on your paper.

1. What can you store using bookmarks?

2. Why would you want to use bookmarks?

3. What does *download* mean?

4. What should you always do before downloading information from the Internet?

5. What is one thing you should do to make sure information you find on the Internet is reliable?

Choose the correct answer and write it on your paper.

1. You can use a _____ to save a Web site that you use often.

   A domain name   **C** download

   B bookmark   **D** data

2. When using a _____, you type in key words to help you find a list of Web sites.

   A search engine   **C** bookmark

   B information superhighway   **D** domain name

3. A school or college would most often use _____ in its Web site address?

   A *org*   **C** *net*

   B *com*   **D** *edu*

Write the word or words on your paper that complete each sentence correctly.

4. A _____ is software that helps you search, find, and save information from the Internet.

5. An ISP is an _____.

6. Information that you find on the Internet is _____.

7. A _____ is the part of a Web site address that tells you who owns the address.

Write the key words you would use in a search engine to find information on the Internet on the following topics.

8. the climate in Costa Rica

9. the tallest building in Europe

10. pizza recipes

Chapter 1   R E V I E W

Part A Write the missing word on your paper.

1. An _____ lists topics in alphabetical order.
2. The different parts of a book are *chapters*
3. A _____ is a word with the same meaning as another word.
4. _____ tell you what can be found on a particular page.
5. The list of chapters or sections of a book is the _____ .
6. A _____ contains facts about a particular topic.
7. A topic that is part of a larger topic is a _____ .
8. A _____ names what you want to find out about.
9. The order of the letters of the alphabet is *alphabetical order*
10. What you want to find out about is your _____ .
11. An introduction to a book is the _____ .
12. A *search engine* tells you who owns a Web site address.
13. A _____ would direct you to another part of a book.
14. _____ charge a fee to give you Internet access.
15. A _____ is similar to your topic.
16. The _____ is a network of computers linked together.
17. An address on the Internet at which a page of information can be found is a _____ .
18. Information that you find on the Internet is *browser*
19. To _____ means to transfer data to your computer.
20. A _____ allows you to save your favorite Web site addresses.
21. You are _____ when you are communicating by computer.
22. A Web site that helps you find information online is a _____ .
23. Software that provides a way to find and store information on the Internet is a _____ .

Part B Rewrite the following list of words in alphabetical order on your paper.

24. you've   you   shade   brook   loose
seventy   brooks   seven   wrote   we're

Part C Write the letters of the words that would appear on the page with each set of guide words or guide letters.

25. package—pickles
    A pack   **B** passenger   **C** pillows   **D** pail

26. sh—sw
    A shadow   **B** sleigh   **C** soap   **D** seal

Part D Write at least two key words and a synonym or related topic on your paper for each question.

27. What is the population of Vancouver, British Columbia?

28. Which baseball team won the World Series six years in a row?

Part E Choose the correct answer and write it on your paper.

29. Which book part gives a list of chapter titles?
    A cross reference   **C** the table of contents
    B an index   **D** guide words

30. Where is the table of contents located?
    A in the back   **C** beginning of each chapter
    B in the front   **D** in the middle

Test-Taking Tip Sometimes it is easier to learn new vocabulary words if you make them a part of your speaking and writing in other discussions and subject areas.

Using Dictionaries

Dictionaries come in all sizes. There are very large dictionaries with hundreds of thousands of words. There are smaller dictionaries that include only the most commonly used words. Every dictionary, however, contains words and information about those words.

No dictionary is ever totally complete. New words and meanings are always being added. Most of the dictionaries that you find in classrooms and homes are abridged, or shortened. This means that some words have been left out of these dictionaries. Unabridged, or complete, dictionaries have not been shortened. They are large books, often divided into several volumes. Libraries usually have unabridged dictionaries.

In Chapter 2, you will learn about different features of print and online dictionaries and how to use these features.

Goals for Learning

- ◆ To understand how a dictionary is organized
- ◆ To identify the different parts of a dictionary entry
- ◆ To use a dictionary to find word meanings
- ◆ To use a dictionary to check spelling
- ◆ To use a dictionary as a reference book
- ◆ To use an online dictionary

A **dictionary** is a book that lists words and some facts about the words. Every dictionary has **entries,** guide words, and **keys.** An entry is a word described in the dictionary. A key explains symbols and abbreviations that appear in each entry. Here is a sample dictionary page.

Dictionary

A book that contains an alphabetical listing of words and their meanings

Entry

A listing in a dictionary. An entry provides facts about a word.

Key

A guide to the symbols and abbreviations used in each entry

guide words

mouth 314 **music**

mouth (mouth), *n., pl.,* **mouths** (mouthz). **1.** an opening through which a human or animal takes in food. **2.** a part of a river where its water empties into a larger body: *the mouth of the Nile.* [German *mund*] **mouth´less,** *adj.*

mov•ie (mōō´vē), *n.* **1.** See **motion picture. 2.** a motion-picture theater: *The movie is next to the drugstore.* **3. movies,** motion pictures: *The people go to the movies.*

Mu•si•al (myōō´ zē l) *n.* Stanley Frank ("Stan the Man") Born 1920, U.S. baseball player.

mu•sic (myōō´ zik), *n.* **1.** a sound which expresses ideas and feelings using rhythm, melody, and harmony. **2.** a musical work for singing or playing. [Greek *mousikē* (the art) of the Muse]

entries listed in alphabetical order

a - act, ā - āble, â - dâre, ä - ärm, e - ebb, ē - ēven, i - it, ī - īce, o - hot, ō - ōver, ô - ôrder, oi - oil, ŏŏ - bŏŏk, ōō - lōōt, ou - out, u - up, û - ûrge, ch - chief, ng - sing, sh - shoe, th - thin, th - this, zh - vision,   ə = *a* as in *ago.*

pronunciation key

Activity A Use the sample dictionary page above. On your paper, write the word that completes each sentence.

1. The guide words are at the _____ of the page.

2. The first entry on page 314 is _____ .

3. The last entry on the page is _____ .

4. The pronunciation key is at the _____ of the page.

5. There are _____ entries on page 314.

Most dictionary entries contain the same basic features. The entries below provide examples of these features. Many dictionaries include cross references, as indexes do. Looking up cross references can help you get more information about a word.

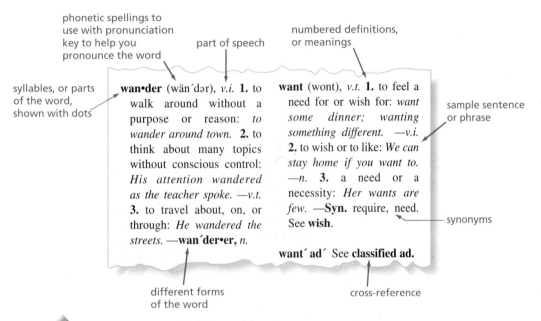

phonetic spellings to use with pronunciation key to help you pronounce the word

part of speech

numbered definitions, or meanings

syllables, or parts of the word, shown with dots

sample sentence or phrase

wan•der (wän´dər), *v.i.* **1.** to walk around without a purpose or reason: *to wander around town.* **2.** to think about many topics without conscious control: *His attention wandered as the teacher spoke.* —*v.t.* **3.** to travel about, on, or through: *He wandered the streets.* —**wan´der•er,** *n.*

want (wont), *v.t.* **1.** to feel a need for or wish for: *want some dinner; wanting something different.* —*v.i.* **2.** to wish or to like: *We can stay home if you want to.* —*n.* **3.** a need or a necessity: *Her wants are few.* —**Syn.** require, need. See **wish.**

want´ ad´ See **classified ad.**

synonyms

different forms of the word

cross-reference

The first pages of most dictionaries contain a chart that explains all the features of the entries.

Activity B Use the sample entries above and the pronunciation key on page 36 to answer the questions that follow. Write your answers on your paper.

1. How many meanings does *wander* have?

2. What are two synonyms for *want?*

3. What is another form of the verb *wander?*

4. Does the *a* in *wander* have the same sound as the *a* in *want?*

5. Which two entries have cross-references?

Syllable

*A part of a word with
one vowel sound*

Accent mark

*A mark that shows
which part of a word to
stress when pronouncing
the word*

Stress

*To pronounce a syllable
with more emphasis
than the other syllables
in the word*

Pronouncing a Word

You may look up a word in a dictionary to find out how to pronounce it. A dictionary entry has three features to help you.

- The word appears in **syllables** separated by dots. A syllable is a part of a word with one vowel sound.

- One of the syllables has an **accent mark** (´). This mark shows which syllable to **stress** when pronouncing the word.

- Each entry gives the phonetic spelling for the word. Match the vowel sound in the pronunciation key with the vowel sound in the entry word.

EXAMPLE

mu•si•cal (myo͞o′zi kəl)

a - act, ā - āble, â - dâre, ä - ärm, e - ebb, ē - ēven, i - it, ī - īce,
o - hot, ō - ōver, ô - ôrder, oi - oil, o͝o - bo͝ok, o͞o - lo͞ot, ou - out,
u - up, û - ûrge, ch - chief, ng - sing, sh - shoe, th - thin, th - this,
zh - vision,   ə = a as in *ago*.

The phonetic spelling of *musical* shows that the vowel sound in the third syllable is the same as the *a* sound in *ago*. This vowel sound is a *schwa*. It appears with its symbol ə.

as•sem•bly (ə sem′ blē)

Activity C Look at the sample dictionary entry and pronunciation key. Then answer these questions.

1. How many syllables does *assembly* have? How do you know?

2. Which syllable do you stress when pronouncing *assembly*?

3. How can you tell which syllable to stress?

4. What vowel sound does the first syllable have?

5. What vowel sound does the last syllable have?

Parts of Speech

Abbreviation
A shortened form of a written word

An **abbreviation** is a shortened form of a written word. An abbreviation that appears in most entries tells you the word's part of speech. Abbreviations for parts of speech may appear in other parts of the entry if the word can be more than one part of speech.

Here is a list of abbreviations for parts of speech and their meanings.

n.	=	noun: names a person, place, thing, or idea
pron.	=	pronoun: replaces a noun (he, she, me, that, everyone)
adj.	=	adjective: describes a noun or pronoun
v.	=	verb: expresses action or a state of being (run, sing, look, become)
adv.	=	adverb: tells how, when, where, or how much (very, slowly, quickly)
prep.	=	preposition: shows a relationship between a noun or pronoun and another part of the sentence (in, above, near)
conj.	=	conjunction: connects sentences or parts of a sentence (and, because, or)
interj.	=	interjection: a word that expresses feelings (Oh! Wow!)

In most dictionary entries, a verb is labeled either *v.t.* or *v.i.* rather than just *v*. Some verbs are both transitive and intransitive.

v.t.	= verb, transitive: a verb that needs an object to complete its meaning. An object is a noun or a pronoun.
v.i.	= verb, intransitive: a verb that does not have an object.

EXAMPLE

Transitive verb	She throws the baseball. (*Baseball* is the direct object.)
Intransitive verb	She throws hard. (*Hard* is an adverb.)

Singular and Plural

The abbreviation *sing.* means "singular" or "one." Most words become plural, or "more than one," by adding *-s*. If the word you look up forms its plural in a different way, the plural form follows the abbreviation *pl.*

Synonyms

Syn. is another common abbreviation. *Syn.* stands for *synonym,* or a word with a similar meaning to the entry word.

Activity D Use these sample dictionary entries to answer the following questions. Write your answers on your paper.

> **i•vo•ry** (ī′ və rē, ī′ vrē), *n., pl.* **-ies** [ME < OF *ivurie*] **1.** the hard creamy-white dentine that composes the tusks of the elephant, walrus, etc. **2.** the substance used to make carvings, billiard balls, etc. **3.** a yellowish-white color. **4.** something made of ivory (as dice or piano keys) or of a similar substance. –**ivory** *adj.*

> **change** (chānj), *v.t.* **1.** to cause to be different in some way. **2.** to replace with something else. *v.i.* **1.** to become different in some way. **2.** to go from one stage to another. **Syn.** alter, vary, shift –*n.* **1.** a shift from one thing to another.

1. What abbreviations appear in the two entries? Write the abbreviations and their meanings.
2. *Ivory* can be two parts of speech. What are they?
3. What is the plural spelling of *ivory?*
4. Is *change* a transitive or intransitive verb? How do you know?
5. What are three synonyms for *change?*

Lesson 1 REVIEW

Number your paper from 1 to 6. Write the letter of the correct definition beside the number of the term.

1. dictionary
2. entry words
3. plural
4. pronunciation key
5. abbreviation
6. synonym

A Words listed in a dictionary

B Explanation of symbols used in phonetic spelling

C A book that lists words

D More than one

E A shortened form of a written word

F A word that has almost the same meaning as another word

On your paper, write the full word or words for each abbreviation.

7. pl.   8. n.   9. prep.   10. adj.

On your paper, write the answers to these questions.

11. Where do guide words appear in a dictionary?
12. What are syllables?
13. What information does an accent mark give you?
14. Where is the pronunciation key in a dictionary?
15. What is the abbreviation for synonym?

Spelling Builder

Homographs

A *homograph* is a word that has one spelling but more than one meaning and more than one pronunciation. A dictionary entry will give you this information.

Examples
bass—bass

With a short *a* sound, bass is a "kind of fish." With a long *a* sound, bass is a "low singing voice."

Look up the following homographs in a dictionary. Write their parts of speech, definitions, and pronunciations.

bow—bow   contest—contest
lead—lead   sow—sow
suspect—suspect tear—tear
wind—wind   desert—desert

Word Meanings

A dictionary entry gives one or more numbered meanings for each word listed. Look at the word in the sample phrase or sentence, so that you can tell which definition fits.

Using What You've Learned

Write your own dictionary entry for the word *car.* Use the example entry *overcast* as a model. Make sure to include the word, the phonetic spelling, its part of speech, and the definition. Check your definition with a dictionary definition.

EXAMPLE

> **o•ver•cast** (ō´və r kast), *n.* **1.** a covering, esp. of clouds.   **2.** an arch in a mine, supporting an overhead passage.   *–adj.* **3.** cloudy; dark; said of the sky or weather.   **4.** Sewing made with overcasting. *–v.t.* **-cast´, -cast´ing, 5.** to overcloud; darken. **6.** *Sewing* to sew over an edge of material with long, loose stitches so as to prevent raveling.

The number in parentheses after each sentence below matches the number of the meaning in the dictionary entry above.

EXAMPLE   Because the sky was overcast, she grabbed her raincoat. (3)

My aunt showed me how to overcast the edges of the quilt. (6)

The miners knew the overcast would give way in an earthquake. (2)

Activity A   For each sentence below, write the part of speech and meaning of *overcast* as it is used in the sentence.

Example   Yesterday was overcast all day.
(Adjective, cloudy, dark; said of the sky or weather.)

1. The *overcast* fell down and trapped the miners.

2. Mrs. Gomez *overcast* the seams in Asako's shirt.

3. The *overcast* hem would not ravel easily.

4. We had an *overcast* sky on Monday.

5. The *overcast* made everyone feel gloomy.

Etymology
The study of the history of a word
Origin
The beginning of something
Derived
Comes from (many English words are derived from other languages)

Activity B Use a dictionary to find the meanings of the words in bold. Then, rewrite each sentence on your paper. Replace the words in bold with their meanings. You may have to add some words so that the sentence makes sense.

Example   Mr. Robles realized that his daughter Alicia was **precocious.**

Mr. Robles realized that his daughter Alicia was **extremely mature for her age.**

1. The Williams family spent their summer vacation at a **resort.**

2. "I'm doing some **reconnaissance** work," said the pilot.

3. Jada does not **resemble** her twin sister Kalisha in any way.

4. Rafael said that O. Henry wrote under a **pseudonym.**

5. John works for Anita Valdez, a **reputable** attorney.

Word Origins

You may look up a word to learn its history, or **etymology.** A word's spelling, pronunciation, and meaning may change over time. All of these changes are part of the history of the word.

When you look up a word to learn its **origin,** you may see the symbol <. Origin means beginning. The symbol means "**derived** from," or "comes from." The information that follows the symbol < explains the word's history. Some dictionaries use the word *from* or the abbreviation *fr* instead of the symbol <. Here are some other abbreviations you may see when you look up a word's history. They tell the original language of the word.

OE = Old English	ME = Middle English	L = Latin
G = German	Gk = Greek	It = Italian
OF = Old French	F = French	
S = Spanish	Pg = Portuguese	

Other Forms

A dictionary often gives other forms of the entry word followed by their parts of speech.

EXAMPLE

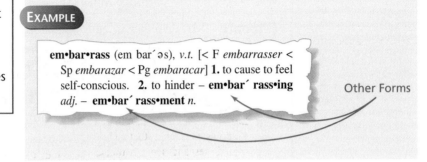

em•bar•rass (em bar´ əs), *v.t.* [< F *embarrasser* < Sp *embarazar* < Pg *embaracar*] **1.** to cause to feel self-conscious. **2.** to hinder – **em•bar´ rass•ing** *adj.* – **em•bar´ rass•ment** *n.*

Other Forms

Activity C Use the sample entry to complete the following. Write your answers on your paper. Use a dictionary for help if you need it.

1. Write the word *embarrass* on your paper.

2. Write the adjective form of *embarrass*.

3. Write the noun form of *embarrass*.

4. Write a sentence for each of the two meanings of *embarrass*.

5. What is the part of speech given for *embarrass*?

Some words in the English language have Greek origins.

Differences in Dictionary Entries

No two dictionaries are exactly alike. An entry for the same word in different dictionaries may contain different information.

EXAMPLE

This word in italic, or slanted type, explains that *home run* is a baseball term.

This symbol means that the word is an Americanism. It is used in American speech and writing.

A

home run *Baseball* a hit that allows the batter to touch all bases and score a run; also (Colloq.) **hom´er** *n.*

B

*****home run** *Baseball* a safe hit that allows the batter to touch all bases and score a run.

C

home run *n*: a hit in baseball that enables the batter to make a circuit of the bases and score a run.

D

home´ run´ *Baseball,* a hit that enables a batter, without the aid of a fielding error, to score a run by making a nonstop circuit of the bases.

This abbreviation stands for *colloquial.* It means that we use the word in informal speech.

Some dictionaries are easier to read than others. School dictionaries often have larger print and more pictures than collegiate or unabridged dictionaries.

Activity D Use the sample entries above to answer the following questions. Write your answers on your paper.

1. Which of the entries is the easiest to understand—A, B, C, or D? Why?

2. Which entry gives extra information? What is that information?

3. What is another term for *home run?*

4. Which entries give the part of speech? What part of speech is *home run?*

5. Why is it helpful to know the informal version of the word?

Cross-references in a dictionary entry lead you to other words and definitions. Looking up cross-references will help you as you write.

Many dictionaries give the same basic information for a word. Some dictionaries give more information, and some give less. Different dictionaries may give information in a different order.

EXAMPLE

A

hock•ey (hȧk´ ē) *n.* [prob.<OFr. *hoquet,* bent stick] **1.** a team game played on ice skates, with curved sticks and a rubber disk (puck). **2.** a similar game played on foot on a field with a small ball.

B

hock•ey (hok´ ē) *n.* **1.** See **ice hockey. 2.** See **field hockey.** [earlier *hockie*]

field´ hockey, a game, played on a rectangular field, having a netted goal at each end, in which two teams of 11 players each compete in driving a small leather-covered ball into the other's goal, each player being equipped with a stick having a curved end or blade that is flat on one side and rounded on the other.

Activity E Use the information in the sample entries to answer these questions. Write your answers on your paper.

1. What is the origin of the word *hockey?*

2. How was *hockey* probably spelled in the past?

3. Which entry has a cross-reference?

4. What is the difference between the playing surfaces in the two kinds of hockey?

5. How many players are on a field hockey team?

Vocabulary Builder

Understanding Prefixes

A prefix is a word part added to the beginning of a word.

A prefix changes a word's meaning. Here are three common prefixes and their meanings.

trans- (across, beyond)
dia- (through, across)
anti- (against, opposing)

Use a dictionary to find two words with each prefix. List the words and their definitions. Write a sentence using each word.

Read each entry carefully. On your paper, write the answers to the questions.

> **con•fet•ti** (kən fet´ ē)   *n.* [It. pl. of *confetto,* sweetmeat] bits of colored paper or ribbon for throwing around at celebrations.

 1. How many syllables does the word *confetti* have?

 2. What vowel sound do you hear in the first syllable?

 3. What part of speech is the word *confetti?*

 4. What is the origin of the word *confetti?*

 5. What would you do with confetti?

> **in•voice** (in´vois), *n.* [prob. <MF *envois* messages] a list of goods shipped to a buyer stating prices. – *v.t.* **in•voiced, invoic•ing** to present an invoice for goods sold or services provided to someone.

 6. Can you use *invoice* as a verb?

 7. What did the word *invoice* mean in Middle French? What was its spelling?

 8. When would you expect to get an invoice?

> **e•mo•tion•al** (i mō´shən əl), *adj.* [< L *e-* out + *movere* to move] **1.** showing strong feeling. **2.** appealing to the emotions. – **e•mo•tion•al•ly** *adv.*

 9. What is the meaning of the word *emotional* in these sentences—meaning 1 or meaning 2?

   A This music is very emotional.

   B Max gets emotional during sad movies.

 10. What language does the word *emotional* come from?

Always check a dictionary to be sure of a word's spelling. You may wonder how you can look up a word if you cannot spell it. In this lesson, you will learn some general rules to help you spell words.

Spelling the Plurals of Nouns

Form the plural of most nouns by adding *-s* or *-es*.

> **EXAMPLE** pencil—pencils   sock—socks
> leash—leashes   bus—buses

If a noun does not follow the *-s* or *-es* rule for forming its plural, look at the dictionary entry to find the plural form.

> **EXAMPLE**
>
> **child** (child) *n. pl.* **chil•dren** [ME>OE *cild*] **1.** a young girl or boy between the age of infancy and teens. *adj.* childlike.

Here are some other nouns that do not follow the *-s* or *-es* rule.

> **EXAMPLE** ox—oxen   moose—moose
> man—men   medium—media

Activity A Look up each of the following words in a dictionary. On your paper, write the plural form. Write *Yes* beside each word if the word follows the *-s* or *-es* rule. Write *No* if it does not.

1. ferry   **6.** sheep

2. umbrella   **7.** cage

3. woman   **8.** class

4. city   **9.** puppy

5. shelf   **10.** turkey

Adding Endings to Words

Double the final consonant of some words before adding an ending. Check a dictionary if you are not sure about doubling the final consonant.

EXAMPLE

slip	+	ed	=	slipped
hop	+	ing	=	hopping
grant	+	ed	=	granted

For some words that end with a silent -e, drop the e before adding an ending. Check a dictionary if you are not sure about dropping the final e.

EXAMPLE

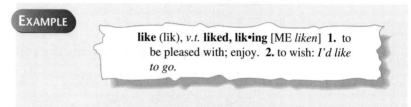

like (līk), *v.t.* **liked, lik•ing** [ME *liken*] **1.** to be pleased with; enjoy. **2.** to wish: *I'd like to go.*

Activity B Add the endings in parentheses to these words. On your paper, write the words with the endings. Then, use a dictionary to check your spelling.

1. bake (ed)

2. charge (ing)

3. use (ful)

4. safe (ty)

5. write (er)

6. step (ing)

7. tall (est)

8. plan (ed)

9. hum (ing)

10. drop (ed)

Spelling Verbs

Add -ed to regular verbs to make their past or past participle forms.

EXAMPLE
| I jump. | I jumped. | I have jumped. |
| He washes. | He washed. | He has washed. |

Form the past or past participle of irregular verbs in other ways. The dictionary entry will show you the past and sometimes the past participle for irregular verbs, along with the present participle.

EXAMPLE   begin   began   begun   beginning

Activity C On your paper, write the answers to the questions about the entries below.

catch (kach), *v.t.* **caught, catch•ing** [L *capere* take] to capture or take.

cost (kost), *v.t.* **cost, cost•ing** [L *constare,* to stand firm] to have a price of.

creep (krēp), *v.i.* **crept, creep•ing** [ME *crepen*] to move along with the body close to the ground.

draw (drô), *v.t.* **drew, drawn, draw•ing** [ME *drawen*] **1.** to pull: *to draw in a horse.* **2.** to make lines or pictures.

en•joy (en joi´), *v.t.* [ME *enjoyen* to make joyful] to take pleasure in. **–en•joy•a•ble** *adj.* **–en•joy•ment** *n.*

1. Which verb is regular? How do you know?

2. Which verb does not add an ending to make the past form?

3. Which entry shows four different forms for the verb?

4. Write the past form of *creep.*

5. Write the past form of *catch.*

Activity D On your paper, write the past or past participle form of the verb in parentheses. Then check your spelling with the entries on page 50.

1. Elio (draw) a picture in art class.
2. The turtle (creep) across the road.
3. That car (cost) them a lot!
4. Lisa (enjoy) the movie.
5. Juan has (catch) the ball.

Homonyms and Sound-Alike Words

Homonyms are words that sound alike but that have different spellings and different meanings.

> **EXAMPLE**   to   too   two
> They went to the movies. (preposition)
> Joe wanted to go, too. (adverb)
> They are meeting two friends. (adjective)

Words that sound almost alike can cause spelling problems. Read the meanings in a dictionary to find out which word you need.

> **EXAMPLE**   loose   lose
> My belt is loose. (adjective)
> Did you lose your watch? (verb)
> close   clothes
> Please close the door. (verb)
> We bought new clothes for school. (noun)

Homonym

A word that sounds exactly like another word but is spelled differently and has a different meaning

Activity E On your paper, write the word that correctly completes each sentence. Use the dictionary entries to be sure you have used the correct word.

> **its** (its) *pron.* of or relating to it. (used as an adjective)
>
> **it's** (its) **1.** a contraction of *it is.* **2.** a contraction of *it has.*

1. Here is my book. Have you seen _____ cover?

2. _____ been a nice day today.

3. I wonder what _____ name is.

4. _____ a quarter past two.

5. _____ time to go now.

Activity F Number your paper from 1 to 15. Use a dictionary to help you find 15 spelling errors in the paragraph below. On your paper, write the corrected words. If you have word processing equipment available, try typing in the paragraph and using the spell checker. Do you get the same results with the spell checker?

> Next Wedesday, I'll call my freind in the country. I'll invite him too visit me and my fammily for the weekend. We always find the same things intresting, witch is why we like each other's compeny. We like baskitball, and their's a grate court near my house. Its in the park just down the street. We usualy get about the same number of pionts each game. He's on the teem, but I'm knot.

Use a dictionary to find the correct spelling for each word in bold. If you have word processing equipment available, type in the paragraph, and use the spell checker. Then, on your paper write the paragraph with all of the words spelled correctly.

The **Basball** Hall of Fame is in Cooperstown, New York. It was **dedecated** in 1939. People like to visit the **musuem.** The Hall of Fame is called "The shrine of **orgonized** baseball." A shrine is a **wholly** place!

Thirteen of the words in bold are misspelled. Check the spelling of all the bold words in a dictionary. On your paper, write the 13 misspelled words correctly. If the word is correct, write *correct.*

1. The **foremans** on Roberto's job have a meeting every **Wensday.**

2. A friend of mine has two **calfs** for sale.

3. Maria's club **planed** the **Thanxsgiving** party.

4. "Is all that noise **nessessary?**" asked Mr. Williams.

5. "I'm **to** tired for this **comotion!**" he said.

6. Jamal would rather see a movie **than** watch TV.

7. "Where is **your** homework?" asked the teacher.

8. He **beleives** that everyone deserves a chance to **suceed.**

9. I need peace and **quite** to do my homework.

10. "Do you **realy** need a **hole** pizza?" asked Pierre.

Where To Find It

Computer Spell Checkers

A computer's spell check feature is helpful, but it does not check a word's meaning. For example, you might not know which word to use in the following sentence:

The (beach, beech) tree produces nuts that you can eat.

If you make a spelling error and write *beesh,* the spell checker will catch the error.

However, the spell checker can check only spelling. If you used *beach* instead of *beech,* the spelling would be correct, even though the word would be wrong. If there is a spelling error, the spell checker will give you a list of words such as *beach, beech,* and *bench.* Use an online or print dictionary to check the meanings of the word choices.

You can use a dictionary to find out interesting and important facts. Here are some kinds of facts you might find in a dictionary.

- Facts about real people
- Facts about fictional characters
- Facts about cities, rivers, states, and countries
- The meaning of foreign words

EXAMPLE

Columbus, Christopher. 1451–1506. Italian, served Spain as an explorer. First European to discover America (1492) in an attempt to sail to Asia from Europe.

Activity A Look up the following words in a dictionary. On your paper, write one fact you learn about each item. Write *no entry* if your dictionary does not contain an entry for a word. Look up the word in a different dictionary later.

1. hors d'oeuvres

2. Dakota

3. Marconi

4. Robinson Crusoe

5. impressionism

6. pomegranate

7. otter

8. Montreal

9. NASA

10. O'Keeffe

Different Kinds of Dictionaries

Some dictionaries provide special information.

A **geographical dictionary** has a list of rivers, mountains, cities, and other geographical features of the world. A **biographical** dictionary has a list of famous people and some facts about their lives.

A dictionary of synonyms and **antonyms** has a list of words with other words that have the same meanings and words that have opposite meanings.

Activity B On your paper, write the type of dictionary that would probably have the information listed in each item below. Write *geographical, biographical,* or *synonyms and antonyms.*

1. Information about your town or city
2. A word that means the same as *nice*
3. The date that Calvin Coolidge became president
4. A word that means the opposite of *large*
5. A list of some of Thomas Edison's inventions
6. The height of Mt. Everest
7. Information about the climate of Peru
8. A biography of Abigail Adams
9. Animals that live in Antarctica
10. Pierre Trudeau's term as prime minister of Canada

You can get
writing ideas
simply by
skimming a
dictionary and
opening it to any
page. Write five
factual sentences
about five
random words
from a dictionary.

Activity C Use the information in the entries below to answer these questions.

---

au gra·tin (ō grät´ən), *adj.* [F *with scrapings*] made with a crust of bread crumbs and cheese.

Ba·con (bā´kən), *n.* **Francis, 1561–1626,** English philosopher and writer.

ba·gel (bā´ gəl), *n.* [Yiddish] a hard bread roll shaped like a small doughnut.

Bagh·dad (bag´ dad), *n.* capital city of Iraq; pop. about 1,000,000. also **Bagdad.**

ban·shee (ban´ shē), *n.* (in Irish folklore) a female spirit whose loud screams warn of a coming death.

bant·am·weight (bant´ əm wāt), *n.* a boxer or wrestler weighing 113 to 118 pounds.

Bar·num (bär´ nəm), *n.* **P(hineas) T(aylor),** 1810–91, U.S. showman and circus owner.

chop su·ey (chop soō´ ē), *n.* a Chinese-American dish of meat, bean sprouts, etc., served with rice.

C.O.D. *abbr.* **1.** cash on delivery. **2.** collect on delivery.

Doyle (doil), *n.* **Sir Arthur Conan** (kō´nə n), 1859–1930, British physician and novelist: known for his Sherlock Holmes stories.

flib·ber·ti·gib·bet (flib´ ər tə jib´ it), *n.* an irresponsible flighty person.

leap year *n.* a year of 366 days, occurring every fourth year; the extra day is on February 29: a leap year is a year whose number can be divided by 4.

L.P.N. *abbr.* licensed practical nurse.

pop. (pop) *abbr.* **1.** popular. **2.** population.

R.N. *abbr.* **1.** registered nurse. **2.** Royal Navy.

Sher·lock Holmes (shûr´ lok hōmz´), *n.* a fictional British detective with great powers of deduction, the main character in many stories by A. Conan Doyle.

Yo·sem·i·te Falls (yō sem´ə tē), *n.* [AmInd name of the Valley Indians, lit. *grizzly bears, killers*] series of waterfalls in Yosemite National Park in California: upper falls, 1,430 ft.; lower falls, 320 ft.; total drop: 2,526 ft.

---

a - act, ā - āble, â - dâre, ä - ärm, e - ebb, ē - ēven, i - it, ī - īce,
o - hot, ō - ōver, ô - ôrder, oi - oil, ōō - bŏŏk, ōō - lōŏt, ou - out,
u - up, û - ûrge, ch - chief, ng - sing, sh - shoe, th - thin, <u>th</u> - <u>th</u>is,
zh - vision,   ə = *a* as in *ago*.

---

1. List the entries that are foreign words.

2. List the names of real people.

3. List the entries that are abbreviations.

4. Tell what each abbreviation means.

5. List the geographical locations.

Online Dictionaries

Like print dictionaries, online dictionaries will help you find the right word. Type the key word *dictionary* into a search engine to find an online dictionary. Look for cross references that take you to other Web pages.

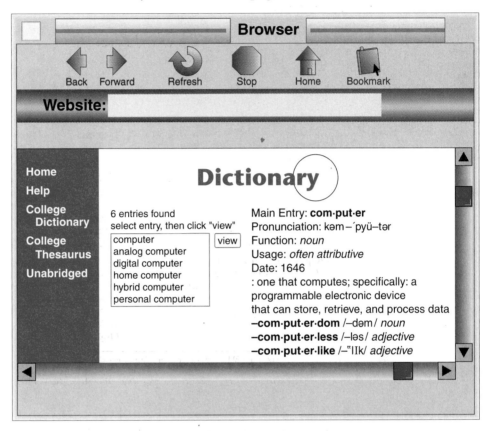

Activity D Use the information above to answer the following questions. Write each answer on your paper.

1. How many entries did the search find for "computer?"

2. Where else could you look for "computer" on this Web site besides the regular dictionary?

3. What is the function of the word *computer*?

4. What is the definition of *computer*?

5. What are three other words given with *computer* in part of each word?

More About Online Dictionaries

You may also find online foreign language dictionaries and dictionaries of commonly misspelled words. Specialty dictionaries provide lists of words related to particular research fields such as science, history, and sports. Many online dictionaries contain so many pages that it would be impossible for us to read them all. Always check a few different dictionaries when looking for a definition. Online dictionaries give us many places to look.

Activity E Write three sentences about some of the differences between online and print dictionaries. Include why it might be a good idea to check both.

The local library is an excellent place to find online dictionaries and other online resources.

Use the entries below to answer the questions that follow. On your paper, write your answers.

Ak•ron (ak´ rə n), *n.* a city in N.E. Ohio: pop. 275,425.

Al•ex•an•der the Great (al´ ig zən´ d r), 356–323 B.C.; king of Macedonia, 336–323; conqueror.

an•cient (ān´ sha nt), *adj.* [< L *ante* before] **1.** of times long past. **2.** very old.

At•lan•tis (at lan´ tis), *n.* a mythical island in the Atlantic Ocean west of Gibralter, that was swallowed up by the sea.

B.C. *abbr.* **1.** before Christ. **2.** British Columbia.

e•qui•nox (e´ kw noks´), *n.* [< L *aequus* equal *ə nox* night] the time when the sun crosses the equator, making night and day an equal length in all parts of the earth.

Leip•zig (lip´ sig), *n.* a city in Germany; pop. 596,000.

N. *abbr.* **1.** north. **2.** northern.

1. Which city has more people—Akron or Leipzig?

2. Was Alexander the Great a real person? How do you know?

3. Twice each year, day and night are equal in Norway. Are they equal on these same days where you live?

4. What is the original meaning of *ancient?*

5. Petra's parents live in B.C. What is the full name of that place?

6. How old was Alexander the Great when he became King of Macedonia?

7. Can tourists visit the island of Atlantis?

On your paper, answer the following questions.

8. Why would someone use an online dictionary?

9. What do some online dictionaries have that print dictionaries do not have?

10. Why is it a good idea to check a few different dictionaries for definitions?

Chapter 2   R E V I E W

Word Bank

abbreviation

accent mark

antonym

biographical
dictionary

derived

dictionary

entry

etymology

geographical
dictionary

homonym

key

origin

stress

syllable

Part A Write the missing word on your paper.

1. A _____ lists words and facts about words.
2. An _____ is a listing in a dictionary that provides facts about a word.
3. A guide to symbols and abbreviations is a _____ .
4. A _____ is a part of a word with one vowel sound.
5. An _____ shows you which syllable to stress.
6. When you _____ a syllable, you emphasize it.
7. An _____ is a shortened form of a written word.
8. The study of the history of a word is its _____ .
9. The beginning of something is its _____ .
10. A word that comes from another word is _____ from that word.
11. A _____ sounds like another word but has a different spelling and a different meaning.
12. A _____ lists rivers and other features.
13. A _____ lists famous people.
14. An _____ is the opposite of another word.

Part B Write the answers to these questions on your paper.

15. Where do you find the guide words in a dictionary?
16. Which part of the entry does the pronunciation key explain?
17. What does each of these abbreviations or symbols mean?
    A v.i.   **B** prep.   **C** adj.   **D** <   **E** pl.   **F** L
18. What does the abbreviation *Syn.* mean?
    A suffix   **B** syllable   **C** stress mark   **D** synonym
19. What words might computer spell checkers miss?
    A antonyms   **C** homonyms
    B hard words   **D** entry words
20. Where do you usually find a pronunciation key?
    A in the index   **C** after each entry word
    B the bottom of the page   **D** in the etymology section

Part C Use the entry below to answer the questions that follow. On your paper, write the answers.

> **com•pas•sion** (kəm păsh´ ən), *n.* [ME>L. *compati,* to suffer, bear pain. See PATIENT.] **1.** the feeling of another's pain or sorrow. **Syn.** pity, concern

21. How many syllables does *compassion* have?

22. What part of speech is *compassion*?

23. What is the origin of *compassion*?

Part D Rewrite each bold word correctly, if it is misspelled. Use a dictionary to check your answers.

24. I **beleive** that he has lived in five **different citys.**

25. The **safety** of the **childrens** was her **bigest** concern.

26. **There** going to **except** the prize **instead** of us.

Part E Use these entries to answer the questions. On your paper, write the answers.

27. How many U.S. presidents were named Johnson?

28. Who was James Weldon Johnson?

29. What kind of book does a lexicographer write?

30. Who was the city of Louisville named after?

> **John•son** (jon´sən), *n.* **1. Andrew** 1808-75; 17th president of the U.S. 1865-69. **2. James Weldon** (wel´ dən), 1871-1938; U.S. writer. **3. Lyn•don Baines** (lin´ dən bānz), 1908-73; 36th U.S. president 1963-69. **4. Samuel** 1709-84; Eng. lexicographer and writer.
>
> **lex•i•cog•ra•pher** (lek´ sə kog´ rə fər), *n.* a person who writes a dictionary.
>
> **Lou•is** (lōō´ is), **Joe** (born *Joseph Louis Barrow*) 1914-81; U.S. boxer: world heavyweight champion 1937-49.
>
> **Lou•is•ville** (lōō´ ē vil´), *n.* (after Louis XVI) city in Northern Kentucky on the Ohio river: pop. 361,958.

Test-Taking Tip Read test questions carefully to identify those questions that require more than one answer.

3

Other Sources of Information

Have you ever needed to know how to fix a leaky faucet? Find a recipe for a special dessert? Or get to a place you wanted to visit? Books, magazines, the Internet, and other references can help you find the answers you are looking for. You just need to know which reference has the information you need and where to find the reference. Then you need to know how to use the information you find.

In Chapter 3, you will learn how to find and use everyday references.

Goals for Learning

◆ To discover the kinds of information in an almanac

◆ To understand and use the contents of an atlas

◆ To use a map to locate places

◆ To locate information in an encyclopedia

◆ To locate cooking resources

◆ To understand food labels and package directions

◆ To follow directions in a how-to book

◆ To recognize and find different kinds of information in magazines

Farmer's almanac

An annual calendar of days, weeks, and months with weather predictions and astronomical facts

General information almanac

An almanac that contains facts and figures about a variety of subjects from the previous year and from the past

An almanac is a book of facts published once a year. Two kinds of almanacs are **farmer's almanacs** and **general information almanacs.** Some almanacs appear on CD-ROM, which you use on a computer.

Farmer's Almanacs

A farmer's almanac is a yearly calendar of days, weeks, and months with weather forecasts and facts about astronomy. The weather forecasts help farmers decide when to plant or harvest crops. Because the moon affects tides, mariners use the astronomy information in a farmer's almanac to determine when the tide will be high or low. Farmer's almanacs provide other information helpful for farm and home care.

Activity A On your paper, write the answers to these questions.

1. What are two kinds of almanacs?

2. Would you expect to find a calendar in a farmer's almanac?

3. Why would a ship's navigator want to know about the phases of the moon?

4. What form of almanac can you use on a computer?

5. Name two kinds of information found in a farmer's almanac.

Phases of the Moon

New Moon   First Quarter   Full Moon   Last Quarter

General Information Almanacs

A general information almanac has facts and figures about many subjects from the most recent year and from the past. Most general information almanacs appear once a year. Look in the index to find the topics that the almanac covers. Unlike most other reference books, the index of an almanac is usually in the front.

Here are topics you might find in a general information almanac:

Biographies of U.S. presidents	Agricultural facts
Facts about the United States	Awards and prizes
Facts about other countries	Events of the last year
Facts about Social Security	History of Canada
Number of calories in foods	Income tax information
Populations of U.S. cities	Names of U.S. colleges
Supreme Court decisions	People in Congress
ZIP codes and area codes	Sports facts

Activity B Write complete sentences on your paper to answer these questions.

1. Would you expect to find information about early Canadian history in a general information almanac?

2. How is the index in an almanac different from indexes in other reference books?

3. What time periods do general information almanacs cover?

4. What are three types of facts you might find in a general information almanac?

5. A statistic is a numerical fact. Write three statistics from this almanac account:

> William Henry Harrison was the ninth president of the United States. He was president only 31 days. He got pneumonia during the inauguration and died on April 4, 1841.

An almanac can be very useful in your everyday life; for example,

- if you are on a special diet, you can find facts about calories and nutrition.

- if you want information about a college, you can find the names, addresses, number of students, and number of teachers in most of the colleges and universities in the United States.

- if you are interested in sports, you can find facts about nearly every sport and sporting event.

- if you are writing a letter, most almanacs list the ZIP codes for each area of the United States.

- if you have bought a product that doesn't work, you can find the addresses of many large companies.

- if you are interested in choosing a career with plenty of job openings, almanacs list the most rapidly growing careers.

- if you want information about recent world events, almanacs list that information.

An almanac often has facts about the year before its title date. For example, the 2001 almanac includes many facts about 2000. To learn facts about 2001, you would have to check the 2002 almanac.

To find more current information, use a publication that appears more often. For instance, magazines come out every week or every month. The most up-to-date facts are in the daily newspaper or on Web sites on the Internet.

Activity C Use these facts from a 2001 almanac to answer the questions that follow. Write your answers on your paper.

2001 Almanac

Awards — Medals — Prizes

<u>2000 Nobel Prize Winners</u>

Physics	A.F. Ioffe, Russia
	Herbert Kroemer, Germany
	Jack S. Kilby, U.S.
Chemistry	Alan J. Heeger, U.S.
	Alan G. MacDiarmid, U.S.
	Hideki Shirakawa, Japan
Physiology/Medicine	Avid Carlsson, Sweden
	Paul Greengard, U.S.
	Eric R. Kandel, U.S.

<u>2000 Nobel Prize Winners</u>

| Literature | Gao Xingjian, France |
| Peace | Kim Dae Jung, South Korea |

<u>Pulitzer Prize in Journalism, Letters, & Music</u>

Journalism

2000	Washington Post
1999	Washington Post
1998	Grand Forks (ND) Herald

National Reporting

2000	Wall Street Journal
1999	NY Times staff
1998	Russell Carollo, Jeff Nesmith,
	Dayton (OH) Daily News

<u>Miss America Winners</u>

2000	Heather Renee French, Maysville, Kentucky
1999	Nicole Johnson, Roanoke, Virginia
1998	Kate Shindle, Evanston, Illinois

123

---

1. Who won the 2000 Nobel Prize in literature? From what country was the winner?

2. From what country was the 2000 Nobel Peace Prize winner?

3. What newspaper did the top national reporters in 1998 work for? How do you know?

4. Who is Eric R. Kandel?

5. What newspaper won the Pulitzer Prize in journalism in 2000?

Electronic Almanacs

Electronic almanac
Almanac that is on a CD-ROM or at an Internet Web site

Almanacs on CD-ROM or at an Internet Web site are **electronic almanacs.** Electronic almanacs are usually up-to-date, free, and reliable. They are often more current than printed almanacs.

The index of an electronic almanac usually appears on the home page of the almanac's Web site. This page has a search box into which you type the name of what you are looking for. The almanac may list its subjects by countries and maps. When you click on a country, the Web page may show you a map as well as information on population and geography.

Electronic almanacs cover various topics, from the weather to the Olympics to literature to snowfall around the world. To find an online almanac, conduct a search using the key word *almanac.* You also can search by using the key words *electronic AND almanac.* Be sure to capitalize the word *AND* in your two-word search. A list of almanac Web sites will appear on your screen. Then click on the almanac that you would like to visit. Check the year of the almanac to make sure that you are getting the most recent information.

The Central Intelligence Agency (CIA) has a reliable online almanac. At the CIA electronic almanac Web site, you can find current information about any country in the world. The almanac is at the following site:

http://www.odci.gov/cia/publications/factbook/

Activity D Write the word on your paper that completes each sentence correctly.

1. An _____ almanac is available on CD-ROM.

2. The _____ of an electronic almanac usually appears on the almanac's home page.

3. You could find information about the _____ of the world at the CIA almanac Web site.

4. To get current information, you should check the _____ an almanac was published.

5. Electronic almanacs are usually up-to-date, _____, and reliable.

Lesson 1   R E V I E W

Write complete sentences on your paper to answer these questions.

1. What are two kinds of information that appear in a farmer's almanac?
2. What kinds of facts would you find in a general information almanac? Give two examples.
3. What is a statistic?
4. How often are most almanacs published?
5. Where would you look to find out whether an almanac has information about a certain country?

Number your paper from 6 to 11. Next to each number write *FA* if you can find the answer to the question in a farmer's almanac or *GIA* if you can find the answer to the question in a general information almanac. Write *B* if you could find the information in both.

6. When will the next full moon be?
7. If fish are biting best at high tide, what time should you go fishing?
8. Who won the World Series in 1960?
9. When should I set out my tomato plants this year?
10. Who won the Pulitzer Prize for journalism in 1997?
11. What is the ZIP code for Boise, Idaho?

On your paper, answer the following questions.

12. Where would you find electronic almanacs?
13. Where is the index on an Internet almanac?
14. What key word(s) would you use to find electronic almanacs?
15. What is a reason to use an electronic almanac instead of a print almanac?

An **atlas** is a book of maps and geographical facts. It is a reference source that you can find in print books and on CD-ROM.

Atlas

A book of maps and geographical facts

Symbol

A sign or mark that stands for something else

Scale

The relationship shown between distances on the map and actual distances

Reading a Map

To use an atlas, you must be able to read a map and understand its **symbols.** A symbol is something that represents something else. The key, or legend, on a map explains the symbols on the map. Artists create maps to **scale.** You can use the scale to find the actual distances shown on the map.

EXAMPLE

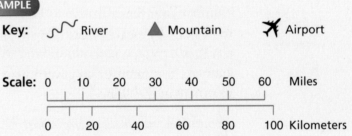

Activity A Use this map to answer these questions. Write the answers on your paper.

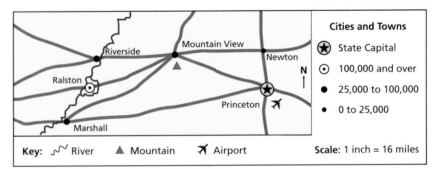

1. How far is the mountain from the river?

2. Which city is the capital?

3. How wide is the area shown on this map?

4. Which city has a population of over 100,000?

5. Which town has fewer than 25,000 people?

How to Use a Gazetteer

A **gazetteer** is a dictionary of geographical place names. It lists in alphabetical order the names of all the places shown on the maps in the atlas. It is like an index to an atlas or to a map. You can find gazetteers in print form or on CD-ROM.

A **grid** is a network of lines on a map that helps locate certain places. The lines go across (**horizontal**) and up and down (**vertical**). A **grid map** is a map with grid lines. The spaces between the vertical lines on a grid map have numbers. The spaces between the horizontal lines have letters.

The letter and number next to a place name in the gazetteer tell you exactly where to look on the map to locate that place.

Online Gazetteer

You can easily locate places using an online gazetteer. Use the search box to type in the name of the town, village, or city, and the state. You can use this government Web site to locate places anywhere in the United States:

http://www.census.gov/cgi-bin/gazetteer

You will first get information about whether the place is a village, town, or city, and its population. Then you can choose to view the map of that location. When the map appears on the screen, you can choose additional information such as the following:

City labels	Parks
Counties	Streets
Highways	Bodies of water

Gazetteer

A dictionary of geographical place names

Grid

A network of lines on a map that makes it possible to locate specific places

Horizontal

Going across

Vertical

Going up and down

Grid map

A map with grid lines

EXAMPLE If you look up Laurensburg in the gazetteer of the atlas for this map, you might see the following:

Laurensburg   C-2

To locate Laurensburg, first find the C along the left or right side of the map. Then find the 2 along the top or bottom of the map. Laurensburg is located in the square next to the C and under the 2.

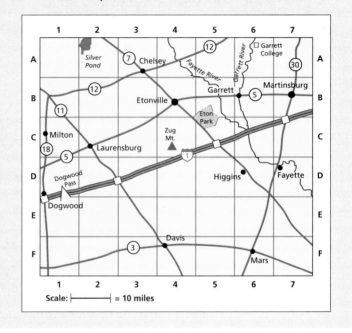

Activity B Locate each of these places on the map in the example box. On your paper, write the letter and number of each location on the grid.

1. Milton

2. Garrett River

3. Dogwood Pass

4. Higgins

5. Chelsey

6. Eton Park

7. Silver Pond ·

8. Garrett College

9. Fayette

10. Davis

Lesson 2   R E V I E W

On your paper, write the answer to these questions.

1. What are two things an atlas contains?

2. What is the difference between a key and a symbol?

3. What does a map scale show?

4. What is a grid?

5. What is a gazetteer?

On your paper, write the name of the place found at each of these locations on the grid map below.

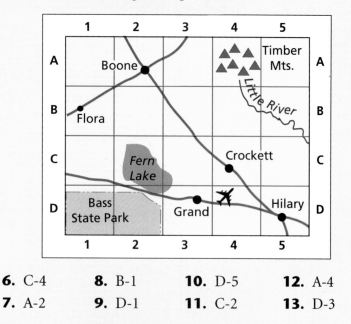

6. C-4	**8.** B-1	**10.** D-5	**12.** A-4
7. A-2	**9.** D-1	**11.** C-2	**13.** D-3

14. How do names appear in a gazetteer?

15. How do you search for a place using an online gazetteer?

Political map

A map that shows the boundaries of states and countries clearly

Physical map

A map that shows the roughness of the earth's surface

Product map

A map that has symbols that show where goods are grown or produced

Road map

A map that shows roads, highways, towns, and other useful travel information

Maps can teach you about history. For example, maps from the 1300s and 1400s show how people thought the world looked. The continents on old maps have different shapes than they do on today's maps.

Kinds of Maps

There are many kinds of maps with different features and purposes. A **political map** shows the boundaries of states and countries. Usually each state or country is a different color. A **physical map** shows the roughness of the earth's surface. It shows mountains, hills, and rivers. A **product map** uses symbols to show where items grow or are produced.

Road Maps

A **road map** shows roads, highways, towns, bodies of water, and other information helpful to a traveler. A road map includes a scale and a key with symbols.

When using a road map, carefully read the map key. The key shows the different kinds of roads on the map. For example, you may see one-lane roads, local roads, toll roads, interstate highways, and railroads on the map.

Here is an example of a road map.

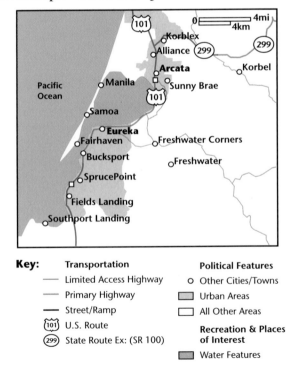

Key:

Transportation		Political Features	
——	Limited Access Highway	○	Other Cities/Towns
——	Primary Highway	▢	Urban Areas
——	Street/Ramp	▢	All Other Areas
🛡101	U.S. Route		**Recreation & Places of Interest**
⬭299	State Route Ex: (SR 100)	▢	Water Features

Writing Tip

When you are writing travel directions, base them on a correct map of the area. Make sure that you use the same street names and symbols that the map uses. Provide estimated distances by using the scale from the map.

Activity A Use the road map on page 74 to answer these questions. Write the answers on your paper.

1. Near what large body of water is Eureka, California?

2. How far is it from Fields Landing to Bucksport?

3. If you were driving from Fields Landing to Arcata, how many towns would you pass through on the way?

4. What kind of road is 101?

5. What kind of recreation does Eureka, California, offer?

Online Road Maps

Road maps of the United States are now available on many Internet Web sites. To find a road map, all you need to know is the city or town. You also can find a map of a street or an intersection. If you need to find a place that is outside city or town limits, you can locate that place by entering a complete address, including the ZIP code. Many Web sites also provide directions to get from one place to another.

Online maps look like printed maps. However, online maps may give you extra information. You can locate services such as restaurants and gas stations that may come in handy when you are traveling. You may want to know where the nearest hospital is if you are traveling far from home.

Here are some businesses and places that you could locate on an online road map:

Lodging	Entertainment	Restaurants	Services	Transportation
Hotels and motels Campgrounds	Movie theaters Museums Stadiums Zoos	Barbecue Chinese Seafood	ATMs Banks Churches Hospitals	Airports Automobile rentals Bus lines Gas stations

Longitude and Latitude

A **globe** is a model of the earth. It shows the continents, islands, and oceans as they actually are. Mapmakers have divided the surface of the globe into parts. They use imaginary lines called longitude lines and latitude lines.

Longitude lines go from north to south (vertically) on a map and globe. They measure the distance from east to west. **Latitude lines** go from east to west (horizontally) on a map and globe. They measure the distance from north to south.

The **equator** is a line of latitude that runs from east to west around the center of the earth. We measure all other lines of latitude from the equator.

Activity B Use the view of the globe below to answer these questions. Write the answers on your paper.

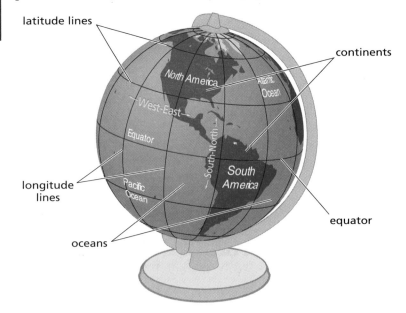

1. What is the name of the latitude line in the center of the globe?

2. What two continents do you see on the globe?

3. Which continent is mostly south of the equator?

4. What two bodies of water do you see on the globe?

5. Which body of water is west of the two continents?

Lesson 3 R E V I E W

Use the road map below to answer the questions that follow.
Write the answers on your paper.

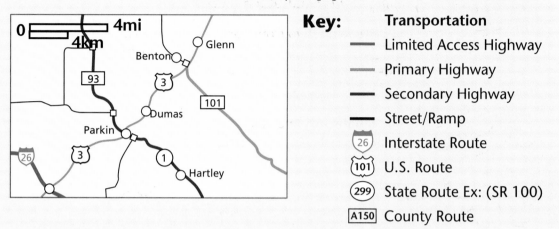

Key: Transportation

— Limited Access Highway
— Primary Highway
— Secondary Highway
— Street/Ramp
🛡26 Interstate Route
🛡101 U.S. Route
🛡299 State Route Ex: (SR 100)
⬜A150 County Route

1. What three kinds of information appear on the map?
2. How many towns appear on this road map?
3. What type of road is Number 26?
4. What road(s) would you take to get from Hartley to Dumas?
5. How are online road maps different from print road maps?

Use the view of the globe below to answer these questions.
Write the answers on your paper.

6. What is the name of the line running west to east in the middle of the globe?
7. Which continent shown is north of the equator?
8. What is the name of the lines that run north to south?
9. What do latitude lines measure?
10. How is a globe different from a road map?

Encyclopedia

A book or set of books with a collection of articles and facts on many subjects, organized in alphabetical order

Volume

A single book, or one book in a set of books

An **encyclopedia** is a very useful type of reference book. An encyclopedia is a book or set of books with facts on many subjects. It usually has a collection of articles in alphabetical order.

Some encyclopedias are only one book, or **volume.** Others have many volumes. Most sets of encyclopedias have similar features, as you can see in the diagram below. These features can help you find the information that you need quickly.

Inside each volume, guide words appear at the top of each page.

Guide letters often appear on each volume.

Each volume has a number on the spine.

The last volume is an index to all the other volumes. Every article and subject in the encyclopedia is listed. Cross references are often given.

Activity A Which volume of the encyclopedia pictured on page 78 would you look in to find facts about each topic listed below? Because some topics may suggest more than one idea, write the volume number or numbers on your paper. Next to each number, write the subject you would look up.

Example   Italy
         Vol. 9— Italy
         Vol. 5— Europe

1. History of Brazil
2. Birds of Antarctica
3. Mammals of the tundra
4. History of Canada
5. Hockey
6. Products of Spain
7. Thomas Edison's inventions
8. Shakespeare
9. United States Congress
10. Mississippi River

Related Topics and Cross-References

When you read about a topic in an encyclopedia, you may find that the article names another related topic. Some articles also give a specific cross-reference to another related topic.

> **HONEY PLANTS,** a group of plants that furnish the nectar from which bees make honey — often also called bee plants.

> **NECTAR** is a sugary liquid produced by many flowers. Besides being the main source of honey, it is also very important in cross-pollination. *See also* **Pollination**.

Activity B Use the encyclopedia entries above to answer these questions. Write the answers on your paper.

1. What is the related topic named in the entry about honey plants?

2. If you were to look up this topic, what guide letter would appear on the correct volume?

3. What is the cross-reference named in the article on nectar?

4. What is another name for honey plants?

5. What guide letter(s) would appear on the volume containing the article about pollination?

Activity **C** Use the examples below to answer the questions that follow. Write the answers on your paper.

EXAMPLE

. . . Boundary arguments with Guatemala were settled in 1933. For Bibliography, *See* **Costa Rica** (History).

HONDURAS, BRITISH. *See* **Belize** (History).
HONDURAS BARK is the bitter bark from a small tropical American shrub, used as a medicine. Also called Cascarilla Bark.

1. What two cross-references appear in the examples above?

2. What related topic would you look up to learn more about Honduras bark?

3. What is a bibliography? Use a dictionary if you need to.

4. The article in *Example 1* has a bibliography. What topic must you look up to find it?

5. Explain what Costa Rica (History) means.

CD-ROM and Online Encyclopedias

You also can find encyclopedias on CD-ROMs and online through the Internet. These electronic encyclopedias present information, including videos and music recordings, in a way that printed encyclopedias cannot. Some people consider these encyclopedias more interesting to use than printed encyclopedias. In some electronic encyclopedias you can listen to historical recordings of speeches by U.S. presidents or view films of sporting events from many years ago.

CD-ROM Encyclopedia Convenience

There are several other advantages to using electronic encyclopedias. Encyclopedias stored on CD-ROM take up very little space. Printed encyclopedias can take up a lot of shelf space and can be heavy to carry. CD-ROMs are easy to carry, easy to store, and easy to access on a computer. Also, encyclopedia CD-ROMs usually cost less than printed encyclopedias.

Online Encyclopedias

You can find online encyclopedias on the Internet. Some online encyclopedias are free, and many companies that publish printed and CD-ROM encyclopedias also offer online encyclopedias. The online encyclopedias that charge a fee are sometimes available on a free trial basis. If you decide that you want to use the online encyclopedia, you can buy a subscription to use the encyclopedia for a certain period of time.

Both CD-ROM and online encyclopedias offer indexes in the form of search boxes in which you type a topic or term. The screen then displays the results. When using electronic encyclopedias, you can find cross-referenced topics by clicking on the highlighted topics within the entry.

Activity D On your paper, answer the following questions.

1. What is one advantage of using an electronic encyclopedia?

2. How do you find a specific topic on a CD-ROM encyclopedia?

3. How does the cost of a printed set of encyclopedias compare with that of an online encyclopedia?

4. Which form of encyclopedia is usually the most up-to-date?

5. How can you find cross-references on online encyclopedias?

Writing Tip

Whether you choose to use online, CD-ROM, or printed encyclopedias for research, use your own words when writing your report. It is illegal to use exact sentences from these resources without telling where you found the information.

Encyclopedias About Special Subjects

You are probably most familiar with large sets of encyclopedias. However, there are many other kinds of encyclopedias. One-volume general encyclopedias have short articles about many different subjects. They are sometimes called "desk" encyclopedias.

There are also encyclopedias about just one subject. In these encyclopedias, all the articles provide details about that subject. For example, a home medical encyclopedia includes only information related to medical topics.

Activity E Write the word on your paper that completes each of the following sentences correctly.

1. An encyclopedia is a collection of _____ on many subjects.

2. The subjects in an encyclopedia are arranged in _____ order.

3. A desk encyclopedia has _____ volume.

4. A _____ is one in a set of books.

5. _____ appear at the top of each page in an encyclopedia.

On your paper, write the answer to these questions.

1. What is one way that dictionaries and encyclopedias are alike?

2. What is one way that almanacs and encyclopedias are alike?

3. How many volumes would you expect a desk encyclopedia to have?

4. Encyclopedia sets have guide letters on the spine of each volume. What else may appear on the spine to help you find the right volume?

5. What do the guide words on each page tell you?

Study the encyclopedia in the picture. In which volume would you look to find each topic below? On your paper, write the number and the guide letters of the volume.

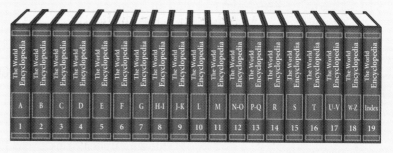

6. President John F. Kennedy

7. the history of Mexico

8. automobile (history)

9. wildlife of China

10. Charles Dickens

11. elephants

On your paper, write the answers to these questions.

12. Where do you find online encyclopedias?

13. What is one difference between book encyclopedias and encyclopedia CD-ROMs?

14. How do you find a specific topic on a CD-ROM encyclopedia?

15. What kinds of articles would you expect to find in a legal encyclopedia?

Cookbooks

A cookbook is a reference book about food. Most cookbooks contain some of the following information:

Cookbooks help you prepare everyday meals.

- Facts about storing foods
- Meal-planning help
- How to carve meat
- Food-shopping advice
- Nutrition facts
- Calorie charts
- Suggestions for a low-fat diet
- How to measure ingredients

General cookbooks focus on a wide range of cooking skills, such as preparing eggs and baking cakes. Specialty cookbooks focus on certain types of food, such as Asian or French cooking, vegetables, salads, or low-fat meals.

Activity A Write *Yes* or *No* on your paper to tell whether a cookbook might answer these questions.

1. How many calories are in a grilled cheese sandwich?

2. How do you carve a turkey?

3. Which store in your town has the best fresh vegetables?

4. What nutrients are in eggs?

5. What foods are good for snacks?

6. What should you eat to get enough vitamins?

7. How do you store fresh fruits?

8. How can you cook chicken breasts?

9. How much do strawberries cost?

10. How long should you roast a 15-pound turkey?

Here are some abbreviations that appear in recipes.

Abbreviations Used in Recipes	
lb. = pound	min. = minute
oz. = ounce	hr. = hour
doz. = dozen	pt. = pint
pkg. = package	qt. = quart
tsp. = teaspoon	F = Fahrenheit
t. = teaspoon	g = gram
tbsp. = tablespoon	c. = cup
T. = tablespoon	sq. = square

Activity B On your paper, write each underlined abbreviation in the recipe below. Next to each abbreviation, write its meaning.

Salsa Cruda

1 16-<u>oz.</u> can of drained and chopped tomatoes
1 4-<u>oz.</u> can of green chili drained, seeded, and diced
1/2 <u>c.</u> of onion, minced
1 <u>T.</u> of vinegar
1 <u>t.</u> of sugar
1/8 <u>tsp.</u> of salt

Blend the following ingredients in a bowl: tomatoes, green chili, and onion. Add vinegar, sugar, and salt to tomato mixture. Keep at room temperature for 30 <u>min.</u> Serve with tacos and enchiladas.

Vocabulary Builder

Measurement Terms

An *ounce* is the unit of measurement for weight in the customary system. This is the system of measuring used in the United States. A *gram* is the unit of measurement for weight in the metric system. Most countries use the metric system for measurement.

Below are units of measurement from the two systems. Use a dictionary to determine which belong to the customary system and which belong to the metric system. Then match similar units from each system.

kilogram	pound	inch	dekameter
mile	foot	meter	kilometer

Finding Recipes on the Internet

You can find recipes from all over the world on the Internet. If you are not sure what recipes you would like, you can begin by typing in the general word "recipes." Then add words to help you narrow your focus. If you know what recipe you want, you may find many varieties of it on different Web sites.

Search by Category

You can find recipes by searching for specific courses, foods, or ingredients. Here are some examples of ways to search for recipes:

Type of course:	soup, salad, bread, side dish, main dish
Specific foods/recipes:	chicken chow mein, curry rice, ravioli
Specific ingredients:	potatoes, mushrooms, spinach

Search by Place

If you search for recipes from a specific country, region, or continent, add the name of that place to your key word search. Examples of place searches include the following:

Country	Region	Continent
India	South Asia	Asia
Mexico	Latin America	North America
Italy	Western Europe	Europe

Activity **C** On your paper, write some key words you would use to find each recipe below.

1. beef stew

2. green vegetable salad

3. Indian curry

4. Swedish meatballs

5. watermelon pickles

Additional Internet Cooking Resources

Cooking resources on the Internet offer additional help for someone who may not know a lot about the recipe. Here are some things to look for on recipe and cooking resources on the Web:

Menus	Help you decide what to cook for a meal, for the day, or for the week
Glossary	Defines or explains cooking terms and ingredients
Alphabetical search	An alphabetical listing of recipes
Advice on cooking techniques	Descriptions of different cooking methods

Activity D Read the recipe below. Then answer the questions that follow.

Curry Couscous   North Africa

2 1/2 c. Water
1 1/2 c. Couscous
1/2 c. Scallions, Chopped
1/4 c. Chopped Almonds
1 clove Garlic, Minced (chopped fine)
2 t. Unsalted Butter
1 t. Olive Oil
1 t. Dried Parsley
1/2 t. Curry Powder

Heat the olive oil in a heavy nonstick skillet over medium heat. Saute the scallions 2–3 minutes until softened. Stir in the curry, almonds, and garlic and saute 2 minutes. Stir in the water, parsley, and butter. Bring to a boil. Stir in the couscous and remove from heat. Cover and let stand 5 minutes or until liquid is absorbed. Fluff with a fork.

1. How much water do you need?

2. What ingredients are chopped?

3. How much olive oil do you heat?

4. How hot should the skillet be when you heat the olive oil?

5. For how long should you let the couscous stand?

Lesson 5 REVIEW

Write *Yes* or *No* on your paper to tell whether a cookbook would have the answers to these questions.

1. How do you defrost a chicken?
2. How many calories are in a cup of yogurt?
3. Where is the best place in your city to buy eggs?
4. How long can you store dough in the freezer?
5. How long should you bake a potato?

Write the meaning of each of these terms on your paper.

6. 15 g
7. 4 oz.
8. 2 pt.
9. 350°F
10. 3/4 pkg.
11. 1 T.
12. 1/4 tsp.
13. 3 hrs.
14. two lbs.
15. 5 qt.

On your paper, write the best answer for each of these questions.

16. On cooking Web sites, which of the following offers meal-planning help?

    A menus   B glossary   C search   D recipes

17. Which of the following key words would you NOT use to search for recipes from India?

    A Indian cooking   C Asian cooking

    B India   D herbs

18. The abbreviation for Fahrenheit is _____.

19. To find what a cooking term means you would look in a _____.

20. What are two ways to search for recipes found on the Internet?

Following Directions on a Package

Packaged foods come in cans, boxes, and sealed plastic bags. We store some packaged foods at room temperature. Some are refrigerated or frozen. Packaged foods are convenient. Almost anyone who can read can prepare them. Simple and easy-to-follow recipes appear on the packages.

Activity A Read these directions from a package of macaroni and cheese. Then write on your paper the answers to the questions that follow.

Directions

Add macaroni and 1 tsp. salt to 6 c. boiling water. Stir. Boil rapidly, stirring occasionally, 7 to 10 minutes or to desired tenderness. Drain. Add 1/4 c. margarine, 1/4 c. milk, and the cheese sauce mix; mix well. Makes 4 1/2 cup servings.

---

1. The box contains dry macaroni and an envelope of cheese sauce mix. What other ingredients do you need to prepare this meal?

2. How long do you cook the macaroni?

3. What do you do first if you are following the directions correctly?

4. What do you do after you drain the macaroni?

5. How large would the servings be if only two people ate this meal?

Preparing Frozen Foods

Frozen vegetables are easy to cook. Like other packaged food, directions for preparing frozen vegetables appear on the package.

Activity B Read these directions from a package of frozen broccoli cuts. Then write on your paper the answers to the questions that follow.

BROCCOLI CUTS

Store in freezer at 0°F.
Keep frozen until ready to use. Do not refreeze.

Microwave: Combine vegetable and 2 tablespoons water in a microwave-safe container. Microwave on high 7-11 minutes, or to desired tenderness, stirring halfway through cooking time. Drain and season to taste.

Stovetop: Bring 1/2 cup water to boiling in saucepan. Add desired amount of frozen vegetable. Bring to second boil. Stir; cover and reduce heat. Simmer 3-6 minutes, or to desired tenderness, stirring occasionally. Drain and season to taste.

Makes 5 servings.

1. Where should you store the package until you are ready to use it?

2. What other ingredients besides broccoli and water do you need to prepare the vegetable?

3. What is the first step of the directions if you are using a microwave?

4. Which is the fastest method of cooking the broccoli?

5. How many servings does one package make?

Food Labels

The label on a food package lists all of the package's ingredients in order of **predominance.** That means that the ingredient with the greatest quantity appears first. The ingredient with the smallest amount appears last. Labels also give nutrition information per serving.

EXAMPLE

MACARONI & CHEESE DINNER

Nutrition Facts

Serving Size 2.5 oz.
(70g / about 1/3 Box)
(Makes about 1 cup)
Servings Per Container about 3

Amount Per Serving	In Box	Prep
Calories	260	390
Calories from Fat	25	150

	% Daily Value**	
Total Fat 2.5g*	4%	26%
Saturated Fat 1g	5%	20%
Cholesterol 10mg	3%	3%
Sodium 560mg	23%	30%
Total Carbohydrate 47g	16%	16%
Dietary Fiber 1g	4%	4%
Sugars 7g		
Protein 11g		
Vitamin A	0%	15%
Vitamin C	0%	0%
Calcium	10%	10%
Iron	15%	15%

* Amount in Box. When prepared with 2% lowfat milk, one serving (about 1 cup) contains an additional 14g total fat (3g sat. fat), 170mg sodium, and 1g total carbohydrate (1g sugars).

** Percent Daily Values are based on a 2,000 calorie diet. Your daily values may be higher or lower depending on your calorie needs:

	Calories:	2,000	2,500
Total Fat	Less than	65g	80g
Sat. Fat	Less than	20g	25g
Cholest	Less than	300mg	300mg
Sodium	Less than	2,400mg	2,400mg
Total Carb		300g	375g
Fiber		25g	30g

INGREDIENTS: ENRICHED MACARONI (ENRICHED FLOUR [FLOUR, NIACIN, FERROUS SULFATE, THIAMINE MONONITRATE, RIBOFLAVIN]); CHEESE SAUCE MIX (WHEY, DEHYDRATED CHEESE [GRANULAR AND CHEDDAR (MILK, CHEESE CULTURE, SALT, ENZYMES)], WHEY PROTEIN CONCENTRATE, SKIM MILK, CONTAINS LESS THAN 2% OF SALT, BUTTERMILK, SODIUM TRIPOLYPHOSPHATE, SODIUM PHOSPHATE, CITRIC ACID, YELLOW 5, YELLOW 6, LACTIC ACID)

CHUNK LIGHT TUNA IN WATER

Nutrition Facts

Serv. Size 2 oz. drained
(56g / about ¼ cup)
Servings about 2.5

Calories 60
Fat Cal. 5

* Percent Daily Values (DV) are based on a 2,000 calorie diet.

Amount/Serving	%DV*	Amount/Serving	%DV*
Total Fat 0.5g	1%	**Total Carb.** 0g	0%
Sat. Fat 0g	0%	Fiber 0g	0%
Cholest. 30mg	10%	Sugars 0g	
Sodium 250mg	10%	**Protein** 13g	23%

Vitamin A 0% • Vitamin C 0% • Calcium 0% • Iron 2%
Niacin 20% • Vitamin B-6 8% • Vitamin B-12 20% • Phosphorus 8%

INGREDIENTS: LIGHT TUNA, WATER, VEGETABE BROTH, HYDROLYZED CASEIN, HYDROLYZED SOY PROTEIN, SALT.

Activity C Study the two food labels on page 91. On your paper, write the answers to the following questions.

1. What is the main ingredient in the macaroni?

2. What is the main ingredient in the can of tuna?

3. Which food has more calories per serving?

4. Which food has been enriched?

5. How many servings are in one can of tuna?

6. How many servings are in the macaroni and cheese?

7. Which food has more protein?

8. Which food has more fat?

9. What happens to the fat content when you use 2% milk to prepare the macaroni and cheese?

10. What percentage of the daily value of vitamin B-12 would you get from a serving of the tuna?

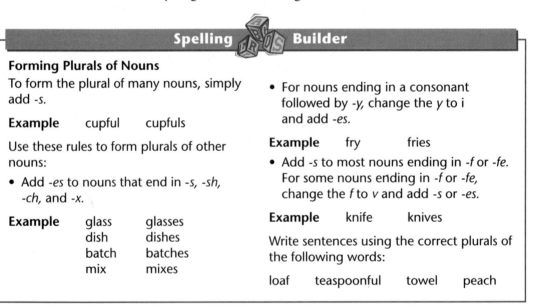

Spelling Builder

Forming Plurals of Nouns

To form the plural of many nouns, simply add -s.

Example   cupful   cupfuls

Use these rules to form plurals of other nouns:

• Add -es to nouns that end in -s, -sh, -ch, and -x.

Example   glass   glasses
                dish   dishes
                batch   batches
                mix   mixes

• For nouns ending in a consonant followed by -y, change the y to i and add -es.

Example   fry   fries

• Add -s to most nouns ending in -f or -fe. For some nouns ending in -f or -fe, change the f to v and add -s or -es.

Example   knife   knives

Write sentences using the correct plurals of the following words:

loaf   teaspoonful   towel   peach

Write the answers to these questions on your paper.

1. What types of containers do packaged foods come in?
2. What directions are on packages of food?
3. What advantage is there to eating frozen foods?
4. How is the order of ingredients listed on the package?
5. What kinds of information do food labels have?

Read the directions from the package of fish pieces. Then answer the questions that follow.

FISH BITES

Store in freezer at 0°F.
Keep frozen until ready to use. Do not refreeze.

Microwave: Place fish bites in a microwave-safe container. Place cover over container, but allow a space for steam to escape. Microwave on high for 5–7 minutes, or to desired doneness. Season to taste.

Oven: Preheat oven to 350°F. Arrange fish bites on cookie sheet so that pieces do not touch one another. Bake in oven for 10–15 minutes. Fish bites are done when batter is lightly browned.

Makes 4 servings.

6. Should you thaw the fish bites before you cook them?
7. What should you do when cooking the fish bites in the microwave?
8. Should you add more ingredients to the fish bites?
9. How long should you bake the fish bites?
10. How do you know when the fish bites are done?

How-to books

Reference books that provide detailed instructions for how to complete specific tasks

Do It Yourself with How-to Books

How-to books tell you how to do something. You probably can find a how-to book to help you do anything you want to do. Some subjects of how-to books include:

All About Rock Collecting	Be Your Own Lawyer
Learning to Play the Piano	How to Design and Make Your Own Skateboard
How to Run a Meeting	Getting Started in Car Repair
Pay Fewer Taxes—Legally!	Improve Your Spelling
Teach Yourself to Speak Russian	Easy Kitchen Remodeling

Many how-to books are available on CD-ROM. You also can find how-to information on the Internet. There are often photos, drawings, or diagrams that show you the steps involved in the process.

When searching on the Internet, you may have to sift through a large amount of information to find what you really need. How-to information is also available on videocassettes that you can get at the library or a video store.

Activity A Decide which of the following books probably tell you how to do something. Write their titles on your paper.

1. *Building a Go-Cart*

2. *Do-It-Yourself Tree Houses*

3. *Building a Model Car*

4. *The Purple Pumpkin*

5. *How to Care for Your Puppy*

Following Directions

A how-to book provides step-by-step instructions that explain how to do or make something. The book lists any materials that you will need to complete the task. Most of the time, the book will have photographs or drawings of the finished product.

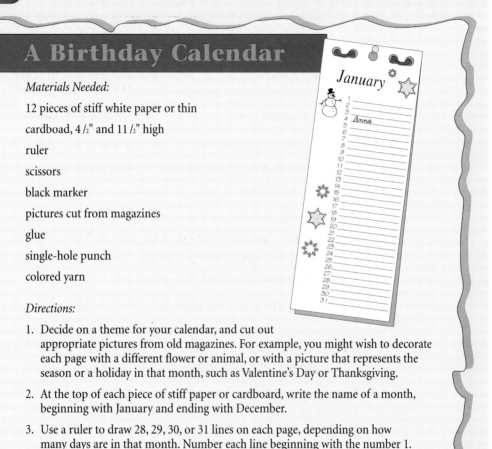

A Birthday Calendar

Materials Needed:

12 pieces of stiff white paper or thin cardboad, 4 1/2" and 11 1/2" high

ruler

scissors

black marker

pictures cut from magazines

glue

single-hole punch

colored yarn

Directions:

1. Decide on a theme for your calendar, and cut out appropriate pictures from old magazines. For example, you might wish to decorate each page with a different flower or animal, or with a picture that represents the season or a holiday in that month, such as Valentine's Day or Thanksgiving.

2. At the top of each piece of stiff paper or cardboard, write the name of a month, beginning with January and ending with December.

3. Use a ruler to draw 28, 29, 30, or 31 lines on each page, depending on how many days are in that month. Number each line beginning with the number 1. (See drawing)

4. Glue magazine pictures to each page, or draw pictures of your own.

5. Put the months in order. Then punch five holes at the top of each piece of paper. Use yarn to bind the pages together as shown in drawing.

6. Write the names of friends and relatives next to their birthdays.

7. Hang up calendar.

Activity B Use the directions on page 95 to answer these questions. Write your answers on your paper.

1. What materials do you need to make the calendar?
2. What are the different tools that you will need?
3. What will you need the tools for?
4. How many pieces of paper do you need? Why?
5. Why should you decide on a theme before beginning?

In some how-to books, writers give the directions in paragraph form rather than step-by-step list form. Within the directions, the writer mentions the materials you will need to complete a project.

Activity C Use these directions to answer the following questions. Write your answers on your paper.

Setting Up an Aquarium

People have set up aquariums for thousands of years. The first aquarium would be as old as the ancient pyramids. In America, raising tropical fish is one of the most popular hobbies.

You will need a fish tank, some lights, a heater and thermometer, a pump, and a filter. You will need some glass wool and charcoal for the filter. On the bottom, you will put some gravel. For cleaning the tank, get an algae scraper and a dip tube. A nylon fish net will be useful. Try some guppies for your first fish. They are very hardy.

1. What do the directions tell you how to do?
2. What materials will you need to buy or borrow to complete this project?
3. What instructions must you follow to complete this project? List the steps in order.
4. What are two ways that these directions are different from the directions on page 95?
5. Are there any suggestions in the directions?

Read the paragraph below. Then write on your paper the answers to the questions that follow.

Hanging a Mirror on a Door

If the door is very smooth, roughen it with sandpaper. Wear rubber gloves, and use a putty knife to spread rubber cement on the back of the mirror. *Be careful not to get the cement on your hands.* Put the cement about half an inch from the four edges. Press the mirror firmly on the door. Allow 24 hours for the cement to set.

1. What does the paragraph tell you how to do?
2. What materials will you need to complete this project?
3. What instructions must you follow to complete this project? List the steps in order.
4. Why would you put cement half an inch from the edges?
5. What do the directions caution against?

Follow the instructions below. Write your answers on your paper.

6. Name a project you have done in the past.
7. Make a drawing of the completed project.
8. Write a list of the materials you used.
9. Write the directions you followed in order.
10. List any cautions you followed.

A **magazine** is a paperback publication. It has stories and articles by several writers. It usually has illustrations and advertisements. **Periodical** is another name for a magazine. A periodical comes out at regular **intervals,** such as daily, weekly, or monthly. An interval is a space of time between events.

Some magazines are on CD-ROM. Many are also available from online computer services, including the Internet. If magazines are not available for reading online, then you often can subscribe to them online. You usually can search for articles in older issues of online magazines. Some online magazines are free, but many charge a fee.

Kinds of Magazines

There are hundreds of different kinds of magazines to choose from. Most magazines have stories and articles for people with special interests.

Magazine Categories		
Business and Finance	Fashion	News
	Gardening	Sports
Cooking and Food		
	Hobbies and Special Interest	Political
Computers		
		Entertainment

Digests

Most people don't have time to read a lot of magazines. That is why digests are so popular. A **digest** is a periodical that has summaries of articles from other magazines.

Many digests contain **condensed** articles from other publications. A condensed article is shortened but keeps the main ideas of the original.

Magazine

A paperback publication with stories and articles on a variety of topics by different writers

Periodical

A magazine published at regular intervals, such as daily, weekly, or monthly

Interval

The space of time between events

Digest

A magazine that contains summaries or condensed articles from other magazines

Condensed

A shorter version of an article but with the same main idea

Publish

To print and distribute magazines, books, newspapers, or other reading materials

Cycle

The period of time between events, such as the publishing of a magazine

Activity A Follow the directions below. Write your answers on your paper.

1. Write a list of all the magazines that you have read or know about. Visit the library or a newsstand to refresh your memory.

2. Next to each title, write the general subject of the magazine. Use the categories on page 96 as a guide.

3. Circle the categories of magazines you subscribe to or read regularly.

4. Share your list with your class.

5. Bring old issues of magazines to class to share if possible.

Publication Cycles

To **publish** means to print and distribute magazines, books, newspapers, or other materials. Most magazines are published monthly. A few magazines are weekly publications. Some are published less often. This is the publication **cycle.** A cycle is the period of time needed for a certain event to repeat itself.

Activity B Match each numbered word on the left with its correct meaning on the right. Write each word and its meaning on your paper. Use a dictionary to help you.

1. daily		**A**	twice a month
2. weekly		**B**	once a year
3. monthly		**C**	every day
4. annually		**D**	every week
5. bimonthly		**E**	once a month

Activity C Answer these questions on your paper. You may need to visit a library or newsstand to answer some of these questions.

1. Name a magazine that is published weekly.

2. Name a magazine that is published monthly.

3. What type of publication appears daily?

4. Name something published annually.

5. Give an example of a publication cycle.

How to Get a Magazine

You can get a magazine in several ways:

- You can read one at the library.
- You can buy one at a newsstand.
- You can subscribe to one.

When you subscribe to a magazine, you fill out an order form to have the magazine sent to you by mail. You may enclose the payment for the **subscription** with the order form, or you may choose to receive a bill later. The subscription rate is often lower than the newsstand rate.

Here is an example of a subscription order form.

Car Digest

One–year subscription (12 issues):	$15.00
Two–year subscription (24 issues):	$27.00

SAVE 30% OVER THE NEWSSTAND RATE!

☐ Payments enclosed. ☑ Bill me later.

Name _Chris Williams_

Address _31 E. Ralston Place_

City/State/Zip _Wilton, Delaware 19999_

Signature _Chris Williams_

Activity D Use the order form above to answer these questions. Write your answers on your paper.

1. How much does each issue of *Car Digest* cost with a one-year subscription?

2. How often is this magazine published?

3. Does the magazine cost less at the newsstand or by subscription?

4. Where might you get this magazine to read at no cost?

5. How much money will you save if you purchase a two-year subscription instead of a one-year subscription?

Finding Articles in Magazines

Look in the magazine's table of contents to find out what kinds of articles are in a magazine. The table of contents is usually near the front of the magazine. In some magazines, several pages of advertisements come before the table of contents. In other magazines, the table of contents appears on the cover.

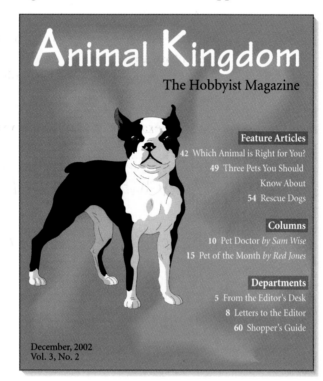

Animal Kingdom
The Hobbyist Magazine

Feature Articles
42 Which Animal is Right for You?
49 Three Pets You Should Know About
54 Rescue Dogs

Columns
10 Pet Doctor *by Sam Wise*
15 Pet of the Month *by Red Jones*

Departments
5 From the Editor's Desk
8 Letters to the Editor
60 Shopper's Guide

December, 2002
Vol. 3, No. 2

Using What You've Learned

Searching for Magazines
Write down three general topics in which you are interested, such as cars, music, or animals. Or, choose from the following topics: sharks, snowboarding, fashion, or mountain bikes.

Use a library's reference section to find a magazine article about each of your topics. Read all three articles, and decide which one would most interest your classmates. Write a one-paragraph summary of that article. Then read your summary to your class.

Activity E Use the sample magazine cover on page 101 to answer these questions. Write your answers on your paper.

1. What is the theme of this magazine?

2. Who is likely to read this magazine?

3. When was this issue of the magazine published?

4. How many feature articles are in this issue?

5. On what page do the letters to the editor begin?

Where To Find It

Finding Magazines on the Internet
Search for a magazine about a favorite topic on the Internet.

First, get online. When the homepage is on the computer screen, go to the search box. Type in key words to search for your subject and magazine. For example, suppose that you want to find a geography magazine. Type in the key words *geography AND magazine.* Be sure to capitalize the word *AND.* The results of your search will appear on your screen. Then, click on the specific magazine you want to sample, find out about, or subscribe to. Some magazines come only in printed form, but some magazines are online.

Some other key words you might want to search for are *auto mechanics AND magazine, careers AND magazine, fashion AND magazine, mountain bikes AND magazine,* and *cooking AND magazine.*

Lesson 8   R E V I E W

On your paper, write your answers to the following questions.

1. What is a periodical?
2. Where can you find electronic versions of magazines?
3. What are some different kinds of magazines? List at least three kinds. If necessary, look at the list on page 98.
4. What kind of periodical has summaries of articles from magazines?
5. Is an encyclopedia a periodical? Explain why or why not.
6. What is a condensed version of an article?
7. Why might someone want to read a condensed version of an original article?
8. Give three examples of a publication cycle.
9. What does it mean for a company to *publish* a magazine?
10. What is the most common interval for magazine publication?
11. Which magazine is published more often—a bimonthly or a monthly?
12. Where can you read magazines at no cost?
13. Which is usually less expensive—buying magazines at a newsstand or having a subscription?
14. Where in a magazine do you look to learn about its articles?
15. What key words would you type for an Internet search for a magazine about tropical fish?

Chapter 3 R E V I E W

Word Bank

atlas

condensed

encyclopedia

gazetteer

general
information
almanac

globe

grid map

how-to books

magazine

periodical

physical map

publish

road map

scale

subscription

Part A Write the missing words on your paper.

1. A _____ is the relationship between distances on the map and actual distances.

2. A _____ is a paperback publication with stories and articles on a variety of topics.

3. You look in a _____ for geographical place names.

4. When you _____, you print and distribute magazines, books, or newspapers.

5. A map with grid lines is a _____.

6. A model of the earth is a _____.

7. A shorter version of an article is _____.

8. Reference books with detailed instructions for completing specific tasks are _____.

9. A magazine published at regular intervals is a _____.

10. A _____ shows the roughness of the earth's surface.

11. A map that shows roads, highways, and towns is a _____.

12. A _____ contains facts and figures about many subjects from the previous year and from the past.

13. You have a _____ when you have a regular order for a magazine or newspaper.

14. A book of maps and geographical facts is an _____.

15. A _____ is a book or a set of books with articles and facts on many subjects.

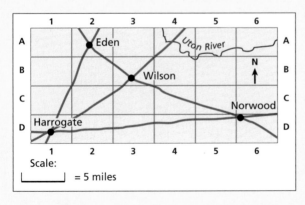

Scale:
⊢_____⊣ = 5 miles

Part B Use this map to answer the questions below.

16. Which city is southwest of Eden?

17. Which city is located at D-6?

18. How many miles is it from Wilson to Norwood?

Part C On your paper, write the answers to these questions.

19. An annual calendar of days, weeks, and months with weather predictions is a _____.

    A cycle   **B** magazine   **C** digest   **D** farmer's almanac

20. Which is a line that circles the center of the earth?

    A equator   **B** longitude line   **C** grid   **D** interval

21. Which type of map shows boundaries of states?

    A political   **B** product   **C** physical   **D** road

Part D On your paper, write the answers to the following questions.

22. Which type of map shows where goods are produced?

23. How do you find cross-references in online encyclopedias?

24. What key word would you use along with *recipes* for an Internet search for Italian recipes?

25. What would you look for on a cooking Web site if you needed to plan meals for the week?

26. How are ingredients listed on a food label?

27. Make up a title of a how-to book.

28. Which type of magazine is published most often—annual or bimonthly?

29. How are online magazines different from printed magazines?

30. Where could you look to find the population of a country?

Test-Taking Tip When studying for a test, you will remember facts and definitions more easily if you write them down on index cards. Practice with a partner, using these as flash cards.

Using the Telephone

What is the difference between a cellular phone and a traditional phone? What are calling cards, and how do they work? Whom do you call with questions about different telephone service providers and toll-free numbers? What is an International Access Code, and how do you use it? Much of this information appears in telephone books and online. Knowing how to use available information resources is a useful and important skill.

In Chapter 4, you will learn about telephones and where to find information about them. You will also learn about the sections of a telephone book, telephone billing options, and cell phones. Some lessons in this chapter deal with different sections of the phone book and some deal with telephone service providers and the services they offer, international calling, telephone bills, cellular phones, and phone cards.

Goals for Learning

◆ To recognize the different sections of a telephone book

◆ To learn how to find numbers in the White Pages of the telephone directory

◆ To learn how to use the Yellow Pages to find information

◆ To learn how to find numbers in the Blue Pages

◆ To learn about telephone service providers and bills

◆ To learn about cell phones and phone cards

Directory

A book that lists in alphabetical order names, addresses, and telephone numbers of people, businesses, and government agencies

White Pages

A part of the telephone book with residential and business listings arranged in alphabetical order

Resident

A person who lives in a certain place

Fee

A charge for a service

Another name for a telephone book is a telephone **directory.** A directory lists names, addresses, and telephone numbers of people, businesses, and government agencies. Names appear in alphabetical order. Most telephone companies publish new directories once a year. Directories are available online.

The White Pages

The **White Pages,** the main part of the telephone book, lists names, phone numbers, addresses of **residents,** businesses, and government agencies. A resident is a person who lives in a certain place. Residential listings appear alphabetically by last name. To find a person's telephone number you need to know his or her last name. Also, it helps to know a person's first name and address, because some people have the same last name.

EXAMPLE

SANDERS Norma 1121 Millstream Dr Earton	**555-0990**
George F 1221 Haworth Av Earton	**555-9876**
Wm H 1288 Juniper Earton	**555-9980**
William & Wilma 2100 So Main Lawton	**555-2101**
SANTORO Kay 2111 Key St Earton	**555-5601**

More About Telephone Listings

- More than one name may appear for a single telephone number. The telephone book's publisher may charge a **fee** to list additional names. A fee is a charge for a service.

- People may request an unlisted or unpublished telephone number. Their names and numbers do not appear in the telephone book. Usually, there is a fee for this service.

- The directory uses many abbreviations without punctuation.

EXAMPLE

Wm	= William	Jr	= Junior
St	= Saint	&	= and

• The directory lists names the way people want them listed.

EXAMPLE Henderson G Wm   Silva Enrique & Susana J

• A name listed with an initial comes before a first name that begins with the same letter.

EXAMPLE Harper A
Harper Abraham

• Some abbreviations follow alphabetical order as if they were spelled out. *St. John* appears in the list as if it were *Saint John.*

EXAMPLE Sacco Renato
St. John Alice
Samson Hilary

Alternative Spellings for Names

Some names have different, or **alternative,** spellings. An alternative offers a choice between two or more possibilities. If you cannot find a name, think of another way to spell the name. Then look up the alternative spelling. Alternative spellings usually have a cross reference.

EXAMPLE SCHWARZ . . . See Also Schwartz, Shwartz, Swartz

Activity A On your paper, write your answers to the following questions.

1. In what order would these names appear—Raymond Mong, Charles Mendes, Maria Mulkern?

2. Which name would appear first—Bob Hogan or B. Hogan?

3. What would be an alternative spelling for the name *Shwartz*?

4. Which last name would come first—St. Clair or Salzberg?

5. What are two ways you could list your name in the telephone book?

The Yellow Pages

The **Yellow Pages** is a classified telephone directory that lists businesses, **products,** and **services** for a city or town and its surrounding area. Products are goods that you can buy. Services are what businesses or individuals do for you. Business listings appear in alphabetical order by the type of business.

> **EXAMPLE** Products: Shoes, Windows, Guitars
> Services: Shoe Repair, Window Installation, Guitar Lessons

Activity B Number your paper from 1 to 5. Write whether the subject heading is a *product* or a *service*.

1. Travel Agents and Bureaus
2. Pianos—Tuning and Repair
3. Automobile Body Repairing
4. Pianos—New and Used
5. Dolls—Retail

To find a number in the Yellow Pages, you need to know only the type of business. Subject listings in the Yellow Pages are helpful because they list types of businesses alphabetically.

Activity C Use the sample Yellow Pages to answer these questions.

Accountants

A E Smith Accountants 18 Wilton Ave Tanner······ 555-2093

ANDERSON DAVID E
Fredrick Bldg Rt 4 ···················· **555-0578**

ARNOLD JACK & SYLVIA
Professional accountants
Ready to serve you
6 days a week 9 to 5
45 W 25th St Sky City ············· **555-6393**

1. What do A. E. Smith, David E. Anderson, and Jack and Sylvia Arnold have in common?

2. What information does the Arnold listing provide that the other two listings do not?

3. Write these three names as they would be listed in the White Pages.

4. What is A. E. Smith's address?

5. What is David E. Anderson's phone number?

Professional Listings

A **profession** is a job, or occupation, that requires special information and academic training. A **professional** is someone who works at a specific profession. Professionals provide a service to people.

Profession

A job that requires special information and academic training

Professional

Someone who works at a specific profession

EXAMPLE	Librarian	Veterinarian	Teacher
	Doctor	Lawyer	Pharmacist

Activity D What service does each of these professionals provide? Write your answer on your paper. You may use a dictionary for this activity.

1. architect

2. accountant

3. attorney

4. pharmacist

5. optometrist

More About Business Listings

Business listings in telephone directories vary in size, length, and style. Many are really advertisements. The larger the listing, the more money it costs to list it. If a business spends a lot of money on its listing, it does not necessarily provide better services.

- Businesses may have their listings highlighted in bold, in extra-large letters, or some other way. There is usually a fee for this service.

- In business listings, the apostrophe (') may be left out.

EXAMPLE	Roy Smythe's Plumbing Service
	Roy Smythes Plumbing Service

- Business names, such as radio stations, that begin with initials are listed at the beginning of each letter section.

EXAMPLE	**W**
	WNBD
	W & S Auto Painting
	Wilton Insurance

- If a business name begins with the word *the*, it appears in alphabetical order according to the first word after *the*.

EXAMPLE	Chan's Asian Market
	Chicken Corner, The

Blue Pages

Some telephone books have a separate section called the **Blue Pages.** The Blue Pages list government agencies.

GOVERNMENT OFFICES

GOVERNMENT – CITY		GOVERNMENT – COUNTY		GOVERNMENT – STATE	
GALESVILLE - CITY OF –		**GALES - COUNTY OF –**		Attorney General	800-555-9801
City Clerk's Office	555-7942	Aging, Department of	555-2222	Dept of Motor Vehicles	800-555-9900
Economic Development	555-6000	Toll Free	800-555-2222		
Fire Dept		Finance Department	555-9810	**GOVERNMENT – FEDERAL**	
Emergency calls Dial 9-1-1		Property Tax	555-1000	Environmental	
or	555-9865	Water & Sewer	555-1001	Protection Agency	202-555-2090
Mayor's Office	555-8740	Information	555-5000	Internal Revenue Service	202-555-1040
Police Dept	555-4000	Sheriff		Social Security Administration	
Crime Solvers	555-4002	Civil Court Process	555-3000	Toll Free	800-555-1213
Drug Hot Line	555-4001	Warrant	555-4000	Hearing Impaired—TDD Only	
Emergency calls Dial 9-1-1		Circuit Court	555-1600	Toll Free	800-555-0778
Public Information	555-6859	Domestic Relations	555-9000	Veterans Administration	800-555-1000

Activity E On your paper, write your answers to the following questions.

1. In which two sections could you find the number for Video Clips, a local video store?

2. Under what letter would you look to find the number for The Fancy Flounder Fish Market?

3. In what order would the business names below appear in the White Pages?

WDMS-AM 1500   WDMS-TV 5

The Jacksons' Sport Center   George Jones Office Supplies

W & A Clothing   Jackson's Plumbing Supplies

Use the sample Blue Pages above to answer these questions.

4. What number would you use to contact the Social Security Administration if you were hard of hearing?

5. What number should a person in Galesville call with information about a crime?

Use the information in the sample directory listings to answer the questions that follow. Write your answers on your paper.

VYSKOCIL Thomas A 58 Gale Pl Norwood	**555-8900**	**WILMINGTON Grace** atty	
Thomas J 4800 48th Pl Westport	**555-8765**	54 Rand Ter Westport	**555-9000**
		WINE A E MD	
W		15 Durham St Suite 10 Southview	**555-6000**
		Answering Service	**555-5609**
WAAS Anne Jones Rt 1 Norwood	**555-8700**	**Arnold Edward MD** 5601 56th Pl Westport	**555-6859**
WBQ TV REPAIR INC		**WINE & CHEESE SHOP** 48 Sand Ln Norwood	**555-4000**
54 Rand Ter Westport	**555-9005**	**Wine Insurance Co**	
WEBB Broadcasting Station		34 Water Blvd Southview	**555-7650**
5617 Webb Road Westport	**555-5600**		

1. What is the phone number of the attorney listed?

2. What is Dr. Wine's home phone number?

3. What number can you call if Dr. Wine is not home or in the office?

4. In which city is Dr. Wine located?

5. What is the last name of Thomas J of 4800 48th Place?

6. What is the profession of Grace Wilmington?

7. Why is WEBB listed after WBQ TV Repair?

8. Which business is located in Southview at 34 Water Blvd.?

9. What type of information appears in the Blue Pages?

10. How do subject listings help you find what you are looking for in the Yellow Pages?

Spelling Builder

Alternative Business Spellings

Some businesses use nonstandard spellings to get attention. These directory listings might be alphabetized according to nonstandard spellings. Read these examples:

Glo Nite Signs (for **Glow Night** Signs)

Aire-Flo Heating (for **Air Flow** Heating)

Tree-O Landscaping (for **Trio** Landscaping)

Write the standard spelling for the following alternative spellings.

1. Kat's Galore Pet Store
2. E-Z Lawn Mowers
3. Hi-Way Paving Company
4. X-Press Pizza
5. Kash-for-Karz Auto Dealer

If you are leaving a message for someone to return a phone call, be sure to include the area code, the phone number, and the caller's name. Also, include the date and time that you took the message.

Using Area Codes

Different parts of the United States have different area codes. Your area code appears in the front of your telephone directory. The directory also has a map that shows area codes for other parts of the United States and Canada. To call people outside your local calling area, you must dial their area code and their telephone number. In most places you must also dial "1" before the area code.

EXAMPLE

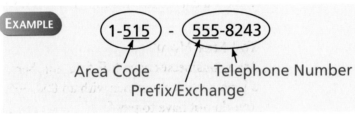

You may have to dial the area code to make some local calls. Check your directory to find out whether local calls require an area code.

Activity A On your paper, write answers to these questions.

1. Where does the area code directory appear in the telephone book?

2. How do you call someone who is not in your local calling area?

3. Which part of this telephone number is the area code— 1-284-555-7890?

4. What is your area code?

5. How could you find out whether you need to dial the area code to call towns or cities in your local calling area?

Directory Assistance

When you know someone's number, you can dial it directly. When you do not know the number, you can look for it in the directory. You may call Directory Assistance if the directory does not list the person or the business. If the number is new, Directory Assistance will give it to you. However, Directory Assistance will not give out an unlisted number.

Remember to dial 411 for Directory Assistance. You will need to know the city in which you're looking for a phone number. An operator will find the number that you need. There is usually a charge for this information service.

Toll-Free Numbers

Many businesses have **toll-free** numbers. A toll-free number is a long-distance number with an 800, 866, 877, or 888 area code. You do not have to pay for the call even though the call is long distance. The people you are calling pay for the call.

Toll-Free Numbers

- can help you get questions answer about a product or service

- can help you get more information about an advertisement

- help businesses attract customers

Activity B On your paper, write the answers to the following questions.

1. What are the area codes for toll-free numbers?

2. What is Directory Assistance?

3. What number do you call to find a new telephone number that does not appear in the directory?

4. Will Directory Assistance give out an unlisted number?

5. What is one reason you would use a toll-free number?

Toll Calls

You will be charged a fee when you make a **toll call.** Toll calls often have a phone number with a 900 or 976 area code. Usually, these numbers are used for entertainment purposes. Examples of these numbers are entertainment services, "chat" lines, or numbers that provide sports scores.

EXAMPLE   1-900-   555-1111

Area Code

Toll number fees are usually higher than long-distance fees. The charge might be a **flat fee.** A flat fee remains the same no matter how long you stay on the line. Otherwise, the call might carry a per-minute charge. Always listen carefully to any instructions at the beginning of the call. Usually, this type of fee will appear separately from local and long-distance charges on your monthly telephone bill.

International Calling

The telephone directory includes directions for making international calls. It also lists calling codes for countries and cities around the world. You may dial foreign countries directly if you know the number and the International Access Code, which connects you to an international line. In the United States, the International Access Code is 011.

EXAMPLE	International Access Code		Country Code		City Code	
Bombay	011	+	91	+	22	+ Local Number
Sao Paulo	011	+	55	+	11	+ Local Number

Calling Canada

To dial directly to Canada, dial "1," the area code, and then the telephone number. Canadian phone numbers do not include an International Access Code.

Dial foreign countries directly if you know the number.

Activity C On your paper, write the word that correctly completes each sentence.

1. A number that has the area code 888 is a _____.

2. "Chat" lines are _____ calls.

3. In order to dial a number in Canada, you must use a _____.

4. Dial _____ for Directory Assistance.

5. When calling a number in Europe or Asia, you must dial _____ before you dial the country code.

Where To Find It

Finding Area Codes and International Access Codes

You will find area codes and international access codes in the front of your local telephone directory. Directions in the telephone directory explain how to use these codes to make international calls.

Also, you can find these telephone codes on the Internet. First, get online. Then, think of a city or country you might call. Type the key words *area codes* or *international call codes* into a search engine.

The computer screen will display Web sites that provide these code numbers.

Choose one of the Web sites by clicking on it. Then, type the name of a city, state, or country. The area code or international code for that area will appear on your computer screen, along with directions for completing the call.

Then, check your local telephone directory, and add any new information that you have found online.

Lesson 2   R E V I E W

On your paper, write the word that correctly completes
each sentence.

1. Each part of the United States has a different area _____.

2. Your area code appears in the _____ of your telephone
   directory.

3. You may call _____ if you cannot find a phone number
   in the telephone directory.

4. Use the _____ when calling a foreign country.

On your paper, write the answers to these questions.

5. What is the difference between flat fees and per-minute
   charges?

6. Why is it important to listen to any instructions at the
   beginning of a toll call?

7. What numbers must you dial when making an
   international call?

8. What number do you dial for local information?

9. Where do you find calling codes for countries and cities
   around the world?

10. Which of the following would be a toll-free call?

    A a sports hotline   C an 800 number

    B a "chat" line   D an international call

Using What You've Learned

Create a personal phone book with
numbers that you call frequently. You may
want to include family members, friends,
doctors, and businesses. Write the names
in alphabetical order. It might be helpful
to include some phone numbers under
two different letters. For example, write
your doctor's phone number under "D"
for *doctor* and again under the first letter of
his or her last name. Include the area code
with each phone number. Make note of
any long-distance or toll-free numbers.
Include the numbers for directory
assistance and local emergency numbers.

> **Telephone service provider**
>
> *Company that provides telephone service to homes and businesses*

A **telephone service provider** supplies telephone service to homes and businesses. Most areas of North America offer a choice of telephone service providers. You can check with your local Better Business Bureau, ask friends and neighbors, or go online to find a reliable provider. An example of an online search for a telephone service provider with the first two results appears below.

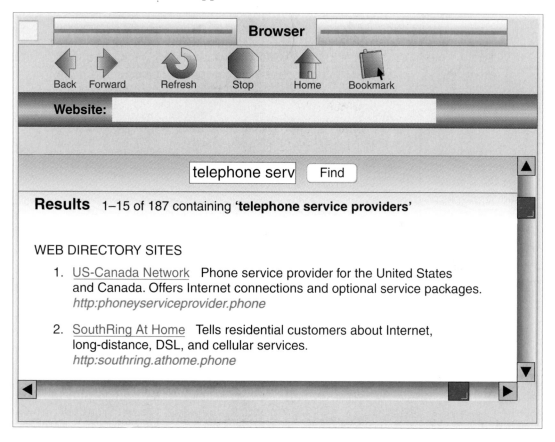

Browser

Back   Forward   Refresh   Stop   Home   Bookmark

Website:

telephone serv   [Find]

Results 1–15 of 187 containing '**telephone service providers**'

WEB DIRECTORY SITES

1. US-Canada Network   Phone service provider for the United States and Canada. Offers Internet connections and optional service packages.
   http:phoneyserviceprovider.phone

2. SouthRing At Home   Tells residential customers about Internet, long-distance, DSL, and cellular services.
   http:southring.athome.phone

Local and Long-Distance Providers

Some telephone service providers offer either local or long-distance telephone service. Some companies provide both services. You may choose the same telephone service provider for both local and long distance if the company provides both services. Also, you may choose different companies for these services, depending on the type of service you need. Different companies charge different fees for their services. You might save money by choosing different local and long-distance providers.

Activity A On your paper, write the answers to the following questions.

1. What is a telephone service provider?
2. How can you find a telephone service provider in your area?
3. What key words would you use to search for a telephone service provider on the Internet?
4. Do some telephone service providers offer both local and long-distance service?
5. Why might you choose different telephone service providers for local and long-distance service?

Basic and Optional Telephone Services

Most telephone service providers offer both basic and optional services. **Basic telephone service** is the least costly. It simply connects your phone to other phones so that you can make and receive calls. If you want more services, you may choose **optional telephone services.** Optional telephone services are additional telephone functions such as call waiting and caller ID. You can read about the options that your current telephone service provider offers by looking in the front of your phone directory or by calling your telephone company. For example, most telephone service providers offer special services for people who are hard of hearing. The chart on page 121 shows some of the most common optional telephone services.

Optional Telephone Services	
Automatic callback	Calls back last incoming call
Voice mail	Takes recorded messages of incoming calls
Caller ID	Shows name and phone number of person calling you
Call waiting	Tells you when you are speaking on the telephone that you have another call
Enhanced repeat dialing	Redials busy phone numbers
Call forwarding	Allows you to send a recorded call from one phone to another
Internet and DSL lines	Connects your computer to the Internet and provides faster Internet access

Activity B On your paper, write answers to the following questions.

1. What is basic telephone service?

2. How might you save money when choosing telephone providers?

3. What does caller ID do?

4. How can you find out what optional telephone services your provider offers?

5. What does call forwarding do?

Telephone Bills

Telephone service providers charge fees for their services. Long-distance calls usually cost more than local calls. Long-distance calls are **itemized,** or listed one by one, on a separate page of the telephone bill. A bill is a request for payment of services.

```
                    CHARLES LEVINE            SEP 24,2004
                    ACCT (701)555-1234


     FROM LAST BILL
        $30.33 LAST BILL
        -30.33 PAYMENTS
           .00 THANK YOU FOR YOUR PAYMENT


     CURRENT CHARGES
        $25.76 LOCAL TELEPHONE CHARGES
         2.68 ITEMIZED CHARGES
         1.79 TAXES/MISC. CHARGES
        $30.23 TOTAL PAY BY OCT 24


        To Call the Business Office Dial (701) 555-3000
```

Activity C Use the sample telephone bill above to answer these questions. Write your answers on your paper.

1. What is Mr. Levine's telephone number?

2. What number should he call if he has questions about the charges on his bill?

3. How much does Mr. Levine owe this month?

4. How much were the long-distance charges?

5. How much were the local charges?

6. How much were the taxes?

7. What is the date of the bill?

8. How much was Mr. Levine's bill last month?

9. Does he still owe money for last month?

10. By what date does he have to pay this bill?

Lesson 3 REVIEW

On your paper, write the word or words that correctly complete each sentence.

1. A _____ offers telephone service to homes.

2. _____ redials busy phone numbers.

3. _____ telephone service usually costs more than basic phone service.

4. Long-distance calls usually cost more than _____ calls.

5. You can find a telephone service provider on the _____ .

Read the following questions. On your paper, write your answers.

6. How do optional telephone services differ from basic services?

7. Name three optional services.

8. What calls are itemized on a telephone bill?

9. What does voice mail do?

10. What does call waiting do?

Vocabulary Builder

Telephone "Tech Talk"

Being familiar with some of today's "tech talk" can help you use new technology. The word *tech* is short for *technology.*

Modem: a device that connects a computer to a telephone line. *The **modem** connected me quickly to the Internet.*

Fax: short for facsimile, a document sent from one machine to a machine at another location through telephone lines, radio waves, or satellite. *I sent her a long **fax.***

Cordless: telephone without a cord and operated by battery. *I walked around the house with a **cordless** phone.*

Complete the following sentences using the "tech talk" words listed above.

1. The _____ machine received a new document through the telephone line.

2. She needed batteries for her _____ phone.

3. My computer was connected to a telephone line by a _____ .

Cellular phone

Telephone operated by radio waves rather than telephone lines or electric wires

Today, **cellular phones** and phone cards offer additional options to telephone users. People want to communicate with others wherever they go. Whether they are at a sports event, in a car, or walking down the street, people can easily "stay connected."

Cellular Phones

Cellular, or cell, phones are telephones that work by using radio waves instead of lines or wires. You can receive or make calls on a cell phone. A cell phone is not connected to a telephone line. You can carry a cell phone with you wherever you go.

Companies that offer cell phone service own cell phone towers. These towers send invisible radio waves between cell phones.

Cell Phones	
Benefits	**Drawbacks**
small	may not work in some areas
easy to carry	need to recharge batteries
useful in an emergency	may cost more than basic phone service

Your telephone service provider's basic or optional service does not cover the use of a cell phone.

Cell phones are small and can be taken almost anywhere.

Activity A On your paper, write B for *benefit* or D for *drawback* for each cell phone statement below.

1. Cell phones are small.

2. Cell phones require batteries.

3. Cell phones are easy to carry.

4. You can use a cell phone in an emergency.

5. Cell phones do not work in all areas.

Cell Phone Plans

Cell phone companies offer different billing options and plans. Some users want only basic service. Some users want special options and discounts if they make calls during certain hours.

Cell phone companies usually bill calls by the minute. However, some plans offer unlimited calls for a flat monthly fee. Usually, calls made from 6:00 A.M. to 6:00 P.M. cost more per minute. These are heavy-use hours. Users can save money by making calls during the evening hours and on weekends. Also, many cell phone companies offer discounted long-distance rates.

Cell Phone Options

Most cell phone companies offer the same options that home and business telephone users have. Voice mail, call waiting, caller ID, and call forwarding are a few of these options. Itemized bills are another option. Some cell phone companies may not itemize bills. Users who want the option pay a fee.

Activity B On your paper, write the word that completes each sentence correctly.

1. Cell phone companies usually bill calls by the _____ .

2. You can save money by calling on weekends or during _____ hours.

3. Cell phone companies offer _____ , like voice mail and caller ID.

4. Some plans offer unlimited calls for a flat _____ fee.

5. Cell phone companies may offer _____ long-distance rates.

Phone Cards

Phone cards and calling cards are convenient phone services. These cards are small plastic cards that provide long-distance service. The instructions on the back of the card tell you how to dial from any telephone. You do not need to call from your home phone when using a phone or calling card. You usually pay less for long distance than you would if you paid with cash or a credit card at a pay phone. Phone and calling cards are also useful when you travel.

Phone Cards	Calling Cards
prepaid	not prepaid
buy at most stores	buy from telephone service providers
often costs less for long-distance	cost of calls appears on monthly bills

Activity C Answer the following questions. Write your answer on your paper.

1. When do people generally use phone or calling cards?

2. Where can you find directions for how to use these cards?

3. What is one difference between a phone card and a calling card?

4. Where can you get a phone card?

5. How do users pay for calls with a calling card?

Lesson 4   R E V I E W

On your paper, write answers for the following questions.

1. How is a cellular phone different from a regular phone?
2. What kinds of calls can you make with a prepaid phone card?
3. What do cell phone towers do?
4. Where can you purchase a phone card?
5. What are two benefits of cell phones?
6. What are three optional features a cell phone may have?
7. What is one drawback of cell phones?
8. What is a phone card?
9. What time is using a cell phone usually the most costly?
10. Where can you buy a calling card?

Chapter 4   R E V I E W

Word Bank

alternative

basic telephone service

Blue Pages

cellular phone

fee

flat fee

International Access Code

itemized

optional telephone services

phone card

products

profession

professional

resident

service

toll-free

toll call

telephone service provider

White Pages

Yellow Pages

Part A Write the missing word on your paper.

1. A telephone operated by radio waves is a _____ .
2. Companies that provide telephone service to homes and businesses are _____ .
3. A _____ is what businesses or individuals can do for you.
4. The _____ lists residential and business numbers.
5. _____ are goods that you can buy.
6. The _____ lists phone numbers of government agencies.
7. Additional telephone functions beyond basic service are _____ .
8. _____ means "listed one by one."
9. A person who lives in a certain place is a _____ .
10. Telephone service that connects one phone to other phones is _____ .
11. A _____ gives you prepaid telephone calls.
12. A _____ is a charge for service.
13. A _____ number has an 800 or 888 area code and is free to the caller.
14. Someone who works at a specific profession is a _____ .
15. A _____ is a job that requires special information and training.
16. The _____ lists businesses, products, and services.
17. A choice between two or more possibilities is an _____ .
18. A _____ is the same amount no matter how long you stay on the telephone.
19. A call to a 900 number is a _____.
20. The _____ connects you to an international line.

Part B Use the sample directory page below to answer the following questions. Answer in complete sentences.

D'ZMURA T 15 Eaton Ln Denton 555-4321	**EDGE Wm C** 80 W St Jackson 555-0837
DZWONCHYK Martha Rt 4 Selby 555-7654	**EDGERION John & Susan** 24 Tulip Dr Denton .. 555-3410
E	**EDISON M K MD** 3 Howard Plaza Selby 555-5400
	If no answer call 555-1740
EJ's Pizza Rt 4 Selby 555-8700	**EDISON Inc. contractors**
E Smith Inc 601 Rouse Way Jackson 555-0837	140 Town Hwy Jackson 555-9090
EDDY R Frank 39 Wither Av Denton 555-0426	**EDWARDS C Attorney** 4 Howard Plaza Selby 555-4000

21. What is M. K. Edison's profession? How can you tell?

22. What is the number of EJ's pizza.

23. Which of these listings might appear in the Yellow Pages?

Part C Write the correct answer on your paper.

24. Why do many businesses have toll-free numbers?

    A They want to charge you later.

    B They are required by law.

    C Businesses do not have to pay for them.

    D The toll-free number encourages people to call them.

25. Why does basic telephone service cost less?

    A Basic telephone service is more popular.

    B Basic telephone service has fewer features.

    C Basic telephone service does not itemize bills.

    D Basic telephone service is less reliable.

Test-Taking Tip Make sure you have the same number of answers on your paper as there are items on the test.

5 Using a Library

The library is a good place to look for information. Nowhere else is so much information on so many different subjects in one place. At first glance, you may think that the library is too big and has too much information. How will you ever find what you are looking for? All libraries, big and small, follow a similar plan for arranging books and other resources. You can understand that plan. It will help you find the information you are looking for.

In Chapter 5, you will learn about libraries. You will understand the kinds of resources libraries have. You will learn how those resources are organized. You will learn how to find the information you need.

Goals for Learning

◆ To learn how to find information in a library

◆ To learn about the types of materials available in a library

◆ To learn to recognize and find fiction materials

◆ To learn how to find nonfiction books using the Dewey Decimal System

When people think about libraries, they usually think about books. Today, however, libraries have a wide variety of audiovisual materials and equipment as well as print materials. Because of this, some libraries today are called media centers.

Print Materials in a Library

Here are some of the print materials you will find in most libraries.

Libraries are investing in CD-ROMs, DVDs, and other electronic sources that take up less shelf space than books do. They also weigh little and last longer than paper materials.

Hardback books	Books in hardcover include fiction and nonfiction. You can check out most of these books.
Paperback books	Most libraries have collections of paperback, or softcover, books that you can check out.
Reference books	The reference section has encyclopedias, atlases, and other books. You usually cannot check out these books. You must use these books in the library.
Magazines	Libraries subscribe to many kinds of magazines. The most recent issues usually are displayed on a rack. Libraries keep old issues on separate shelves. You often have to ask the librarian to get them for you.
Newspapers	Most libraries subscribe to all the local newspapers. Some get newspapers from other cities. The library keeps old issues on file. Ask your librarian for help.
Telephone books	You can find local telephone books in your library. Some libraries have copies of telephone books from other cities.
Guides	Libraries have many kinds of guides and handbooks. You can look in guides to colleges and vocational schools to find out about their programs and requirements.

Activity A What kind of print material would you look for in the library for each situation? Write your answers on your paper.

1. You need the number of a service to help you move to a new city.

2. You plan to go to the community college in the fall and want to know whether it offers courses in electronics.

3. You want to read an article in last February's *Car Times*.

4. You want to find a part-time job.

5. You want to look at a map of Canada.

Audiovisual Materials in a Library

Here are some of the audiovisual materials that you will find in most libraries.

Videotapes	Videotape cassettes store movies, nonfiction documentaries, training programs, or other productions on tape. Videotapes are played on VCRs.
Compact discs (CDs) and CD-ROMs	CDs store music. CD-ROMs store computer information. (ROM stands for "Read Only Memory.") One CD-ROM can hold an entire encyclopedia with color photographs, video, sound, and text. You need a computer with a CD-ROM drive to access information on a CD-ROM.
Digital Video Discs (DVDs)	DVDs are similar to CDs, but they have much more storage space. To view a DVD, you need a DVD player.
Other materials	Libraries also may have other items. These may include copy machines, personal computers and software, VCRs, DVD players, televisions, filmstrips, audiocassettes, and vinyl records. Ask the librarian for available resources.

Other Libraries

To borrow books from a public library, you usually need a library card. In some cities and towns, you must be a resident to get a library card. In other places, you only must be a resident of the state. You can get a library card by filling out a simple application. The library may ask you for your Social Security number, your driver's license, or some other form of identification. If you do not have one of these, you may need an adult who already has a card to sponsor you.

In most places, the city or county government operates the local public library. Depending on where you live, your county library may have one **branch** or many branches. A branch is one of the libraries in a system. If your library is part of a system, you can use your card to borrow books and other materials from any of the branches in the system.

Students find libraries useful for doing research and studying for classes.

Finding Material in a Library

Libraries have thousands of different books and other materials. To make these materials easy to find, libraries list them in **catalogs.** Here are some kinds of catalogs in a library.

Library catalog	A **library catalog** lists most of the materials in a library. It may list the materials on index cards, it may store them on a computer, or it may list them on **microfiche.** Microfiche contains large amounts of reduced information on film. The materials may include fiction and nonfiction books, videotapes, CD-ROMs, and other types of materials. There are three types of listings: title, author, and subject.
Magazine catalog	A **magazine catalog** lists all the magazines a library subscribes to. It identifies the issues the library has.
Newspapers	A library has a list of the newspapers it subscribes to and all of the old issues it has. It may store old issues of some newspapers on microfilm or microfiche.
Audiovisual catalog	An **audiovisual catalog** lists by title or subject all the films, catalog videotapes, CD-ROMs, and DVDs that a library owns.

Activity B For each item, decide which catalog each person should look at. On your paper, write your answers.

1. Ramon wants to find a nonfiction book about volcanoes.

2. Chan wants to know whether the library has a copy of the December 1994 issue of *Personal Computing.*

3. Beth wants to know whether the library has the movie *City Kids.*

4. Mr. Miller wants to know whether the library has any books of Jack London's short stories.

5. Haimi would like to read an article in the sports section of the September 25, 1995, issue of the *Fieldstone Daily News.*

Electronic Library Resources

Database

A large collection of information stored for quick research

Many libraries have electronic **databases.** A database is a large collection of information that you can access quickly through the computer. You often can read the entire text online.

You can use all of the library's databases at the library. You can usually view some of the collections from a home or a school computer. To get information from a library's electronic database, type in your library card number. Then you can choose from a variety of sources that may include the following:

Periodicals	Electronic issues of local newspapers, newspapers from specific regions of the United States, special newspapers for students, magazines
Encyclopedias	Large electronic encyclopedias
Auto Repair Information	Information about car and truck upkeep
Health Information	Updated information in electronic books, information about health providers, expert advice to your questions

Using What You've Learned

Electronic Library Sources

Use a library computer to find a local or national newspaper database. Sometimes library Web pages have small icons, or pictures, of the different databases that you can click on to read. If not, search for the newspaper database by either typing the name of the newspaper or searching for it on the Web page. Then, search the newspaper database to find the following:

1. the name of a comic strip that appears in that newspaper
2. the title of an article about a recent sporting event
3. information about an upcoming concert
4. the name of famous person in the news
5. two job listings that interest you

On your paper, write the answers to these items.

1. Because of the kinds of materials they have, what are libraries sometimes called today?

2. Name at least two types of print materials other than books that you would find in most libraries.

3. Name two types of audiovisual materials that many libraries have today.

4. Name two other kinds of equipment that you might find in a library.

5. What is the name for lists of materials in libraries?

For each of the following items, decide what kind of material each person should look for at the library. On your paper, write your answers.

6. Sean wants the telephone number of an organization in another city.

7. Ben wants to listen to music by Mozart.

8. Feng would like to watch her favorite movie.

9. Ossie needs extra help learning Spanish. It would help if he could hear the correct pronunciation of words.

10. Juan wants to know the entrance requirements at the local community college.

11. Jana is interested in finding out about a major earthquake that occurred a year ago.

12. Tim would like information about how to fix his truck.

13. Angela wants stories that her whole family can enjoy on their car trip this summer.

14. Wyatt needs to find an article in his local newspaper from two weeks ago.

15. Carolina would like to watch an aerobics workout.

Fiction

An imaginary story

Nonfiction

Based on facts

Novel

A long, complex story

Short story

A story that usually can be read in one sitting

Biography

A nonfiction book about a real person that someone else writes

Dialogue

Conversation

Autobiography

A story of a real person's life written by that person

Biographical novel

A fictional account of a real person's life

History book

A nonfiction book about real people and events of the past

Historical novel

A fictional story about real people and events

Fiction is an imaginary story. **Nonfiction** is based on facts.

Novels and **short stories** are two kinds of fiction. A novel is a long story with many characters and events. Usually, the story has several twists and turns before the final outcome. Most novels are several hundred pages long. Others have fewer than 100 pages. People sometimes call short novels *novellas*.

A **short story** may be only one or two pages long. It also may be as long as 20 or 30 pages. Magazines may contain short stories. You also may find collections of short stories in a book. Literature textbooks often have short stories.

Most fiction is about imaginary people and events. Sometimes, however, authors include real people and events in their stories. They might use people's actual words. Sometimes authors make up people's words. Authors also combine facts and imagination to write about events.

Here are five kinds of fiction and nonfiction books.

Biography	A **biography** is a book about a real person that someone else writes. All of the events actually happened. If there is **dialogue,** or conversation, it is the people's exact words.
Autobiography	An **autobiography** is a story that a real person writes about himself or herself.
Biographical novel	A **biographical novel** is a story about a real person. The author adds imaginary dialogue and imaginary events.
History book	A **history book** is nonfiction about real people and events of the past.
Historical novel	A **historical novel** is a story about real people and events. The author adds imaginary dialogue and events.

If you are not sure whether a book is fiction or nonfiction, do the following:

- Look for the word *novel* or *short story* on the cover or on the title page.
- Check to see whether the book is marked with an *F* or *FIC* for fiction. If it is, the library stores it in the fiction section.

Activity A Make two columns on your paper. Write *Fiction* at the top of one column and *Nonfiction* at the top of the other. Look over the five kinds of books described on page 138. List them in the correct columns. Next to each type of book, write a title of a real book that is an example of that type. You may need to go to your school library to complete this activity.

How Libraries Arrange Fiction Books

All libraries arrange fiction books in alphabetical order according to the authors' last names. Some authors have written many books. Libraries group these books together and arrange them in alphabetical order by title. The words *the, a,* and *an* are not used to alphabetize titles.

> **EXAMPLE** These books by John Steinbeck would appear in the following order:
> *Cannery Row*
> *The Grapes of Wrath*
> *Of Mice and Men*
> *The Red Pony*

If two authors share the same last name, the library arranges their books in alphabetical order according to the authors' first names.

> **EXAMPLE** *The Count of Monte Cristo* by Alexandre Dumas
> *Jonoah and the Green Stone* by Henry Dumas

Some libraries group certain types of fiction books together. For example, they might put all the mystery books in one section. They might put all the science fiction books in another section. As with other fiction books, these books will be arranged in alphabetical order. The order will be according to the authors' last names within that section.

Activity B Arrange these fiction books in the order that they would appear on a shelf in a library. On your paper, write the books in order.

1. *The Outsiders* by S. E. Hinton
2. *White Fang* by Jack London
3. *Hawaii* by James Michener
4. *The Pigman* by Paul Zindel
5. *Seventeenth Summer* by Maureen Daly
6. *Call of the Wild* by Jack London
7. *Huckleberry Finn* by Mark Twain
8. *Wuthering Heights* by Emily Brontë
9. *Jane Eyre* by Charlotte Brontë
10. *Treasure Island* by Robert Louis Stevenson
11. *Watership Down* by Richard Adams
12. *Mowgli's Brothers* by Rudyard Kipling
13. *The Wrestling Match* by Rudyard Kipling
14. *The Dog of Pompeii* by Louis Untermeyer
15. *Kidnapped* by Robert Louis Stevenson

Finding a Fiction Book in a Library

Finding a fiction book in the library can be easy if you remember the following guidelines:

- To find a fiction book on the library shelf, you need to know the author's last name and the title of the book.

- To find a fiction book when you know the title but not the author's name, use the library catalog. The library catalog has records for each book. Each book has an author record and a title record. Some fiction books have subject records. If you look up the title or the subject of the book, you will find the author's name.

- If you search for a book on a computer catalog, type the author's name, the title, or the subject. The computer catalog will list all of the books by that author that the library has. It also will list the books that have that title or are about that subject.

Activity **C** Decide whether you would look up the title record, author record, or subject record for each item in the library catalog. On your paper, write *A* for author, *T* for title, or *S* for subject.

1. *Gone With the Wind*
2. Margaret Mitchell
3. the Civil War
4. *Huckleberry Finn*
5. Mark Twain
6. adventure and adventurers
7. sailing
8. *Treasure Island*
9. Robert Louis Stevenson
10. ocean travel

What is a nonfiction book?

A nonfiction book is about real people, real events, facts, or people's ideas.

How can I recognize a nonfiction book?

Nonfiction books often have a reference list or **bibliography.** These are the books and articles the author consulted when writing the book. Look for these references in the back of the book.

Nonfiction books often have indexes. An index is an alphabetical list of the topics included in the book. Look at the index at the end of this book.

In a library, a nonfiction book has a number on the binding. The first one or two letters of the author's last name are under the number.

Biographies and travel books are examples of nonfiction.

Lesson 2   R E V I E W

On your paper, write the answers to the following questions.

1. Here are some famous fiction stories. Are they novels or short stories?
   A "The Tell-Tale Heart" by Edgar Allan Poe (9 pages)
   B *20,000 Leagues Under the Sea* by Jules Verne (447 pages)
   C "The Most Dangerous Game" by Richard Connell (13 pages)

2. Write the following book titles in the order that they would appear on a shelf in the fiction section of the library.
   The Kitchen God's Wife by Amy Tan
   The Grapes of Wrath by John Steinbeck
   The Joy Luck Club by Amy Tan
   Ceremony by Leslie Marmon Silko

3. What do you need to know to find a fiction book on a library shelf?

4. How can you find a fiction book when you know the title, but you don't know the author's name?

Match each type of book with its description. On your paper, write the item number and the matching letter.

5. History

6. Biography

7. Biographical novel

8. Autobiography

A a book that someone writes about his or her life

B a book about a real person that someone else writes

C a fictional story about a real person

D a book about real people and events of the past

On your paper, write the answers to the following questions.

9. What is a nonfiction book?

10. What is a bibliography?

Dewey Decimal System

A system that libraries use to classify and organize books

Call number

The numbers and letters assigned to a library book—they determine where the book will be placed on the shelf

Who was Dewey?

Melvil Dewey was a librarian who lived from 1851 to 1931. In 1876, he invented a system for arranging books in a library. Today, we know this system as the **Dewey Decimal System.** Dewey also started the first school for training librarians. He taught his system to his students.

What is a decimal system?

Decimals are based on the number ten. Dewey divided the information in books into ten main subject areas. He used the numbers from 000 to 999 to cover the fields of general knowledge. He used decimals and letters to fit special subjects within each group. The **call number** on the spine of a book shows these numbers and letters.

Each book has three numbers before the decimal point. It may have several numbers after the decimal point. Libraries alphabetize books by the author's last name when they share the same number.

Melvil Dewey invented the Dewey Decimal System in 1876.

Nonfiction Books and the Dewey Decimal System

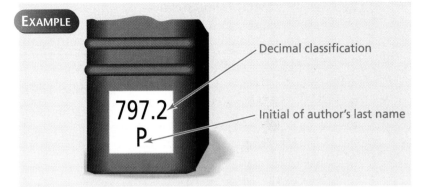

EXAMPLE

Decimal classification

797.2
P

Initial of author's last name

Writing Tip

After you find the nonfiction book in the library catalog, write the book's title, author, and call number on a slip of paper. Check the information on this paper as you locate the book on the shelves.

How can the Dewey Decimal System help me?

To find a book in the library catalog, use one of these three things:

- the title
- the author's name
- the subject

The record in the catalog gives the Dewey Decimal numbers, or call number. Suppose that a book has the call number 797.2/P. First find the 700 shelves in the nonfiction section of the library. Skim the shelves, looking for the 790s. Then find the books with 797.2. Finally, look for the books with the letter P.

What if the book I want isn't there?

All of the books with the same number are about the same subject. If you know the number that matches your subject, you can find other books on that subject.

Do I need to memorize the whole Dewey Decimal System?

Because the call numbers are on the catalog records, it is not necessary to memorize the numbers. However, it is helpful to know the system's ten main groups.

What are the ten main categories of the Dewey Decimal System?

Numbers	Subjects and Subtopics
000–099	General Works *Encyclopedias, periodicals, library facts*
100–199	Philosophy and Psychology *Logic, mental health*
200–299	Religion *Mythology*
300–399	Social Sciences *Government, education, economics*
400–499	Language *Dictionaries, foreign languages, grammar*
500–599	Pure Sciences *Biology, mathematics, botany, chemistry*
600–699	Technology (Applied Sciences) *Engineering, aviation, home economics*
700–799	Arts and Recreation *Fine art, music, sports, architecture*
800–899	Literature *Poetry, plays, speeches, humor*
900–999	History and Geography *Travel, biography*

How are main topics divided?

The Dewey Decimal System divides each main topic into subtopics.

EXAMPLE	Arts and Recreation	700–799	700–709	General Arts
			710–719	Landscape Art
			720–729	Architecture

How do libraries arrange nonfiction books on the shelf?

Libraries arrange books by number first. Then they put books in order by the author's last name. Study these examples closely:

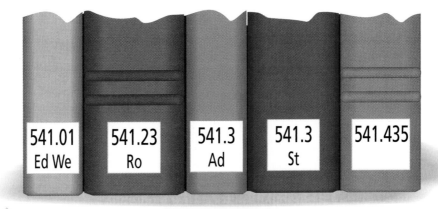

The same book can have different call numbers in different libraries that use the Dewey Decimal System. For example, librarians at different libraries might put the same book into different categories. A librarian might classify a book with the title *Historical Homes* under "History and Geography" in one library and under "Arts and Recreation" in another.

Are there any exceptions to the Dewey Decimal System that I should know about?

The purpose of the system is to help people find books. With biographies, you are more interested in the subject than in the author. The Dewey Decimal System arranges biographies alphabetically according to the person whom the book is about. For example, *My Life* by Golda Meir, an autobiography, would come before *Adlai Stevenson of Illinois* by John Bartlow Martin. Alphabetically, Meir comes before Stevenson.

Activity A Write the main topic heading and numbers of the Dewey Decimal System for each type of book listed below. On your paper, write your answers.

1. Greek mythology
2. Computer science
3. Southwest United States
4. Poetry
5. Sports
6. Mental health care
7. Library science
8. English grammar
9. Advanced math
10. Education in the United States

Activity B Use the facts on pages 144–147 to answer these questions. On your paper, write your answers.

1. Who invented the system that most libraries use to arrange books?

2. Will you find the letter *N* or a call number first on nonfiction books at the library?

3. You need to know at least one of three things to find a nonfiction book in the library catalog. What are these three things?

4. You see the number 920 on a book. What subject is it about?

   A Psychology   **B** Biology   **C** Biography   **D** Religion

5. In which category would you expect to find an encyclopedia?

   A Pure Sciences   **C** History

   B General Works   **D** Social Sciences

6. What is the purpose of the Dewey Decimal System?

7. You want to read *The Babe Ruth Story* by Howard Smith. Should you look for Smith or Ruth alphabetically on the shelf?

8. What are the numbers of the category for a book about early airplanes and aviation?

9. What are the numbers of the category for a book about music of the 1950s?

10. Which of these books would come first on the shelf?

The Dewey Decimal System
- Main Headings -

000–099	General Works
100–199	Philosophy and Psychology
200–299	Religion
300–399	Social Sciences
400–499	Language
500–599	Pure Sciences
600–699	Applied Sciences
700–799	Arts and Recreation
800–899	Literature
900–999	History and Geography

On your paper, write the main heading and numbers that would be used to classify a book on each of the subjects listed below. Use the information on the left and on page 146.

Example   A book about the Spanish language—
Language, 400s

1. A math book
2. A poetry book
3. Shakespeare's play
4. Childhood of Martin Luther King, Jr.
5. Psychology
6. An atlas
7. A book about the Dewey Decimal System
8. A cookbook
9. How to build a ship
10. Famous paintings
11. Football rules
12. How to build a computer
13. Traveling in Europe
14. O. Henry's short stories
15. Life story of Hank Aaron
16. Growing vegetables
17. A geometry book
18. *Life Skills English*
19. *World Almanac*
20. A dictionary

Spelling Builder

Computer Catalog Searches

Some libraries allow you to type only a few words of the title or a few letters of the author's last name when you search for an author or a title. The search result may list several matches. You then can read through the list to find the item you want.

However, when doing a subject search, be aware that you might get more results if you spell out more information, such as the word ending -s or -ing. For example, you will get more search results by searching for *voting* instead of *vote.*

Search a library computer catalog using the following subjects and parts of author names and titles. Write down some of your search results.

1. James and the gi
2. skating
3. vote
4. Steinb
5. boats

Current issue

The most recently published issue of a magazine

Back issue

An issue that was published in the past

Finding Magazines in the Library

In the magazine catalog you can find all of the periodicals, or magazines, that your library has. A periodical, such as a magazine, is published every week, every month, or at some other regular interval. Each magazine is called an "issue." All of the issues in one year make one "volume."

The **current issue** of a magazine is the most recent issue. It is displayed on a library shelf. A **back issue** is a past issue of a magazine. Some back issues may be kept on the shelves. Usually, issues more than six or twelve months old are kept somewhere else in the library. To look at a back issue, you sometimes must put in a written request. Request forms usually ask for the name of the magazine, the publication date, the volume number, and the issue number.

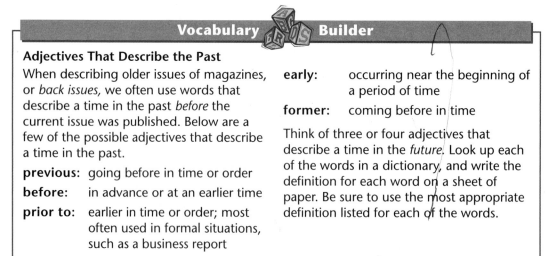

Vocabulary Builder

Adjectives That Describe the Past

When describing older issues of magazines, or *back issues,* we often use words that describe a time in the past *before* the current issue was published. Below are a few of the possible adjectives that describe a time in the past.

previous: going before in time or order

before: in advance or at an earlier time

prior to: earlier in time or order; most often used in formal situations, such as a business report

early: occurring near the beginning of a period of time

former: coming before in time

Think of three or four adjectives that describe a time in the *future.* Look up each of the words in a dictionary, and write the definition for each word on a sheet of paper. Be sure to use the most appropriate definition listed for each of the words.

September 2002 — Month and year of publication
Volume XX
Number 9 — Volume number
— Issue number

Activity A Use the magazine pictured above to answer these questions. On your paper, write your answers.

1. What is the volume number of this magazine?

2. What is the issue number?

3. What is the name of the magazine?

4. When was it published?

5. If you went to the library in September 2003, would this magazine still be on the shelf?

The Readers' Guide to Periodical Literature

When you wish to find magazine articles on a specific subject, you can use *The Readers' Guide to Periodical Literature. The Readers' Guide* lists articles and stories from major general interest magazines. It lists articles by subject and author. It lists stories by author and title. *The Readers' Guide* is published every month and bound into a volume each year. Some libraries have a guide on computer to help you locate magazine articles.

Here are some sample entries in *The Readers' Guide:*

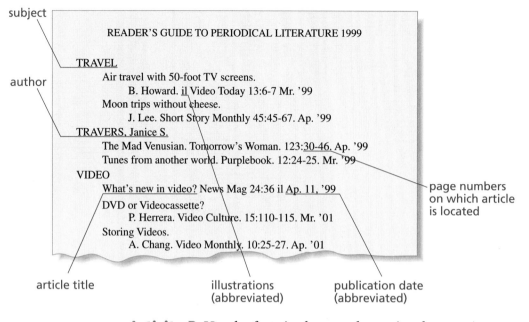

subject

author

READER'S GUIDE TO PERIODICAL LITERATURE 1999

TRAVEL
    Air travel with 50-foot TV screens.
        B. Howard. il Video Today 13:6-7 Mr. '99
    Moon trips without cheese.
        J. Lee. Short Story Monthly 45:45-67. Ap. '99
TRAVERS, Janice S.
    The Mad Venusian. Tomorrow's Woman. 123:30-46. Ap. '99
    Tunes from another world. Purplebook. 12:24-25. Mr. '99
VIDEO
    What's new in video? News Mag 24:36 il Ap. 11, '99
    DVD or Videocassette?
        P. Herrera. Video Culture. 15:110-115. Mr. '01
    Storing Videos.
        A. Chang. Video Monthly. 10:25-27. Ap. '01

page numbers
on which article
is located

article title

illustrations
(abbreviated)

publication date
(abbreviated)

Activity B Use the facts in the sample entries above to answer these questions. On your paper, write your answers.

1. What is the title of the article by B. Howard?

2. Which magazine includes the article "What's New in Video"?

    A *Purplebook*   **C** *Video Today*

    B *News Magazine*   **D** *Tomorrow's Woman*

3. How many pages are in the story by J. Lee?

4. What is the volume number of *Tomorrow's Woman* in which Janice Travers's story appears?

5. Does the article "What's New in Video?" have pictures?

6. Which article might offer information about keeping old videos?

7. Who wrote the article "DVD or Videocassette"?

8. Does *The Readers' Guide* list the articles "The Mad Venusian" and "Tunes from Another World" by subject or author?

9. From which two months does this *Readers' Guide* list articles?

10. How many pages are in the article by A. Chang?

Audiovisual Catalogs

You can learn about many topics by watching a film, a videocassette, a CD-ROM, or a DVD. Not many people have 16mm film projectors at home, but many have videocassette recorders (VCRs) and computers. Most libraries have videocassette and DVD collections. You also can learn about topics by listening to audiocassettes or *books on tape*. You may be able to check these materials out.

An audiovisual catalog is usually on a computer system or in book form. The catalog groups the materials by subject. It lists titles alphabetically. The catalog entries provide facts you might wish to know before you check out or view the work.

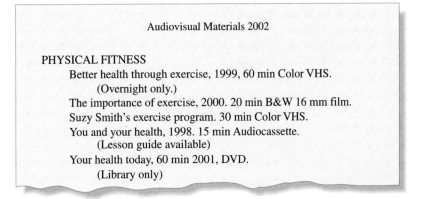

Audiovisual Materials 2002

PHYSICAL FITNESS
    Better health through exercise, 1999, 60 min Color VHS.
        (Overnight only.)
    The importance of exercise, 2000. 20 min B&W 16 mm film.
    Suzy Smith's exercise program. 30 min Color VHS.
    You and your health, 1998. 15 min Audiocassette.
        (Lesson guide available)
    Your health today, 60 min 2001, DVD.
        (Library only)

Activity C Use the information on the audiovisual catalog page above to answer these questions. On your paper, write your answers.

1. How many programs are available on videocassette?

2. Which program is available on 16mm film? Write the title.

3. What equipment will you need to watch "Your Health Today"?

4. What equipment will you need to use "You and Your Health"?

5. Which program would you need to return the day after you checked it out?

Activity D Write the answers to the following questions.

1. What is the title of the film in the film catalog entry below?

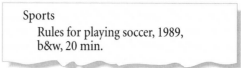

Sports
    Rules for playing soccer, 1989,
    b&w, 20 min.

2. How long is this film?

3. In what year was the film produced?

4. Under what category is the film listed?

5. Is this film in black and white or color?

Video Categories

Libraries arrange videos on the shelf by category in alphabetical order. Read the following list of video caegories:

Film	Films, or movies, like those you find at a video rental store
Documentary	Nonfiction factual subjects ranging from undersea discoveries to the Civil War
Health and Exercise	Exercise, nutrition, and general health
How-To	Help people learn to do or to make things, like building a model boat or getting better grades in school
Young Adult	Fiction of interest to young adults

Activity E Write the answers to the following questions.

1. How do libraries arrange videos on the shelves?

2. Under which category would you look for a video about losing weight?

3. Which category contains videos similar to those you find at a store that rents videos?

4. Under which category would you find a video about the discovery of the North Pole?

5. Under which category would you find a video about starting a small business?

Write the answers to the following questions on your paper.

1. What reference source lists all the magazines that a library has?

2. Which issues of magazines might you have to ask to see?

3. What is the most recent issue of a magazine called?

4. How do you know when a magazine was published?

5. What information should you include when requesting an older magazine issue?

6. How does *The Readers' Guide to Periodical Literature* list magazine articles?

7. How does *The Readers' Guide* list stories?

8. What types of materials can you find in an audiovisual catalog?

9. How do libraries usually arrange entries in an audiovisual catalog?

10. How do libraries arrange videos on the shelves?

Vocabulary Builder

Library Vocabulary

Libraries offer much more than books. Knowing library vocabulary can help you succeed in your search for information.

Create your own Word Bank of library vocabulary and definitions in this lesson. You can make your Word Bank on a single sheet of paper. Include the following terms in your Word Bank: *periodical, current issue, back issue, volume, audiovisual,* and *documentary*. Write the definition and a sample sentence for each term. Add more library terms to your Word Bank as you learn them in this chapter.

Finding information in a library can be easy as long as you follow some simple guidelines. Most libraries have switched from card catalog drawers to a computer catalog. Computer catalogs are easy to use.

At times you may follow these guidelines and still be unable to find what you need. If this happens, ask a librarian for help.

How to Find What You Need
Here's how to find a book in the library using the computer at the library or at your home.

1. If you use your home computer, do a key word search for the name of the library. If you use the computer at the library, click on the *library catalog* on the library's homepage.
2. Type in the title, author, or subject of the book (or other library material). If you search for information by author, you will need to type in the last name first, followed by a comma. Then type the first name: *Becker, Michael*
3. Read the record to find out whether it is the book you want and whether it is available.
4. Copy or print the complete call number for nonfiction books on a piece of paper. For a fiction book, you only need the author's name and title.
5. Find the section of the library that has the book you want. If you are not familiar with the library layout, check with the librarian. Many libraries post a map of the library layout near the checkout desk.
6. Use the call number to find the book on the shelf.

Searching Different Branches
If your library has several branches, you can choose which branch you would like to search for material. Often, the catalog tells you which branch has the material you want. If the material you want is at another branch, you can request that branch to send the material to your library.

Records in the Library Catalog

The entry you choose will appear on the screen in the same way whether you search by subject, author, or title.

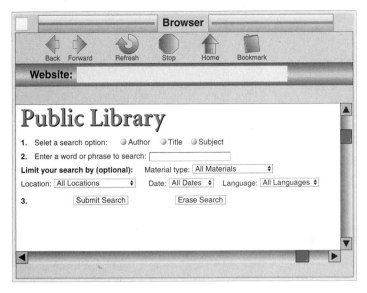

Writing Tip

When you have your search results, take the information with you to find the materials. Most libraries allow you to print this information. Some libraries let you have the printout for free. Some charge a small fee.

When you type the title, author, or subject of your search into the catalog, be sure to select all necessary information. For example, you may be able to choose the library location and the language of the material (for materials that come in languages other than English). At some libraries, it is possible to renew books online.

Understanding Call Numbers

The Dewey Decimal number appears on the back of each nonfiction book. You may see other letters before the number:

   R = Reference   Y or YA = Young Adult   J = Juvenile

An *F* or *FIC* sometimes labels fiction books. A special label may also appear:

   M = Mystery   SS = Short Story Collection
   R = Romance   SF = Science Fiction

Other Facts in a Record

The record also provides the place the book was published, the publisher's name, the copyright date, the number of pages in the book, whether the book is illustrated, and other subject headings the book is listed under.

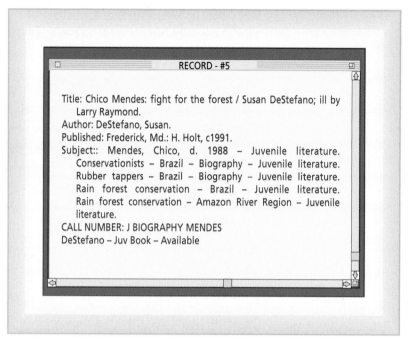

```
RECORD - #5

Title: Chico Mendes: fight for the forest / Susan DeStefano; ill by
    Larry Raymond.
Author: DeStefano, Susan.
Published: Frederick, Md.: H. Holt, c1991.
Subject:: Mendes, Chico, d. 1988 – Juvenile literature.
    Conservationists – Brazil – Biography – Juvenile literature.
    Rubber tappers – Brazil – Biography – Juvenile literature.
    Rain forest conservation – Brazil – Juvenile literature.
    Rain forest conservation – Amazon River Region – Juvenile
    literature.
CALL NUMBER: J BIOGRAPHY MENDES
DeStefano – Juv Book – Available
```

Activity A Use the information above to answer these
questions. On your paper, write your answers.

1. What is the complete title of the book?

2. Who is the author of the book?

3. Is this book fiction or nonfiction?

4. What is the complete call number of this book?

5. Is a copy of this book available to check out of the library?

Activity B Use the information in the entry above to answer
these questions. On your paper, write your answers.

1. Where and when was this book published?

2. Who is the publisher?

3. Does this entry show how many pages the book has?

4. Does this book have pictures?

5. Name two subject headings this book is listed under.

Edit

To get written material ready for publication

Circulate

Can be taken out of the library

You also may see the notation *ed* before or after a person's name in a record. This means that the person has edited the book. To **edit** means to prepare written material for publication.

Now you know about the information on a library catalog Web page. Look at the diagram below of a library's layout.

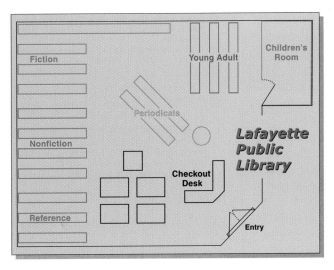

The Reference Section

To find specific information, use the reference section of the library. Encyclopedias, atlases, and handbooks are types of reference books you often will find in the reference section. Check for additional subject headings on the library Web page for *reference* to find out whether the book you want is in the reference section.

The books in the reference section usually do not **circulate.** This means you cannot check them out. As a result, these books are always available to the people who need to use them.

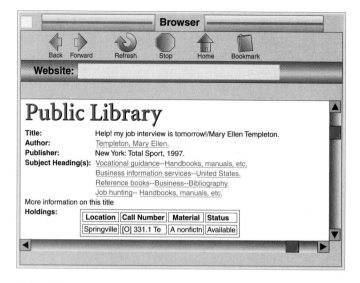

Activity C Use the entry above to answer these questions. On your paper, write your answers.

1. How do you know that this is a reference book?
2. What was Mary Ellen Templeton's job on this book?
3. What is the complete call number for this book?
4. Can you check this book out of the library?
5. What is the subject of this book?

Vertical File

A **vertical file** contains pamphlets and other material too small or too large to put on a library shelf. Libraries arrange materials in the vertical file in alphabetical order according to subject. These materials are often current, and come from a variety of sources, including

- Government agencies
- Colleges
- Museums
- Embassies
- Businesses
- Organizations

Activity D On your paper, write which of these materials might you find in the vertical file.

1. world almanac
2. pamphlet on Indiana parks
3. copy of a speech by the town mayor
4. biography of Malcolm X
5. "Growing Vegetables" by the U.S. Department of Agriculture

Lesson 5 REVIEW

On your paper, write your answers to the following questions.

1. What are the three kinds of records in a library catalog?

2. How do you type an author's name when searching by author?

3. Which of these call numbers are nonfiction?

A Fr	B 346.03	C 92	D 003.1
F	Ho	Ru	To

4. Which of these books would be in the reference section?

   A a literature book   C a mystery novel

   B an almanac   D a math book

5. What do you use to locate a book on the shelf?

6. Where would you look to find a pamphlet about France?

Use the facts on the library catalog Web page to answer the questions that follow. Write your answers on your paper.

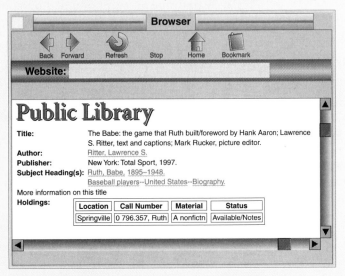

7. What kind of record is shown—subject, title, or author?

8. What subject headings does this record show?

9. What is the call number of the book?

10. In which section would you find *The Babe*?

    A History   C Biography

    B Arts and Recreation   D Social Sciences

Chapter 5   R E V I E W

Word Bank

audiovisual catalog

autobiography

bibliography

biographical novel

biography

branch

call number

catalog

circulate

database

Dewey Decimal System

edit

fiction

historical novel

history

library catalog

magazine catalog

microfiche

nonfiction

novel

The Readers' Guide to Periodical Literature

short story

vertical file

Part A   For each sentence below, write the correct word on your paper.

1. A _____ is a list of information.
2. An imaginary story is _____.
3. One of the libraries in a system of libraries is a _____.
4. A _____ is a long, complex story.
5. Libraries classify books according to the _____.
6. An _____ lists films, videotapes, CD-ROMs, and DVDs by subject or title.
7. A list of books and articles that an author used as references to write a book is a _____.
8. You can usually read a _____ in one sitting.
9. _____ is a film card that stores many pages of reduced copy.
10. A fictional account of a real person's life is a _____.
11. A _____ lists all the magazines that a library subscribes to and identifies the issues that a library has.
12. A true story that a person writes about himself or herself is an _____.
13. The _____ determines where the book will be placed on the library's shelf.
14. A fictional story about real people and events is a _____.
15. A _____ lists most of the library's materials.
16. A _____ book is based on facts.
17. A nonfiction book about a real person that someone else writes is a _____.
18. A _____ contains pamphlets and other small print items.
19. _____ lists articles from many magazines.
20. You can take home library materials that _____ .
21. A large collection of stored information is a _____ .
22. To _____ is to get material ready for publication.

Part B Which of the subjects in each group is a main category in the Dewey Decimal system? Write your answers on your paper.

23. travel, climate, biography, history

24. government, education, social sciences, economics

Part C On your paper, write the answer to these questions.

25. What are three kinds of records in a library catalog?

26. Which of these types of books are fiction? Which are nonfiction? Make two lists on your paper.

    A Biography   **C** Biographical novel   **E** Historical novel

    B Autobiography   **D** History book   **F** Short story

27. In what reference book would you look to find a list of magazine articles on a specific subject?

Part D Write the answers to these questions on your paper.

28. In which section would you look for a pamphlet about the Falkland Islands?

    A reference   **B** the vertical file   **C** nonfiction   **D** fiction

29. Which of these usually do not circulate in most libraries?

    A short story collections   **B** fiction books

    B books from the reference section   **D** nonfiction books

30. Which of these might be the call number of a biography of Thomas Jefferson by R. Hernandez?

    A 921 Je   **B** 921 He   **C** 921 Th   **D** 921 R

Test-Taking Tip When studying for a test, use a marker to highlight important facts and terms in your notes. For a final review, read over highlighted areas.

6

Finding Information from the Media

When someone has a message for one or two people, a letter or a telephone call is the best means of communication. When someone has a message for the general public, the best means of communication is mass media. Mass media, which include television, radio, newspapers, and magazines, reach the most people at one time.

In Chapter 6, you will learn about three types of media: newspapers, television, and radio. Each lesson focuses on the characteristics of the different types of mass media and how you can use them to find information.

Goals for Learning

◆ To learn about information from three types of media: newspapers, television, and radio

◆ To learn about the parts of a newspaper

◆ To learn about reading a newspaper for information

◆ To learn how to use the classified advertising section

◆ To learn how to use the help wanted section of the classified ads

◆ To learn how to use television and radio for information

Mass media

A way to communicate with the most people at one time; for example, television, radio, newspapers, and magazines

Broadcast

To send radio or television signals through the air to receivers in the home, the car, or another location

Television is part of the **mass media.** Television has changed the way we get information about the world. Instead of reading about important events in the newspaper after they occur, we see these events or hear about them *as they happen.*

Television stations **broadcast,** or send, signals through the air to receivers in the home, the car, or wherever we are. Signals also come to us from satellites orbiting the earth. They come into our homes through cables and satellite dishes.

Broadcast television is free to anyone who has a television set and an antenna. To receive information using other methods, people purchase or rent a cable box or satellite dish. They also pay a monthly fee.

Cable television has increased the number of television channels from a few to hundreds. More than 70 million households have cable TV. The number is increasing each year.

Activity A On your paper, write the answers to these questions.

   1. How has television changed the way we get information?

   2. Name three ways that television signals reach receivers.

   3. Name at least two ways that people use television other than for watching TV programs.

   4. How many households in the United States have cable TV?

   5. What does *broadcast* mean?

Television Literacy

Television viewing plays an important part in our lives. In the United States, nearly every household has at least one color television set. If you want to use television as an information tool, you need to understand the television industry.

Kinds of TV Stations

NETWORK TELEVISION

A network is a large television corporation that has member stations. It broadcasts its signal over the airways to these member stations. Network member stations are **affiliates.** Each affiliate carries network programming and other **local** programming. Affiliates provide local news, weather, sports, and other shows directed at a small part of the country.

Each network earns money by selling airtime to advertisers. Affiliates sell airtime to local advertisers. Affiliates have call letters. A local station might use WXYZ as its call letters.

INDEPENDENT STATIONS

This group of small television companies may own one or several stations. Independent stations also sell advertising time. They may produce some original programs, but they usually buy programs from other companies. Many independent stations broadcast old movies, game shows, and reruns of shows first shown on network stations.

PUBLIC TELEVISION

This network of educational television stations does not accept advertisements. Public television stations get much of their money from people who watch the station and send in **donations.** A donation is a gift of money or other items of value. Businesses also donate money as a public service. The federal government and some state governments also give money to public television stations. These stations offer college courses, news, entertainment programming, children's programming, and **documentaries.**

Activity B On your paper, write *N* for *network,* *I* for *independent,* or *P* for *public* for each television description.

1. gets funding from donations
2. has affiliates
3. large television corporation
4. does not accept advertisements
5. small group of television companies

EDUCATIONAL TELEVISION STATIONS

Today, many stations besides public television show educational programs. Some subjects you may find on these channels include the following:

EXAMPLE
Computer skills	How to paint
How to cook	How to do your taxes
How to invest your money	Home repair

Public television stations and educational stations also have new programming that focuses on the government and stock market.

CABLE NETWORKS

These corporations send program signals by cable or satellite dish to local cable companies. The local cable company sells these programs to its customers, or **subscribers,** by providing cable service. There are many cable networks.

The major cable networks have many subscribers. Most cable networks focus on one type of programming, such as sports, news, or music videos. These networks sell advertising time. Advertisers and subscription fees pay for the programming.

Television is a source of information and entertainment.

PREMIUM CABLE NETWORKS AND PAY-PER-VIEW TELEVISION

These networks do not have advertisements. Subscribers pay extra fees that cover the cost of this programming. These stations show mainly movies. Sometimes these channels have special features and other types of programming. On pay-per-view TV channels, people call the local cable company and order programs. They pay a fee for each program they request. Pay-per-view television offers current movies and special sports programming.

SYNDICATES

A **syndicate** is a company or organization that sells television programs to television stations. The syndicate buys the programming from other producers. Game shows, talk shows, and old network shows, or reruns, are popular syndicated programs. They appear on different channels in different cities.

Television Web Sites

Most major networks have Web sites. These sites provide behind-the-scenes information about the television shows on that network. You may find information about television stars and upcoming shows.

Television Scheduling Sites

Several Web sites provide information about television schedules. These sites tell you what time the stations broadcast their programs. The sites that list different television shows also list information about the actors and the characters they play. You also will find movie guides and information about the latest shows. Some sites provide games and television trivia.

Activity C Use the information on pages 168–169 to answer the following questions. Write your answers on your paper.

1. Name three kinds of programs on educational television.

2. What is pay-per-view television?

3. Name two popular types of syndicated programs.

4. Where can you find online television listings?

5. What information would you find on a TV Web site?

The newspaper schedule usually lists your local television stations. Some may also include cable listings. A television program guide on sale at newsstands has a complete listing. The listing below shows one time slot on a certain evening.

11:30 P.M.	② ❹	Talk Show Live
	❺	Television Personalities
	❼	Late News
	⑨	Funny Home Movies
	⑪	Sci-Fi Adventure
	⑳	Travel Express
	㉜	Late News
	㊿	Concert: In the Park

Activity D Use the information in the programming guide above to answer the following questions. Write your answers on your paper.

1. Which two channels broadcast late news at 11:30?

2. What is on Channel 9 at 11:30?

3. What is on Channel 20 at 11:30?

4. What is on Channel 32 at 11:30?

5. What channel is Concert: In the Park on at 11:30?

Using What You've Learned

Compare and contrast your local public television station with a cable television station of your choice. Choose a station that you have watched in the past. If you have not watched a cable station, visit a cable station's Web site to find out more about it. Tell how the two stations are similar and how they are different. For example, what kinds of shows does each station offer? How does each station make money? Which station do you prefer? Write a paragraph that answers these questions.

Lesson 1   R E V I E W

On your paper, write the answers to these questions.

1. What do you need to receive broadcast television service?
2. How do the owners of television stations and television networks earn money?
3. What are affiliates?
4. What does *mass media* mean?
5. What are two ways that public television stations receive money?
6. What are stations that do not belong to a network?
7. What is a documentary?
8. How are pay-per-view television stations different from network stations?
9. Do public television stations accept commercial advertising?
10. What are syndicates?
11. Can you check television listings online?
12. Do most major networks have Web sites?
13. Do newspaper schedules list every television station?
14. Where can you find complete listings?
15. What information would you find on a network Web site?

Federal Communications Commission (FCC)

A government agency that provides licenses to people or companies to operate television and radio stations

Radio plays a major role in people's lives. People listen to radio for music, news, weather, and traffic reports. People call in and discuss their opinions or ask questions on talk radio programs. People with Citizens Band (CB) receivers in their cars and homes may talk to people within a radius of 30 miles.

Radio Broadcasting

Each radio station usually has a special type of programming, such as all news, rock, country, or classical music.

Although radio stations also belong to networks, their programs are different in each area. You usually can find more local news on the radio than on television. Many stations have a news broadcast every hour. Radio offers up-to-the-minute news.

The Federal Communications Commission

The Federal Communications Commission (FCC) is a government agency that gives licenses to people or companies to operate television and radio stations. The FCC also makes rules for these stations. The rules indicate how much airtime stations can sell to commercial advertisers.

Radio stations, like television stations, broadcast their signals over the air. The airways belong to the public, which is why the government controls their use. Each station must broadcast over a specific frequency. A CB radio also has a certain frequency. The word *band* means a certain range of frequencies.

Activity A On your paper, write the answer to each of the following questions.

1. What are four things people listen to the radio for?
2. What does a CB receiver allow people to do?
3. What is the FCC?
4. How do radio stations broadcast their signals?
5. What does *band* mean?

Types of Radio Stations

Radio stations follow various **formats,** or program styles. Stations attract certain types of listeners. For example, a radio talk show might try to inform its listeners about various issues. Or, it might try to persuade listeners to think in a certain way.

A news station might provide up-to-the-minute news coverage. It also has interviews with experts in various fields.

A music radio station's purpose is to entertain. Music stations play a particular type of music most of the time. For example, some stations play country music, and others play jazz. The scheduled list of music that a station plays is its **playlist.**

Radio Advertising

A privately owned radio station's goal is to make a profit. In the early years of radio, most stations were small and locally owned. They broadcast music and local issues to their communities. Today, large corporations own many radio stations. Several **multimedia** companies that own television and newspaper syndicates also own radio stations.

For-profit radio stations sell on-air advertising time to businesses. The commercials help the station make money.

Public radio networks are major suppliers of nonprofit, commercial-free radio. Organizations such as universities and religious organizations operate commercial-free radio stations, too. Public, or nonprofit, radio stations pay their expenses through donations and government grants. Public radio offers a variety of programs, from music to news to specific subject areas.

Activity B Read the following questions. Write your answers on your paper.

1. What does *format* mean?
2. What kind of radio station might have interviews with experts?
3. What types of programs do radio stations offer?
4. What is a playlist?
5. How do public radio stations pay their expenses?

Tape-delayed

Program that is not live but is taped and played later

Internet Radio

Some radio stations broadcast over both the airways and the Internet. You can listen online to these radio programs as they air. You can get programming schedules and music playlists. You can check to see whether the radio station has a Web site that includes its music playlist.

Many radio stations run only **tape-delayed** programs. Tape-delayed programs are not broadcast live. They are taped and played later. Other radio station Web sites offer live video so that listeners also can watch as the radio program airs.

Activity C On your paper, write the word that correctly completes each statement.

1. Some radio stations _____ over the Internet.

2. A station's Web site might provide its music _____ .

3. A _____ program is not offered live.

4. Some stations offer live _____ that you can watch on the Internet as a program airs.

5. You can get a programming _____ at a station's Web site.

Lesson 2   R E V I E W

Copy the following list of terms on your paper. Next to each term, write the letter of its meaning.

Terms	Meanings
1. FCC	**A** list of scheduled music on a radio station
2. playlist	**B** program that is not live but is taped and played later
3. format	**C** agency that licenses radio stations
4. tape-delayed	**D** a combination of television, radio, and newspapers, for example
5. multimedia	**E** the type of programming that a radio station offers

On your paper, write your answers to these questions.

6. What is a CB radio?

7. What does *band* mean?

8. How do for-profit radio stations make money?

9. How do nonprofit and public radio stations pay operating expenses?

10. What are three kinds of radio station formats?

11. Where can radio listeners get a music station's playlist?

12. What is the purpose of a music radio station?

13. What kind of radio station would have up-to-the-minute news?

14. Why do radio stations follow formats?

15. What are two organizations that might run a nonprofit radio station?

Newspapers are also part of the mass media. Everyone who reads a newspaper receives the same information. There are two main kinds of newspapers: **daily** and weekly.

Daily newspapers are published and distributed every day. They have the most current, or up-to-the-present, news. They usually have more **national** and world news than weekly papers have. National news has to do with what is happening in a nation. Generally, daily newspapers have more regular readers than weekly papers have.

Weekly newspapers are often small town newspapers. They usually focus on local news. Local news has to do with one certain place.

Daily

Every day

Current

Up to the present

National

Having to do with a whole country, or nation

Parts of a Newspaper and Kinds of News

Newspapers have parts, or sections. Each part has a different kind of news: national and world news, local news, sports news, business news, regular features, and classified advertisements. Most newspapers follow a similar plan.

- National and world news appears in the front section of most large city newspapers. They usually continue to another page or section of the newspaper. Local newspapers that serve suburbs of large cities may not carry national and world news.

- Local news is information about local events of interest. Local news frequently has its own section of the newspaper. Sometimes it follows the national and world news section. Another name for local news is regional news.

- Sports news is information about sports. Most newspapers have a special sports section. These pages have results from recent sporting events, articles about sports personalities, and general sports news.

- Business news is information about the stock market and events affecting businesses large and small. Many newspapers have a separate section for business news.

Column

A regular newspaper feature about recent events, current political and social issues, and other topics of interest to readers

Regular features are **columns** and articles with information of interest to the public, such as gardening, health, advice, cooking, or celebrities. Comics, television and movie schedules, and announcements about weddings and engagements are also regular features of the newspaper.

Activity A Use the information that begins on page 176 to answer these questions. Write your answers on your paper.

1. Which type of news would you expect to find on the front pages of a big city newspaper?

2. Which section of the paper would you check to find the score of last night's basketball game?

3. Which section of the paper would you check for information about engagements?

4. Which section of the newspaper would you check for information about a company that was sold?

5. Which section of the newspaper would you check for information about a new post office in town?

Reading the newspaper will help you stay informed.

Activity B Decide whether you would look in a daily paper or a local weekly paper to find the answer to each of the following questions. Write *Daily* or *Local* for each item on your paper.

1. What time will the high school theater production begin Friday evening?

2. Where did the president meet with world leaders to discuss the environment?

3. Who won the city championship in baseball last week?

4. What are the win-loss records of teams in the National Football Conference?

5. When is the Calverton City Council's next meeting?

Editorial Pages

The **editorial** section of the paper often appears on the last two pages of the front section of the newspaper. Editorials express opinions about events in the news. Editorial writers work for the newspaper. The editorial pages also usually have letters to the editor, political cartoons, and opinion columns.

People who read the newspaper write letters to the editor. Anyone may write a letter to the editor of any newspaper. The letters are often readers' opinions in response to news editorials, feature articles, columns, and even photographs in the newspaper.

Political **cartoons** show an artist's opinion about current events. A cartoon is usually a single drawing in which an artist tells a joke or expresses an idea.

Political columns tell about recent events, current political and social issues, and other topics of interest to readers. People who write editorials or political columns explain events and issues in the news from their points of view. They often give their opinions about how problems can be solved.

Activity C Use the information given above to answer these questions. Write your answers on your paper.

1. Where will you usually find the editorial pages in a newspaper?

2. What kinds of information will you find in the editorial section of the newspaper?

3. What is the purpose of an editorial?

4. Who writes the letters to the editor and why?

5. What do people who write political columns write about?

Writing On Your Own

The editorial section of a newspaper features letters from readers. Readers can write about current issues that interest them. Readers might want to respond to an article in an earlier issue of the paper. Write a letter to the editor of your local paper about a current local, national, or international issue.

Online Newspapers

There are thousands of online newspapers that provide current news. Often, you must subscribe by providing your e-mail address and name. These Web sites will inform you about the latest news around the world. Many of these online newspapers have the same features as print newspapers.

Other Parts of a Newspaper

Obituary

A short article about someone who has recently died

Death notice

Information about a person's death and details about the funeral arrangements

Comic strip

A series of cartoon frames that tell a story

Newspapers contain many other kinds of information. Most newspaper contain the television-programming directory, which lists the names, times, and channels of programs scheduled for that day.

The movie section of the newspaper lists local movie theaters with the names of movies and show times. Information about television programs, movies, and other arts and entertainment events is often in a separate section of the paper. This section may be titled *Living, Arts & Entertainment,* or simply *Entertainment.*

Obituaries and **death notices** appear in another section. This section may be called *Obituaries* or *Deaths.* An obituary is a brief article about someone who has recently died. A death notice gives information about a person's death and funeral arrangements.

Columns related to fashion, sports, television, new movies, bridge, chess, gardening, or health appear in different sections of the newspaper. Some columnists give advice to readers about how to improve some aspect of their lives.

Comic strips and cartoons are in a special section of the newspaper. A comic strip is a series of cartoons that tell a story.

Activity D Use the information on page 178 and above to answer these questions. Write your answer on your paper.

1. Jake wants to see a movie at a local theater. Which part of the newspaper will tell him what time the movie begins?

2. Latisha enjoys reruns of old television programs. What newspaper feature would tell her when she could watch them?

3. Which part of the paper lists the names of people who have recently died?

4. Eddie enjoys cartoons. In which section of the paper should he look to read them?

5. How can you subscribe to an online newspaper?

News Stories

News stories are the result of the combined efforts of newspaper **reporters** and their **editors.** A reporter finds facts and writes stories, or articles, for a newspaper. An editor decides which stories to report to the public. An editor also may rearrange and correct the information in a reporter's story.

Most news stories begin with a strong first paragraph called a **lead.** The lead is a summary of the most important facts in the story. It answers the questions *Who? What? Where?* and *When?* Other paragraphs in the story explain more about the news event and answer questions such as: *Why did the event happen?* and *How did the event happen?*

Reporters arrange facts and details in paragraphs in order of importance. They usually put the least important facts in the last paragraph. Editors know how much space is available for each story. When there is not enough room for the entire story, an editor may cut the last paragraphs.

Activity E Read the news story below. On your paper, write your answers to the questions that follow.

Sabatino to Open Pizza Parlor

Beginning Wednesday, March 8, you can eat Rosa Sabatino's pizza at a new location. Rosa's Pizza Parlor is opening in the Fairmont Shopping Center. Mrs. Sabatino said that the demand for her pizza had outgrown her small kitchen and she had to open a larger restaurant.

1. Who is the story about?

2. What will happen?

3. When will it happen?

4. Why is it happening?

5. Where will the event happen?

Lesson 3   REVIEW

On your paper, write your answers to the following questions.

1. What four questions do newspaper stories usually answer in the first paragraph?

2. Which newspaper worker finds facts and writes the stories?

3. Who decides which stories to print?

4. What are editorials?

5. What are some reasons people read newspapers?

Copy the following list of terms on your paper. Beside each term, write the letter of its meaning.

Terms	Meanings
6. Cartoon	**A** Column that offers an opinion
7. Editorial	**B** A regular feature about recent events
	C An article about someone who has just died
8. National news	
9. Obituary	**D** A drawing that expresses an idea
10. Column	**E** An event of interest to people in a whole country

Where To Find It

Newspaper Archives

How can you read an old news story if you no longer have a copy of the newspaper? To find the information you need, you can do one of the following:

- Call or write to the newspaper, and request a copy of the news story or information you need.
- Use a microfiche reader at a library to access reduced copies of old newspapers.
- Go to the newspaper's Internet Web site. Search the newspaper's online archives.

Most newspapers charge a small fee for these services. Many libraries provide microfiche readers free but charge for printing or copying articles.

Use one of the three methods above to locate a newspaper article that is at least ten years old. The article can be about a topic of your choice, such as sports, politics, or local events. Share your archived article with the class.

Advertise

To announce something to the public through the media

Advertisement

A public notice, usually about a product or service for sale

Getting Information from Advertisements

Businesses **advertise** in newspapers, on television, on the radio, and online. People pay to have the public see or hear their **advertisements.** An advertisement is a public notice, often about something for sale. People advertise so that you will buy their goods or services. People or businesses that advertise are announcing something to the public through the media. Newspaper ads give you information that you might find useful.

Activity A On your paper, write your answers to these questions about the ad for Rosa's Pizza Parlor.

1. How will the advertisement help Rosa's Pizza Parlor?

2. When will Rosa's Pizza Parlor open for business?

3. Where is the Pizza Parlor located?

4. What do you have to do to get a free pizza?

5. When will the coupon offer end?

Gimmick

An important feature about something that is kept secret

Slogan

A word or phrase that is repeated over and over again that expresses the main idea of a product, business, political group, or other organization

Advertisements often have **gimmicks** and **slogans** that can mislead consumers. A gimmick is an important feature about something that is kept secret. Another name for a gimmick is a catch.

A slogan is a word or phrase expressing the main idea of a product, business, political group, or other organization. Businesses repeat their slogans over and over again.

 EXAMPLE

Activity B Study the two ads. On your paper, write your answers to the following questions.

1. What is the slogan of Dawson's Department Store?

2. List the facts in the Dawson ad.

3. What important piece of information is missing about the price of the coats? Why does this make the ad misleading?

4. What is the slogan of The Auto Center?

5. List the facts in the Auto Center ad.

Television Advertising

Much of what we see on television is commercial advertising. Audience viewing habits are important to the television industry and especially to companies that advertise on television. Obviously, the more people who see an advertisement the better. Advertisers spend billions of dollars each year on television advertising.

Radio and Internet Advertising

Advertisers use radio to sell products, too. Advertisements on radio can come from local advertisers or national advertisers. Radio advertisers must be aware of listeners' habits. Advertisers want their messages to air when a particular audience is most likely to tune in.

Like television advertisers, Internet advertisers rely on images to sell products. Advertisers use two basic types of images: banner ads and pop-up ads. Banner ads appear as part of the Web site. Pop-up ads appear in a new browser window. Advertisers will place these ads on Internet sites that they believe will draw a particular audience.

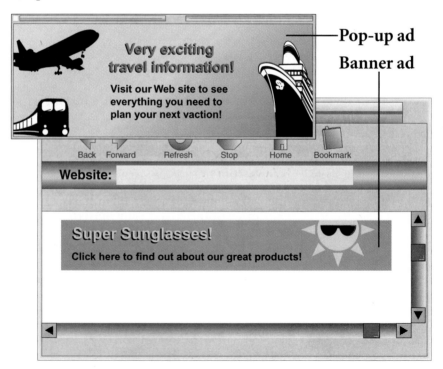

Lesson 4 R E V I E W

On your paper, write the answers to the following questions.

1. What is an advertisement?
2. Why do businesses advertise?
3. What kind of information do ads contain?
4. How can ads mislead people?
5. What is a slogan?
6. What is a gimmick?
7. How do the owners of television stations and television networks make money?
8. What are two types of Internet advertisements?
9. Why must advertisers be aware of listener's habits?
10. When did Internet advertisement begin?

Vocabulary Builder

Advertising Lingo

Specialized fields, such as advertising, have their own vocabulary, or *lingo*. Examples of advertising lingo include the following:

jingle	*a short, catchy tune that gets your attention*
pitch	*sales pitch; what is told to customers about a product or service*
copywriter	*a person who makes a career of writing advertisements*

Write a short paragraph using each of the advertising words defined above.

Classified advertisements

Short public notices (items for sale, apartments or houses for rent, help wanted)

Large businesses use newspaper ads, television, radio, magazines, and the Internet to advertise their products and services. **Classified advertisements,** or ads, are short public notices that offer items for sale. This section of the paper includes houses for sale, apartments for rent, and help-wanted ads that announce available jobs.

You can reach a lot of people at one time if you advertise in the classified section of a daily or weekly newspaper. When we classify things, we divide them into groups. In the classified section of the newspaper, short announcements about job openings or items for sale are arranged, or classified, into sections. Often an index at the beginning of the classified ads lists each section. Usually there are guidewords, numbers, or both at the top of each column to help people find what they are looking for quickly.

EXAMPLE

CLASSIFIED INDEX

100 – 199	Announcements and Notices
200 – 299	Personal and Business Services
300 – 399	Recreation and Leisure
400 – 499	Gourmet and Hosting
500 – 599	Home Repairs and Services
600 – 699	Pets and Animals
700 – 799	Merchandise
800 – 899	Instruction
900 – 999	Employment
1000 – 1099	Rentals
1100 – 1199	Real Estate
1200 – 1299	Business and Business Real Estate
1300 – 1399	Financial
1400 – 1499	Transportation

To advertise in most papers, you have to pay a fee. The amount of the fee will depend on the size of your ad. Some newspapers have special programs that charge a fee only after your ad gets results.

Activity A Use the Classified Index on page 186 to answer these questions. Write the numbers and the title of each topic on your paper.

  1. Under which classification would you find a truck for sale?

  2. Under which classification would you expect to find a house for sale?

  3. Where would you expect to find job openings?

  4. Where would you look if you wanted to get a cat?

  5. If you wanted to take a class, what would you look under?

Activity B Use the classified index on page 186. Write the section where you would probably find the following products or services listed.

  1. Poodle groomers
  2. Institutions that lend money
  3. A computer training school
  4. Help with income taxes
  5. Party planners
  6. A list of jobs
  7. A bricklayer
  8. Apartments for rent
  9. Automobiles for sale
  10. Houses for sale

Activity C Sort the following advertisements into two sections that you might see in the classified ads in the newspaper—*Furniture* and *Business Equipment.* Write *F* on your paper if an item should be listed in the Furniture section or *BE* if the item should be listed in the Business Equipment section.

BEDROOM SET New $1995. Moving; must sacrifice. $650 or best offer. 555-4212.

SOFA Green brushed twill in good condition. $650. Call 555-0984. Ask for Marlene.

CASH REGISTER New in sealed carton, $129. Calvert Cash Register Co. 555-0900.

DESK AND CHAIR Solid wood. Good condition, $450. Call evenings. 555-4039.

COPIERS Reconditioned. All sizes. Like new. Bargain priced $399 and up. Call 555-4835 between 8 and 5.

DINETTE, RECLINER, LAMPS, and more. We're moving south and everything must go. Call 555-9864.

Reading Classified Ads

The number of lines in the ad usually determines the price of a classified ad. Abbreviations keep the ad short and the price down. You will have an easier time finding what you want in the classifieds if you know the meaning of some of these abbreviations.

Abbreviations Used in Automobile Advertisements	
a/c	— air conditioning
air	— air conditioned
am/fm	— AM/FM radio
auto	— automatic transmission
cass	— cassette tape player
CD	— compact disc player
conv	— convertible
6 cyl	— 6 cylinder engine
4 dr	— 4 door
eng	— engine
excl/cond	— excellent condition
fact. warr.	— factory warranty
int	— interior (refers to upholstery)
inte	— interior
lo mi	— low mileage
74K	— 74,000 miles
pb	— power brakes
pl	— power locks
ps	— power steering
pw	— power windows
pwr	— power
rear defr	— rear window defroster
5 spd	— 5-speed transmission
sunrf	— sunroof
4wd	— four-wheel drive

Activity D Study the sample automobile ads. Use the information on page 188 to answer the questions that follow. Write your answers on your paper.

AUTOMOBILES

AUDI '95 4000S. Auto. 4 dr excel. body & int. Needs eng. work. Best offer. 809-555-1021.

CHEVY '02 Cavalier, 5 spd, AC, PS, PB, AM/FM cass, 61K mi. Call today for special sale price. JACK'S CHEVROLET. 201-555-9800.

DODGE '99 Intrepid, loaded, fact. warr., lo mi. A steal if you buy today. 890-555-8000. Ask for Sam.

FORD '01 Taurus, 4 dr auto a/c ps pb, CD, rear defr. Today's bargain prices. 800-555-9088.

HONDA '01 Civic LX, 4 dr coupe. 5 spd, a/c, CD, pwr windows & sunrf, low miles. LIKE NEW! Call 703-555-0920.

NISSAN '99 Altima, AC, cass., 5 spd, blue met., $10,995. 901-555-1000.

PORSCHE '00, 944S 11 Cabriolet, triple black. Cruise, pwr. top, airbags, alarm, leather. Loaded. Fact. warr. 1 owner. Only 3450 mi. Listed for $51,000. Make offer. Save thousands! 809-555-0102.

1. Name three kinds of information contained in every ad.
2. Which car needs engine work?
3. What does "lo mi" mean?
4. What does "4 spd" mean?
5. What does "4 dr" mean?
6. Which cars come with a factory warranty?
7. Which cars have air conditioning?
8. What does "auto" mean?
9. Which cars have power steering and power brakes?
10. Write the ad for the Porsche. Spell out each abbreviated word.

Placing Classified Ads

If you place a classified ad in the paper or online, you want people to find it. You want people to know what you are selling or advertising. The newspaper's classified ad representative can help you write the ad and place it in the most appropriate section of the classifieds.

EXAMPLE   Mr. Nakagawa wanted to buy a used car. He looked under Merchandise (things for sale). First, he looked for the word *Car.* Then he looked for the word *Transportation.* He found a car for sale.

Rosa Sabatino wanted to rent a place for an Italian restaurant. She looked under Rentals and Real Estate. She found only apartments and houses. Then she looked under Business Property. She found a place to rent in a shopping center.

Activity E On your paper, rewrite the ad below so that someone looking for a CD player might find it in the classifieds. In brackets [ ] after the ad, write the section of the classifieds in which you think the ad should appear.

FOR SALE   CD player. Almost new, with 10 CDs. $75. Call 555-9800 and ask for Sue.

Lesson 5   R E V I E W

Use the classified index on page 186. On your paper, write the section where you would find these items listed.

1. Used cars for sale
2. Used furniture for sale
3. Apartments for rent
4. Houses for sale
5. Business property to rent

Read these ads. On your paper, write your answers to the questions that follow.

RECREATION AND LEISURE   (300)
VACATION in Bermuda! 7 days, 6 nights, air, hotel, meals incl. $1300. Mac's Travel Services, 555-8009.

PETS AND ANIMALS/CATS   (610)
KITTEN Free. 10 wks., F. b&w, short hair, litter-trained. Suzy, 555-9849.

MERCHANDISE   (700)
DIAMOND RING Perf. cond. Cost $500. Make offer, 555-0982. Ask for Ralph.

6. What color is the kitten? Is it a male or a female?
7. What person should you ask for if you call about the diamond ring?
8. How much did the diamond ring originally cost?
9. What travel agency is offering the Bermuda vacation?
10. What does the price of the Bermuda vacation include?

Spelling Builder

Abbreviations

Sometimes different abbreviations for the same words appear in newspaper classifieds. For example, the abbreviation for *bedroom* might appear as *BR* or *bdrm,* and the abbreviation for *experienced* might appear as *exp.* or *expd.*

Remember that abbreviations are short forms of words with vowels left out.

Write your own classified ad offering an apartment for rent or an item for sale. Use different abbreviations in your ad. In parentheses, write out the complete word.

Many people read the help-wanted section of the classified ads to find jobs. People who run businesses use this section of the classifieds to advertise job openings.

Business owners also place help-wanted ads online. By using an Internet search engine and typing the key words *job boards,* you will find many job listings online.

Sunday, October 25   *The Daily Banner*   G-1

CLASSIFIED ADVERTISING
Employment

EMPLOYMENT SERVICES (901)

JOB RESUME
$15 & UP
Writing/Editing/Typing
While You Wait. 555-6916

CAREER TRAINING (903)

THE MEDIC SCHOOL. Train med. dental asst. 555-5222.

HELP WANTED (905)

ACCOUNTING CLERK Part time. Entry level position, incls. invoicing, filing, accurate typing, 45/50 WPM. Permanent position, 20-25 hrs. per wk. Security area. Call bet. 9 & 1, 555-4706.

HELP WANTED (905)

ADMINISTRATIVE SECY. $25,500 fee paid. This top Co. needs polished sect'l. talents! Good skills and figure aptitude. 555-0778.

AIR COND & Heat Pump Mechanic fully exp. only. Call Frosty Refrig. 555-2024.

AUTO SALESPERSON Sell and make big money on cars and trucks. Salary plus comm. Benefits. 555-1320.

BOOKKEEPER With aptitude for computerized bkkp. Dependable. 555-1118

CASHIER/CLERK Some exp. req'd. All shifts avail. Apply 100 S. Broad bet 9 & 12 noon.

HELP WANTED (905)

CHEF PASTRY 4 yrs. exp. required, knowledge of European pastry pref. Send résumé to Box CS 47822.

CLERICAL If you love to type, my firm needs your skills. Excellent Salary & Benefits. Call Lisa 555-5804.

CLERK TYPIST General office work, 5 days, vic. Smallwood St. 555-5806.

COMPUTER OPERATOR To work part time eves. Must love to type. WP exp. pref. Pleasant atmosphere, free parking. Call 9-5 at 555-TYPE.

Activity A Use the sample help-wanted ads to answer these questions. Write your answers on your paper.

1. Where can you get training as a dental assistant?

2. What kind of job is open at Frosty Refrigeration?

3. Which jobs require or prefer some experience?

4. What number could you call to get your résumé typed?

5. How are job titles organized in the help-wanted section?

Understanding Abbreviations in the Help-Wanted Ads

Job titles and other information in the help-wanted ads are often abbreviations. The same words may be abbreviated in different ways.

 EXAMPLE
- Admin. Assistant
- Administrative Assist.
- Admin. Asst.

An administrative assistant helps an administrator. An administrator is a supervisor or manager of an office or a company.

Activity B On your paper, write every abbreviation in the following help-wanted ads. Beside each abbreviation, write its meaning. Use the words in the list below to help you figure out the meanings of the abbreviations.

ADMIN ASSISTANT Opp'ty w/CPA firm. Typing 60 wpm, control logs, gen. ofc. exper. req. Résumé to WPR, POB 551, Fairmont.

ADMIN. ASSIST. Printing co. needs qual. indiv. immed. Good salary & benefits. Respond to POB 456, Wesleyville.

ADMIN. ASST. Exec. level. Typing & attention to detail req'd. Also Windows 6.1 and Lotus 1-2-3. Excell. sal., benefits. Call Mr. Kim, 555-8000.

administrative	executive	qualified
and	experience	required
assistance	general	salary
Certified Public	immediately	with
Accountant	office	words per minute
company	opportunity	
excellent	Post Office Box	

Words to Know in the Help-Wanted Ads

When looking for a job, you should know certain terms. Some of these words describe requirements for specific jobs. Many will appear in the want ads. Others may come up during a job interview. Knowing what these words mean will help you determine whether you are qualified for the advertised job.

benefits	what workers receive in addition to wages, such as health insurance and vacations
executive	a manager, a supervisor, or an administrator
experience	the same kind of work that you have done before
full time	a job that requires approximately 40 hours per week, or 8 hours a day for 5 days
part time	a job that requires less than 40 hours per week
permanent	expected to last a long time
qualifications	your skills and work experience
references	people who know about your work and who will recommend you for a job
reliable	dependable; workers who do what they are expected to do
temporary	a limited amount of time

Activity C Use the words from the list to complete these sentences. Write the words on your paper.

1. Ellis Electronics needs a worker for three weeks. This is a _____ position.

2. Rosa Sabatino needs a server who will be at work on time every day. The person must be _____.

3. Rosa wants a server who has worked at a pizza parlor. She wants someone with _____.

4. Rosa will give her workers these _____: full health insurance and a paid vacation.

5. Dan would like a _____ job working weekday evenings.

Job Titles

The same type of job may have different names. For example, a teacher may be called an instructor or a trainer. Office workers with typing skills have many job titles. They may be called administrative assistants, typists, clerk/typists, or word processors.

The way people do their work has changed because of new technology. Job descriptions and titles also have changed. For example, people who type documents today often are called word processors because they use computers and word processing programs. What these workers type has not changed, but how they type has changed.

Activity D Read these job descriptions. On your paper, write your answers to the questions that follow.

WORD PROCESSING ASSISTANT Must type 75 WPM minimum and be reliable. Full time, permanent position. Knowledge of word processing helpful but not necessary. Salary depends on experience. Send references with résumé to Wilson, Inc., 4500 Westfield St., Kingsport.

ADMINISTRATIVE ASSISTANT Responsibilities include supervision of a small staff of office workers. Experience with computers and computer spreadsheet programs required. 60 wpm typing required. Call 555-7598 for appointment.

1. What skill does each of these jobs require?

2. Both of these workers will do word processing. Which company will train the worker?

3. Which job requires recommendations from previous employers?

4. Which job would you apply for if you had computer experience?

5. Why would salary depend on experience?

Activity E Use the information in the help wanted ads below to answer the questions that follow. Write your answers on your paper.

ALARM INSTALLER Trainee position electronics or elec. background. Call 555-5433.

ARTIST Full time job with fast growing advertising agency. 2 yrs exper. req. Must be able to illustrate quickly on a computer. Exp. with typesetting machine or willing to learn. Send résumé to Daily Banner, Box 45A.

ASST. CATALOGER Qualifications: Exper. with Dewey Decimal classification system. Degree from 2-yr or 4-yr college highly desirable. Call the Library. 555-9800.

ASST. OFFICE MGR Small but growing Property Mgt. firm on easy-to-learn computer. F/T. Starting salary $25,000. Send résumé to Daily Banner, Box 87D.

BOOKKEEPER 4 yrs exper. in automated accounting data. Accounting degree preferred. 23,000 plus benefits. Send résumé to Daily Banner, Box 35C.

AUTO BODY REPAIR PERSON & HELPER Must have own tools. Ask for Julian. 555-0988.

BAKER, PASTRY CHEF Exper'd for excell. European bakery. Perm. position. Call 555-3210.

CABINETMAKERS Apprentices only. Will train. Countertop shop. Start immed. 555-9870.

CASHIER Full time position for person with one year exper. Good with figures. Call Sue. 555-0983.

CLERICAL Dependable, exper. worker to handle warehouse inventory, shipping and receiving, & various office clerical work. Call 555-8450 bet. 9 & 12 for appt.

DATA ENTRY Immed. opening, 50 wpm, quick learner, phone manners. Sal. negotiable. Free parking and other benefits. Call Ms. Samaki 8 to 12 for appt. 555-9800.

1. Choose four of the positions. List the qualifications required for each job.

2. Write the abbreviations that match each of these terms.

A full time	**D** words per minute
B permanent	**E** salary
C appointment	**F** immediately

3. In which jobs will workers receive on-the-job training?

4. Which jobs require education beyond high school?

5. Which jobs will cover health care premiums?

On your paper, write the answers to these questions.

1. What word would you look for in the newspaper index to find the help-wanted ads?
2. Put these job titles in the order that you would expect to find them in the help-wanted ads.

   A Computer Operator   **B** Machinist   **C** Accountant
3. What does it mean if an ad says that a job is *open*?
4. About how many hours would you expect to work each week in a full-time job?
5. What is a benefit an employer might offer besides wages?

List all of the abbreviations in these ads on your paper. Beside each abbreviation, write the word or words that the abbreviation stands for.

DATA DISTRIBUTION SPECIALIST Entry level pos. in our mail room. If you have good organizational skills, your own trans., and are able to lift 50 lb., we want to talk to you. Typ. is helpful. Call Mrs. Verney, 555-9800.

BOOKKEEPER/PAYROLL Reliable individual w/exper. working computerized payroll. Needed immed. Good sal. & benefits. Call 555-0984.

CARPET MECHANIC Excellent opp. Must have truck & tools. Apply in person. CarpetTown, 1200 Eastern Avenue, Milton.

BOOK STORE F/T sales/cashier pos. Previous exper. Call 555-0939 for appt.

STYLIST F/T or P/T. Exp. pref. Start immed. Call Joy. 555-4900.

Chapter 6 REVIEW

Word Bank

advertisement

advertise

affiliate

broadcast

classified advertisements

column

death notice

documentary

donation

editorial

Federal Communications Commission (FCC)

format

lead

local

mass media

multimedia

national

obituary

reporter

subscriber

syndicate

tape-delayed

Part A On your paper, write the word that correctly completes each definition.

1. The _____ is the government agency that provides licenses to companies to operate television and radio stations.

2. To _____ means to announce to the public through the media.

3. An _____ is an opinion about an issue written by a newspaper's staff.

4. Television, radio, newspapers, and magazines are _____.

5. _____ means "having to do with a certain place."

6. _____ news is about the whole country.

7. _____ are short public notices.

8. An _____ is about someone who has died recently.

9. A _____ paragraph is the first paragraph of a news story.

10. A _____ is a gift of money or other items of value.

11. A _____ is a customer of a local cable television company.

12. A _____ is a nonfiction film or television program.

13. To _____ is to send radio or television signals through the air to receivers in the home, the car, or other locations.

14. An _____ is a member station that carries a large television station's programs.

15. A _____ is a newspaper feature about recent events.

16. A _____ is information about someone's funeral arrangements.

17. A _____ is a person who researches facts and writes stories for a newspaper.

18. An _____ tells about a product or service for sale.

19. A _____ sells programs to TV stations.

20. _____ is the programming of a radio station.

21. _____ is a combination of television, radio, newspaper, magazines, and the Internet.

22. A _____ program is taped and played later.

Part B Write the best answer for each question on your paper.

23. Which are mass media?

    A newspapers   **C** telephone calls

    B letters   **D** personal photos

24. Which of these media has the most facts about job openings?

    A television   **B** radio   **C** newspaper   **D** magazines

25. Which section of a newspaper has opinions about current events?

    A front page   **B** classified   **C** editorial   **D** entertainment

26. Who decides which stories to print and how long they will be—the reporter or the editor?

27. Which type of television network has programming without commercial advertising?

Part C On your paper, write your answers to these questions.

28. Is broadcast television free?

29. What are four parts, or sections, of a newspaper?

Part D On your paper, write all of the abbreviations in these ads. Beside each abbreviation, write its meaning.

30.
> **JACKSON HEIGHTS** 2 BR apt., A/C, 5 min. walk to bus. $675 + elec. 555-9871

> **CHEVETTE** 91, 4 dr., 4 cyl., ps, pb, red w/white int. Best offer. 555-7109.

> **CLERK** F/T, 50 wpm, exper. req. Sal. $21,000 to start. Send résumé to Daily Banner, POB 34D.

Test-Taking Tip When studying for a test, use the titles and subtitles in the chapter to help you recall the information.

7

Finding Expert Help

What is an expert? An expert is a person who has training and knowledge about a certain subject. An expert may be able to perform a special service for you. For example, an electrician is an expert on electrical wiring. An electrician can install or repair an electrical system.

An expert also can give you advice. For example, an attorney is an expert on matters related to the law. An attorney can give you legal advice or speak for you in a court of law.

In Chapter 7, you will learn how to find expert help. Each lesson will help you know where to go and whom to ask for expert help.

Goals for Learning

◆ To learn how to find expert help when you need it

◆ To learn about nonprofessional experts and how they can help you

◆ To identify organizations that can help you find skilled workers

Expert
A person with training and knowledge about a specific subject

Credentials
Proof that a person is an expert in a certain area of work

Occupation
The regular work or business a person does

Associate's degree
A degree from a two-year college or a community college

Bachelor's degree
A degree from a four-year college or university

Master's degree
An advanced degree, beyond a bachelor's degree, from a graduate school or university

You can find expert help when you need it. An **expert** is a person who has training and knowledge about a certain subject. One group of experts are professionals. A profession is a job that requires special information and often long training. Examples of professionals are architects, engineers, physicians, attorneys, and pharmacists.

A person who is an expert has certain professional **credentials.** Credentials are proof that a person is an expert in a certain **occupation.** An occupation is the regular work or business of an individual.

A person's credentials may include a college degree in a certain field, a degree from a professional school, a license or certificate, experience, and references.

Understanding College Degrees

Colleges and universities offer different degrees that acknowledge a person's study of a particular subject area, such as math or science. Various degrees require different numbers of years of study.

Associate's Degree: A degree from a two-year college or a community college. For example

　　　AA—Associate in Arts

Bachelor's Degree: A degree from a four-year college or university. Many professional occupations require this degree. The most common of these degrees are

　　　BA—Bachelor of Arts
　　　BS—Bachelor of Science

Master's Degree: A degree from a graduate school or a university. This degree means that the person has had advanced training after a bachelor's degree. Some examples are

　　　MBA—Master of Business Administration
　　　MEd.—Master of Education
　　　MS—Master of Science

Doctoral degree

The highest degree awarded by a university or professional school

> **Doctoral Degree:** The highest degree that a university or professional school may award. Many medical professionals and college professors have this degree. Some examples are
>
> MD—Doctor of Medicine
>
> PhD—Doctor of Philosophy

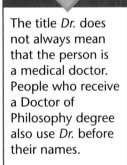

The title *Dr.* does not always mean that the person is a medical doctor. People who receive a Doctor of Philosophy degree also use *Dr.* before their names.

Activity A Match the degree with the best definition. Write each number and matching letter on your paper.

1. Associate's degree

2. Bachelor's degree

3. Master's degree

4. Doctoral degree

A Awarded by four-year colleges or universities

B The highest degree a person can receive in a field

C Awarded by community colleges

D Awarded by graduate schools

Professional Schools

Professional schools provide training for certain occupations. For example, a lawyer must graduate from a law school. Often these schools are part of a large university. Most students receive a bachelor's degree before they attend professional schools.

Becoming a Professional

In addition to attending school, professionals must get experience and take an examination. State governments give these State Board Examinations. A person who passes the examination receives a license to practice the profession.

Activity B A person must do the following things to become a professional. Arrange the steps in the order people usually do them. Write them in order on your paper.

1. Get experience under the supervision of another expert.

2. Pass a state board examination.

3. Graduate from a professional school.

4. Graduate from high school.

5. Attend a four-year college or university.

Business and Financial Experts

There are many experts you may go to for advice and service in business and financial matters. Here are some examples:

Bankers loan people money for automobiles, houses, and other purchases. Many bankers have college degrees and years of experience working at various jobs in banking.

Real estate agents and brokers help people buy, sell, and rent property. Agents and brokers must have a license. A broker has more training and experience than an agent. Agents and brokers must pass state examinations.

Accountants prepare financial reports for businesses. They help people with their taxes. They check financial reports to make sure that they are correct. Most accountants have college degrees. Some accountants become certified public accountants, or CPAs. An accountant must have experience and pass a state examination to become a CPA.

Attorneys, or lawyers, graduate from law school. Then they must take a state examination called a bar exam. After they pass this exam, attorneys may practice law in a court and represent other people in court. They can draw up legal papers such as wills and contracts and give advice to people about the law.

Architects graduate from college. Then they must get experience. Finally, they can take a state examination to become certified. Architects design homes and other buildings.

Activity C On your paper, answer these questions.

1. What does CPA stand for?
2. What is the name of the examination attorneys must pass?
3. Which person has more training and experience—a real estate agent or a real estate broker?
4. What kind of professional helps you borrow money for a car or house?
5. Does an architect need a license or certificate to practice his or her profession?

Physicians and Surgeons

There are many kinds of physicians, or medical doctors. Some of these physicians are general practitioners, or family doctors. Other physicians are specialists in certain areas.

EXAMPLE

Name of Specialist	Area of Special Training
Allergist	Allergies
Cardiologist	Heart
Dermatologist	Skin disorders
Internist	Diseases that do not require surgery
Neurosurgeon	Surgery of the brain, spinal cord, or nerve structures
Obstetrician	Pregnancy and childbirth
Oncologist	Cancer
Ophthalmologist	Eyes
Orthopedist	Bones, joints, and muscles
Otolaryngologist	Ear, nose, and throat
Pediatrician	Infants and children
Psychiatrist	Nervous or mental disorders
Radiologist	High-energy radiation (X-rays)
Surgeon	Surgery (operations)

Activity D Which kind of specialist could help with each of these problems? Write your answers on your paper.

1. Mr. Lopez hurt his eye.

2. Jim has a skin rash.

3. Marta has an earache.

4. Mrs. Rosen starts sneezing every time she is near a cat.

5. Mrs. Tsao is pregnant.

6. Leon sprained his ankle playing basketball.

7. Mr. Franklin is depressed and cannot sleep.

8. Ted has to have his appendix removed.

9. Mr. and Mrs. Ashike's baby has a fever.

10. Liz needs a complete physical examination for college.

Other Medical Professionals

Many medical professionals have degrees from a professional school. However, they are not medical doctors. Each of these professionals must pass a state examination to receive a license to practice.

Podiatrists are doctors of podiatric medicine. They specialize in problems related to feet.

Pharmacists fill prescriptions that medical doctors write. They work in drug stores and pharmacies. This job does not require a doctoral degree.

Dentists are doctors of dental surgery. They treat teeth and gums. They may write prescriptions.

Chiropractors treat people by manipulating the spinal column. They prescribe diet, exercise, and rest. They do not write prescriptions or perform surgery.

Optometrists examine eyes and write prescriptions for glasses. They do not treat injuries, perform surgery, or write prescriptions for medicine.

Veterinarians treat animals and perform surgery if needed. They also can prescribe medicines for animals.

Activity E Which kind of medical professional could help with each of these problems? Write your answers on your paper.

1. Della's gums are sore.
2. Carolyn's cat won't eat.
3. Aunt Julia needs to have a prescription filled.
4. Joey is having trouble seeing the board from his seat in the back of the classroom.
5. Mr. Williams's back is aching.

Lesson 1 REVIEW

Write the answers to these questions on your paper.

1. What degrees does a community college give?
2. What is the highest degree a college or university can give?
3. What type of professional worker is a CPA?
4. What is a master's degree?
5. What kind of examination does a lawyer take?

Which professional does the person in each situation need?
Write the letter of the correct answer on your paper.

6. Mr. and Mrs. Weber want to draw up a will.

    A attorney   **B** accountant   **C** podiatrist

7. Aunt Lynn needs to have a filling replaced.

    A allergist   **B** chiropractor   **C** dentist

8. Alan Fowler's hamster is sick.

    A pediatrician   **B** veterinarian   **C** pharmacist

9. Paul Carter wants to start a business. He needs a loan.

    A banker   **B** accountant   **C** real estate agent

10. Anna Walters needs help with her taxes.

    A attorney   **B** accountant   **C** real estate broker

Vocabulary Builder

Word Parts: *Roots* and *Suffixes*

The names of most medical specialists contain root words and common suffixes. Read the following root words, suffixes, and their meanings.

Combine root words and suffixes to name five specialists. Use a dictionary and the list on page 205 to help you with the spellings.

Root words	Meanings	Suffixes	Meaning
dent	tooth	*-ist*	One who specializes in _____
psych	mind	*-ologist*	One who specializes in _____
cardio	heart	*-ologist*	One who specializes in _____
derma	skin	*-ologist*	One who specializes in _____
ped	child	*-iatrician*	One who specializes in _____

Experts learn their skills in many different ways. They may attend technical or vocational schools, or they may go to business schools. They may participate in internship programs or get on-the-job training.

Becoming an Expert

Skilled workers develop skills through a combination of training and experience.

1. They go to school to learn facts about the work.

2. They get experience on the job, where an experienced person carefully supervises them. This applies to both professionals and nonprofessionals.

> **EXAMPLE** An intern is a recent medical school graduate who practices medicine under the supervision of an experienced doctor.

Many non-medical fields such as accounting, journalism, advertising, public relations, and government, offer internships to students and recent graduates. Student teaching too, is similar to an internship.

3. After the training period, workers usually take an examination. The exam may be written, oral, or practical.

4. Workers are then able to do their jobs on their own. They still have a boss, but no one closely supervises them.

Activity A On your paper, write the definition for each of the following.

1. skilled worker
2. intern
3. professional
4. nonprofessional
5. expert

Choosing an Expert

There is more than one way to get a job done. You can do it yourself. You can find a friend to help you. You can hire an expert. People often hire other experts to do work for them, such as cutting hair or fixing a television set.

When you hire an expert to do a job, you have the right to expect expert work. To ensure that you receive expert work, check the person's credentials. Remember that credentials are proof that the person has trained to do the job.

Credentials can include these things:
A license issued by your state government
A certificate or degree from a school
Recommendations from other people
A written guarantee from the worker

Experts in the Trades

A **trade** is an occupation that requires manual or mechanical skill. Examples are plumber, electrician, carpenter, auto mechanic, and printer.

An **apprentice** is a worker who is learning from an experienced and skilled person.

A **journeyman** has completed an apprenticeship and passed a test.

A **master's level** worker has more experience than a journeyman and has passed another test. This worker has a master's license.

A **foreman** is a supervisor or boss.

A **contractor** agrees to perform work or to provide supplies. Contractors may not be skilled workers themselves, but they hire other people with skills.

Independent contractors are people in business for themselves. They do not work for just one company or corporation.

Trade
An occupation that requires manual or mechanical skill

Apprentice
A worker being trained by an experienced and skilled person

Journeyman
A worker who has completed an apprenticeship and passed a test

Master's level
A worker who has more experience than a journeyman and has passed another test. This worker has earned a master's license

Foreman
A supervisor or boss

Contractor
A person who agrees to perform work or to provide supplies for a job

Independent contractors
People in business for themselves

Look through a Sunday newspaper. Skim the classified ads and the employment section. Find one example of each of the following experts: contractor, master level worker, and foreman. Describe to the class the types of jobs you found. Tell which of these experts you have received help from in the past and why.

Activity B On your paper, write the missing words to complete these sentences. Refer to page 209.

1. An _____ is a worker who is learning a skill from someone with more experience or credentials.

2. Contractors agree to perform _____ .

3. A foreman is a _____ or _____ .

4. A worker who has completed an apprenticeship is a _____ .

5. A journeyman must take another test to receive a _____ license.

Skilled workers are always in demand.

**Writing
On Your
Own**

Compare and contrast a professional and a nonprofessional. Think of a professional and a nonprofessional whose services you have used. Write a paragraph that tells how one professional job and one nonprofessional job are similar and how they are different.

Activity C Read about these workers. Then write on your paper the answers to the questions that follow.

A Mr. Johnson repairs appliances such as washing machines and stoves. He goes to people's houses to do his work. He has an apprentice who helps him.

B The Franklin Appliance Company sells appliances. You also can hire the company to fix appliances. Skilled workers and apprentices work there.

C Ralph Attaway is a piano tuner. He was an apprentice at the Fine Music Store for four years. Now he is in business for himself. He will come to your house to tune or repair your piano.

D Carlotta Rios is an emergency medical technician. She works for the fire department. You can get her help by calling for the Rescue Squad. Her training included special medical emergency courses and many hours of experience.

E Fred Collins works for Mac's Service Station. He is an auto mechanic. He was an apprentice to an auto dealer for four years. Now he is a head mechanic. There are two part-time workers who help him.

F Andrea Brown is an air conditioning specialist. She works for Young's Heating and Air Conditioning, Inc. Her company sent her to evening classes for several years. Now she trains new workers.

1. Which worker does not charge a fee for services?

2. Which workers are independent contractors?

3. If you hire Fred Collins to repair your car, who is actually responsible for his work—Fred or Mac's Service Station?

4. Where did Ralph Attaway work as an apprentice?

5. Andrea Brown trains new workers. What is the name for these workers?

Activity D Choose an expert from the list to help with each problem described below. Write your answers on your paper.

auto body mechanic	firefighter	roofer
auto mechanic	ironworker	surveyor
baker	jeweler	tilesetter
barber	locksmith	travel agent
beautician	musician	watchmaker

1. Sandy wants an expert to cut and color her hair.

2. Harold Williams had a car accident. His fender has a dent. He needs someone who is skilled in this kind of repair work.

3. Lyn wants to fly to Chicago. She could call an airline herself, or she could call someone to make reservations for her.

4. Jane Anderson wants to order a wedding cake.

5. Mrs. West bought a ring that is too small. She needs to have it made larger.

6. Mr. Cosby locked his keys inside his car and cannot get them out.

7. Kim Williams admired her sister's tile floor. Now Kim wants new flooring in her bathroom.

8. The Andersons' roof is leaking.

9. The Rosen family found some land that they really like. Before they buy it, they must find a worker who can measure the land and mark the boundaries.

10. The Garcias want to hire a good dance band for their daughter's wedding.

Lesson 2   R E V I E W

On your paper, write the answer for each item.

1. A plumber who is learning the trade is an _____ .

2. The most skilled craftsperson is a _____ .

3. Which of the following can be considered credentials?

   A a license   **C** a written guarantee

   B a recommendation   **D** all of the above

4. Which worker can help you plan a trip?

   A a jeweler   **B** a travel agent   **C** a locksmith

5. Which worker must go to college to learn the job?

   A an insurance agent   **C** a jeweler

   B a travel agent   **D** none of the above

Write your response to each item.

6. How is an independent contractor different from a contractor?

7. Name at least two ways to identify an expert.

8. List the steps needed to become an expert in a trade.

9. Why are an expert's credentials important?

10. Where would a medical school graduate find on-the-job training?

Spelling Builder

-Er or -Or?

The suffixes -er and -or both mean "one who." There is no spelling rule for telling which occupations end in which of these suffixes. You must memorize them as you use them over time. Look at the following names of professionals and nonprofessionals.

Use the information in this chapter and a dictionary to decide whether to add -er or -or to each word.

jewel___   contract___   plumb___   roof___

teach___   doct___   garden___   act___

survey___ may___   profess___ danc___

Organization

A group of people united for a common cause

Bureau

A specialized group or department that focuses on one area or one main topic

---

You already have learned one important skill to help you find expert help. You can use the Yellow Pages of your telephone directory. You also have learned ways to check for the credentials experts should have.

There is another way to check the credentials of people you wish to hire. You can get help from **organizations** or **bureaus.** An organization is a group of people united for a common cause. A bureau is a specialized group or department that focuses on one main topic.

The following are some organizations and bureaus. You or a member of your family may have received help from one or more of them sometime in the past.

1. **The Medical Bureau or the Medical Society**

   If you need a doctor, this group can help. Representatives can give names of doctors near your home who are taking new patients.

2. **The Better Business Bureau**

   People at the Better Business Bureau can help by giving you information about the services and service record of a certain company. You can use your own judgment about whether to use the company. You can find the telephone number of the Better Business Bureau in the telephone directory.

   BETTER BUSINESS BUREAU OF YOUR CITY
   General Information 1223 Main St 555-9000
   Complaint Service 1223 Main St 555-9020

3. **Welcome Wagon or Welcome, Neighbor**

   If you are new in town, you can call a group that welcomes people to the community. Local businesses support these groups. Groups like the Welcome Wagon give facts about shopping, schools, hospitals, and doctors in your town.

---

4. The Chamber of Commerce

Business people from the community belong to this organization. You can write to the Chamber of Commerce of any city or town in the United States to request information about places to visit, hotels, restaurants, and other businesses in the city or town.

5. Travelers Aid or Travelers Assistance

If you are visiting a new place and need help with a travel-related problem, you can call this group. For example, if you lose your wallet or need to find a doctor, this kind of group may be able to help. However, a group such as Travelers Aid is not a travel agent. Look for this organization in the telephone book, or call the operator for help.

Where To Find It

Finding Reputable Organizations

You can find reputable, or honest, organizations through the Better Business Bureau. You also can find reputable organizations by asking friends, family members, and professionals about their personal experiences with organizations. Before getting help from or contributing to an organization, ask the organization for referrals. You might be looking for information about a particular charity to which you want to contribute clothing. Ask specific questions of the organization, such as "Who can receive the clothing?" "Where and when do you distribute the clothing?"

Complete the following activities.

1. Find the name of an organization in your town that feeds people in need.
2. Ask three people whether they have heard of the organization or have had any personal experience with it.
3. Write three questions to ask the organization.
4. Call the organization, and ask your three specific questions.
5. Share your findings with the class. Do you think the organization is reputable? Why or why not?

6. The Legal Aid Society

Attorneys at the Legal Aid Society will answer your questions on the telephone. They will agree to see you in person for a fee. They also may recommend another attorney who can help you with your problem.

7. The Consumers Union

A **consumer** is a person who buys and uses goods and services. The **Consumers Union** is an organization that tests products and investigates businesses. It publishes the results in a magazine called *Consumer Reports*. You can find this magazine in most libraries.

Your town or city also may have a consumers' group. This group would report about businesses in your area. You may find the name and telephone number in your directory. Your librarian should know about consumer groups.

Use a current telephone directory to find the numbers of organizations and bureaus.

Activity A Use the information on pages 214–216 to answer these questions. Write your answers on your paper.

1. Which group would you call for the name of a pediatrician in your town?

2. Which group would you call to ask whether there have been any complaints about Mac's Service Station?

3. What organization would you call for legal advice?

4. What is a group that gives information to people who are new in town?

5. What organization helps businesses in the community?

Finding Organizations on the Internet

The Internet can provide much more information about an organization than a telephone directory can. Besides giving addresses and telephone numbers, an organization's Web site can tell you what the organization offers. These Web sites usually contain instructions about how to get help from that organization. They also tell how you can help them or make a contribution to their organization. Often organizations' Web sites contain links to other organizations that can help you in related areas.

The Web page of an organization might look like this:

To find an organization on the Internet, type keywords into a search box. For example, if you are looking for help with legal matters, type the words *legal aid* or *legal help.* Using these words results in many Web sites to choose from, including the Legal Aid Society at *www.legalaidsociety.org.*

Another way to find organizations on the Internet is to go directly to the address bar on your computer screen. Type in the Web site that you think would match the organization you are looking for. For example, typing *consumerreports.org* into the address bar and pressing "Enter" takes you directly to the *Consumer Reports* home page. This method will help with most organization names.

Activity B On your paper, write the answer to each of the following questions.

1. Where can you find the most information about an organization?

2. Name two things besides address and phone number that you might find on an organization's Web site.

3. What are two ways you can find an organization on the Internet?

4. What is the Web site address for the Legal Aid Society?

5. What is the Web site address for the *Consumer Reports* home page?

Lesson 3   R E V I E W

Number your paper from 1 to 5. Read about each person's problem and write the name of the group or organization that might help solve that problem. There may be more than one right answer for each question.

1. Justin wants a new car. He would like to know the price of compact cars. He also wants to know some facts about each one.

2. Nick's doctor retired. Nick would like to find a new doctor. Nick wants the office to be near his home.

3. Jack Bevan is planning a trip to Los Angeles, California. He would like to know about interesting places to visit while he is there.

4. Trisha Earle wants to have her washing machine repaired. John's Small Appliance Store is in the Yellow Pages. Trisha wants to find out whether that business is reliable.

5. Mary Franklin is buying a vacuum cleaner. She wants to know which is the most reliable model.

Number your paper from 6 to 10. Write the answer to each question.

6. What does the Legal Aid Society do?

7. What information would you expect to find on an organization's Web site?

8. What information does a city's Chamber of Commerce provide?

9. What is one way to access the home page of *Consumer Reports*?

10. If you need new eyeglasses, what organization could help you find an optometrist?

Chapter 7   R E V I E W

Word Bank

apprentice

associate's degree

bachelor's degree

bureau

consumer

Consumers Union

contractor

credentials

doctoral degree

expert

foreman

independent
contractors

journeyman

master's degree

master's level

occupation

organization

trade

Part A Read each sentence below. Fill in each blank with a vocabulary word that correctly completes each sentence.

1. A _____ worker has more experience than a journeyman and has passed another test.

2. The highest degree awarded by a university or professional school is a _____ .

3. A degree from a four-year college or university is a _____ .

4. A _____ is a person who agrees to perform work or to provide supplies for a job.

5. An advanced degree, beyond a bachelor's degree, from a graduate school or university is a _____ .

6. A _____ requires manual or mechanical skill.

7. A _____ buys and uses goods and services.

8. People in business for themselves are _____ .

9. _____ prove that a person is an expert in a certain area of work.

10. An _____ has training and knowledge about a specific subject.

11. An _____ is a worker being trained by an experienced and skilled person.

12. An _____ is a group of people united for a cause.

13. A two-year college or community college awards an _____ .

14. A _____ is a supervisor or boss.

15. A _____ is a worker who has completed an apprenticeship and passed a test.

16. The _____ tests products and investigates businesses.

17. A _____ is a specialized group or department that focuses on one area or one main topic.

18. A person's regular work is an _____ .

Part B When you have a problem, you need to know the kind of expert who can help. Number your paper from 19 to 23. Write the kind of expert who can help with each problem. Use the Experts list below.

Problems	Experts
19. Sal's car is making a funny noise.	librarian
20. Don's cat needs his annual shots.	pharmacist
21. Jill wants a book about repairing TVs.	mechanic
22. Flora has a stain on her new suit.	dry cleaner
23. Ty needs medicine for poison ivy.	veterinarian

Part C Write on your paper your answers to these questions.

24. Which organization can give you legal advice?

25. Which organization's magazine reports on products and services?

26. Which organization can tell you about a company's reliability?

27. If you needed a doctor, what is one organization you could call?

Part D Write the letter of the word or phrase that correctly answers each question.

28. Which of these professionals is a medical doctor?

   A optometrist   **C** pediatrician

   B pharmacist   **D** electrician

29. Which expert will help you find information on any subject?

   A lawyer   **C** accountant

   B librarian   **D** banker

30. Which professional can help you buy, sell, or rent a house?

   A plumber   **C** accountant

   B real estate broker   **D** veterinarian

Test-Taking Tip Make a short outline of the main ideas of the chapter using the paragraph headings that appear in the text.

8

Filling Out Forms

Throughout your life, you will need to fill out forms. You may have to fill out a form to apply for a job or to obtain a driver's license. You also will need to fill out a form to rent an apartment, open a checking account, or travel to another country. A form is a printed or typed document with spaces to fill in information about you or someone else.

In Chapter 8, you will learn about completing different types of applications and forms. Each lesson focuses on the kinds of information you have to know to fill out forms and the different kinds of forms you may have to fill out.

Goals for Learning

◆ To learn how to fill out applications and other forms correctly and completely

◆ To learn about the kinds of personal information asked for on applications and forms

◆ To learn how to answer questions on job applications

◆ To learn about questions and vocabulary related to loans, credit, and financial forms

Form

A printed or typed document with spaces to fill in information

Personal information

Facts about yourself

Full name

A person's whole legal name

Signature

The name of a person written by that person

Document

A paper that gives information to another person

Almost every **form** you complete asks for **personal information.** Personal information includes facts about yourself. You should know your Social Security number, date and place of birth, home telephone number, and work telephone number (if you have a job).

It is important to know your **full name,** or your legal name.

You must sign most forms with a legal **signature.** A signature is a person's name written by that person. You will use your signature on legal papers such as checks and other **documents.** A document is a paper that gives information to another person. You must always write, not print, your legal signature. You also may use your initials.

On most forms, you will need to provide your complete mailing address. Depending on the form, you may or may not be able to use abbreviations. You probably will need to know the two-letter postal abbreviation for your state. You also will probably need to know your former address (the place you lived before the place you now live).

Activity A Write on your paper these facts about yourself.

1. Your Social Security number
2. Your date of birth (month, day, year)
3. Your place of birth (city, state, country)
4. Your home telephone number, including area code
5. Your mother's full name and your father's full name

Your Name and Your Signature

You probably do not use your full, legal name all the time. People with nicknames, such as Rob for Roberto or Pam for Pamela, often sign their names that way. However, if you buy a house or rent an apartment, you will sign your full, legal name. When you open a checking account you fill out a signature card. You must sign your name on checks exactly as you write it on that card.

Ray D. Ryan
Anna Maria DeMarco
Andy Thomas
Leon Jones-Washington

Activity B Write on your paper the answers to these questions.

1. What is your full, legal name?

2. Write your legal signature. Do not print your signature.

3. What is your complete address? Do not use abbreviations. Follow the example below:

    Ms. Grace Mendez
    6610 Gale Avenue, Apartment 3B
    Dayton, Ohio 45414

4. What is the two-letter postal abbreviation of the state in which you live?

5. What is your work phone number, if you have one?

Where To Find It

Social Security Information

The Social Security Administration provides retirement benefits, health benefits for poor and elderly people, survivor benefits, and disability benefits. You can apply for benefits at a local office or on the Internet at *www.ssa.gov.* You can print and mail the online forms or submit them online. The Web site offers forms and instructions in 16 languages.

Go to the Web site and find the following information.

1. Name two forms available online.

2. List three languages of instruction.

3. What is *Medicaid*?

4. In what year can you retire with full social security benefits?

5. What are *survivor benefits*?

Your Address

Most forms ask for your mailing address. Make sure that you can write your address in the correct form.

 EXAMPLE   Mr. Tony A. Miller
13 East Fifth St.
Apt. 205
Seattle, WA 98109

Postal Codes

The post office has its own method of abbreviating state names. The U.S. Postal Service uses a two-letter postal code. Capitalize both letters, and do not use periods. Use these abbreviations when you write addresses. In other situations, write out the full name of the state.

Activity **C** Write each of these state abbreviations on your paper. Next to the abbreviation, write the name of the state in full. Use a dictionary if necessary.

1. AK	**11.** HI	**21.** ME	**31.** NJ	**41.** SD
2. AL	**12.** IA	**22.** MI	**32.** NM	**42.** TN
3. AR	**13.** ID	**23.** MN	**33.** NV	**43.** TX
4. AZ	**14.** IL	**24.** MS	**34.** NY	**44.** UT
5. CA	**15.** IN	**25.** MO	**35.** OH	**45.** VA
6. CO	**16.** KS	**26.** MT	**36.** OK	**46.** VT
7. CT	**17.** KY	**27.** NC	**37.** OR	**47.** WA
8. DE	**18.** LA	**28.** ND	**38.** PA	**48.** WI
9. FL	**19.** MA	**29.** NE	**39.** RI	**49.** WV
10. GA	**20.** MD	**30.** NH	**40.** SC	**50.** WY

Your Social Security Number

Almost every form and application you will ever fill out will ask for your Social Security number. For example:

- A bank, when you open an account
- Your employer, when you apply for a job
- The government, when you file a tax return
- A stockbroker, if you buy stocks or bonds
- Colleges, if you enroll in courses
- The Social Security Administration, if you apply for benefits

Your parents may have applied for a Social Security card for you when you were born. If you do not have a Social Security card, you can apply for one.

When you apply for a Social Security card, use your full name as you would use it in business. You also will need to supply the names of your parents.

Activity D In your own words, explain in one or two sentences why it is important to have a Social Security card. Write your explanation on your paper.

You can go to a Social Security office to fill out an application for a Social Security card.

Your Birth Certificate

To apply for a Social Security number, you will need an official copy of your birth certificate. An official copy of a birth certificate has a raised seal. A photocopy is not acceptable. If you do not have a copy, contact the capital of the state where you were born. Give them your full name and date of birth, and ask them to send you your birth certificate. In most states, you will have to pay a fee.

If you were born in the United States, you are a United States citizen. If you were born in another country and one of your parents was a U.S. citizen at the time of your birth, you are also a U.S. citizen.

A person who was not born in the United States may apply for citizenship. He or she then becomes a "naturalized" citizen and receives citizenship papers. Naturalized citizens have all of the rights and responsibilities of native citizens.

A person who was not born in the United States and who is not a naturalized citizen must register with the state as an alien. He or she may then apply for a green card. A green card is an official document that allows people who are not citizens to work legally in the United States. Green cards used to be the color green. People still call them green cards even though the cards are no longer that color.

Activity E On your paper, write your answers to these questions. Then discuss your answers with your class.

1. When would you need a birth certificate that proves you were born in the United States?

2. How do you know that a birth certificate is official?

3. When might you have to use your birth certificate to prove your age?

4. What does someone who is not a citizen need in order to work legally in the United States?

5. What city and state would you contact to get a copy of your birth certificate?

Number your paper from 1 to 10. Write the correct letter of the definition next to the number of each word.

Terms	**Meanings**
1. Form	**A** A printed paper with spaces to fill in information
2. Document	**B** 214-45-4501
3. Social Security number	**C** Facts about yourself
	D Name recorded at birth
4. Signature	**E** (931) 555-4592
5. Birth certificate	**F** Your name as you write it
6. Citizen	**G** Person belonging to a country
7. Legal name	**H** Official paper stating when and where a person was born
8. Personal information	**I** A paper with official information
9. Telephone number	**J** Two-letter abbreviation of states
10. Postal code	

On your paper, write your answers to these questions.

11. What is your legal name?

12. What is your signature?

13. What is your mailing address?

14. What documents do you need when you apply for a Social Security number?

15. Write this mailing address on your paper. Put the information in the correct order and spell it correctly.

> Mr. Raul Rivera, Franklin, Pa 15222, 1818 Riverside Ave.

You often will have to complete an **application** form. An application is a form to make a request. A job application form is your request that a company consider you for a job. You will have to provide many kinds of information on application forms.

Here is a list of words you will find on many job application forms.

Words	Meanings
Position	The name of your job
Employer	The person or company that pays you a salary
Employee	A person who works for someone else
Available	The date you can begin a job

Application

A form to make a request

Position

The name of your job

Employer

A person or company that pays you a salary

Employee

A person who works for someone else

Available

Refers to when you can begin a job

Giving complete answers to questions in an interview will help you get the job you want.

Advice for Completing Applications

1. Answer every question. Never leave a question unanswered. The employer will think you forgot or that you cannot answer the question.

2. Some questions may not be **applicable** to you. Applicable means suitable or appropriate. You do not have to answer these questions. Instead, you can write *N/A* in those spaces for "not applicable." The employer will then know that you read the question.

3. Always print or type your answers. Often people do not get a job because the employer can't read their application form.

4. Make sure that your answers are correct. Every fact on your application must be accurate. If the employer tries to call you to offer you the job, you want the correct phone number on your application. Sign the last part of the form to verify that all the information is true and accurate. Any false answer could mean that you will not get the job.

Activity A On your paper, write the answers to the following questions.

1. Why should you never leave the answer to a question blank?

2. What does *N/A* mean?

3. Some employers "grade" a job application. They check the answer to every question and give the application a score. Then they interview the people with the highest scores. What does a neat, complete, and correct job application tells the employer about you?

4. Why should you be very careful that your answers are correct?

5. What is the difference between a "false" answer and a mistake?

Questions About Your Education

Whenever you apply for a job, you will answer questions about your **education.** Education refers to the courses and programs you have taken at any school or college.

Keep your educational records in a special place. You may change jobs several times during your career. Each time you apply for a new job, you will need this information.

Here is a sample of a completed job application form. Notice how many items relate to education.

Job Application Form

Print Name Margaret Louisa Gomez

Address 9301 Watkins Ave., Apt. 101, Wilton, Delaware 19973

Home Phone (264) 555-3881 Business Phone (264) 555-2800

College or University: University of Delaware, Newark, Delaware

Major and specialty: Business Administration, Accounting

Dates attended: From 9/89 To 6/93   Degree received ☑ Yes ☐ No

If yes, give title and date BS 6/89

If no, give number of credit hours completed N/A Years completed: N/A

List pertinent courses completed Accounting, Marketing, Business Administration

Other Training: Wilton Business School, Wilton, Delaware
(Name and Location of School)

Subject studied: Word Processing, Computerized Bookkeeping

Dates attended: From 9/96 To 6/98 Years completed: Day ___ Night 2

Pertinent

Related to the matter at hand

Activity B Use the information in the sample job application form on page 232 to answer these questions. Write your answers on your paper.

1. Name the college that Margaret Louisa Gomez attended.

2. What was her major course of study?

3. Did she graduate from college? If so, when?

4. What kind of degree did she earn?

5. Which of her college courses did Margaret think were pertinent to this job?

Activity C Answer these questions about yourself. Print your answers on your paper.

1. What was the name of the last high school you attended?

2. Where was this school located (city and state)?

3. When did you attend this school (From _____ To _____)?

4. On what date did you graduate or do you expect to graduate?

5. What were the main courses that you took?

Using What You've Learned

Review the definition above for the word *pertinent*. List at least two skills that would be pertinent, or related, to each job.

1. truck driver
2. automobile mechanic
4. electrician
3. bank teller
5. actor

Your Job Skills

Employers want to know about your skills. When you apply for a job, list skills that are **pertinent.** This means that the skills that are related to the job for which you are applying. Here are some machines that office workers often use. A person applying for an office job might list all or some of these on an application.

- copier
- word processor
- document binder
- FAX machine
- telephone
- calculator
- switchboard
- computer
- printer
- videotape recorder, camcorder,
- audiocassette player, CD player
- postage meter

Activity D Answer these questions about yourself. Print your answers on your paper.

1. List any machines that you can operate. Describe in your own words the reason you think being able to operate a specific machine will help you get the job you want.

2. Can you type? If yes, give the number of words per minute (wpm).

3. Can you use a computer? What kinds of computers have you used?

4. Have you ever used a computer for schoolwork? If yes, explain what you used it for.

5. What kinds of software can you use? Examples are word processing, spreadsheet, database management, accounting, graphics, and desktop publishing.

Spelling Builder

Commonly Misspelled Words

It is important to spell words correctly on forms, especially on a job application. For example, make sure that you can spell the new words shown in Lesson 2, such as *education* and *employee.* Before applying for a job, review a list of commonly misspelled words like the ones included below. You can find longer lists in spelling or English textbooks.

definitely	**answer**
address	**accommodate**

Use a dictionary to find the correct spelling for each of the following words. Write each correct spelling on your paper.

1. axcept
2. awright
3. bisness
4. calender
5. merchendice

Lesson 2   R E V I E W

Write the answers to these questions on your paper.

1. What is the purpose of a job application?
2. What do you write in a space if the question does not apply to you?
3. Why is it important to answer every question on a job application form?
4. You may print or type your answers on a job application. What is the one thing that you must write?
5. What does *pertinent* mean?

Match the words with their meanings. On your paper, write the correct letter next to each number.

Words	Meanings
6. Job application	**A** Your school experience
7. Education	**B** The name of your job
8. Position	**C** A form you fill out to ask for a job
9. Employer	**D** Your written legal name
10. Signature	**E** The person or company you work for

When you fill out a job application, you will answer questions about previous jobs that you have had. You will write where you worked, for how long, how much your employer paid you, and answers to other questions.

You will find these words on many job application forms.

Words	Meanings
Supervisor	Your boss
Salary	Amount of money you receive
Previous, former	A time in the past

Here is part of a job application form. You may need to fill one out that looks like this:

Supervisor

A person who is your boss

Salary

The amount of money someone pays you for working

Previous

Refers to a time in the past

Former

Refers to a time in the past

Employer _____

Address _____

Phone ( ) _____

Supervisor _____

Dates employed: from ___/ /___ to ___/ /___

Position title _____

No. hours worked/week _____

Salary: starting $_____ ☐ hourly ☐ weekly ☐ monthly

        ending $_____ ☐ hourly ☐ weekly ☐ monthly

Description of work: _____

_____

_____

_____

Questions About Your Employer and Immediate Supervisor

Your employer and your immediate supervisor can be the same person; however, they usually are different people.

EXAMPLE

Brad Weaver works for Robert J. Workman, Contractors.
Mr. Workman owns the company. He pays Brad for his work.
Mr. Workman is Brad's employer.

Brad is an apprentice plumber for the company. His boss
is a foreman. The foreman's name is Ramon Cruz. Ramon is
Brad's immediate supervisor.

Questions About Your Positions and Job Titles

A position is a job title. It is the name of a job. By knowing job titles, you can find jobs that interest you in the help-wanted ads in the newspaper.

EXAMPLE

apprentice plumber   leasing agent
carpenter   receptionist

Activity A Use the information above and on page 236 to answer these questions. Write your answers on your paper.

1. What is Brad Weaver's job title?
2. Who is Brad Weaver's immediate supervisor?
3. Who is Brad Weaver's employer?
4. What is the position of Brad's immediate supervisor?
5. On your own paper, make a chart of your employment history. Start with the most recent job and work back. Use these headings to create your chart: *Dates of Employment, Position, Employer, Supervisor.*

DATES OF EMPLOYMENT	POSITION	EMPLOYER	SUPERVISOR

More About Your Work Experience

The Standard Form 171 is the name of the federal government job application form. It is also known as a Personal Qualifications Statement. It is a good example of the information you need to know about your experience.

WORK EXPERIENCE *If you have no work experience, write "NONE" and go to 25 on page 3.*

23 May we ask your present employer about your character, qualifications, and work record? *A "NO" will not affect our review of your qualifications. If you answer "NO" and we need to contact your present employer before we can offer you a job, we will contact you first.* . . . .

YES	NO

24 READ **WORK EXPERIENCE** IN THE INSTRUCTIONS BEFORE YOU BEGIN.

- Describe your current or most recent job in Block **A** and work backwards, describing each job you held **during the past 10 years**. If you were **unemployed** for longer than **3 months** within the past 10 years, list the dates and your address(es) in an experience block.
- You may sum up in one block work that you did **more than 10 years ago**. But if that work **is related** to the type of job you are applying for, describe each related job in a separate block.
- INCLUDE VOLUNTEER WORK *(non-paid work)*--**If the work** (or *a part of the work*) **is like the job you are applying for**, complete **all** parts of the experience block just as you would for a paying job. You may receive credit for work experience with religious, community, welfare, service, and other organizations.

- INCLUDE MILITARY SERVICE--You should complete **all** parts of the experience block just as you would for a non-military job, including all supervisory experience. Describe each major change of duties or responsibilities in a separate experience block.
- IF YOU NEED MORE SPACE TO DESCRIBE A JOB--Use sheets of paper the same size as this page (be sure to include **all** information we ask for in **A** and **B** below). On **each** sheet show your name, Social Security Number, and the announcement number or job title.
- IF YOU NEED MORE EXPERIENCE BLOCKS, use the SF 171-A or a sheet of paper.
- IF YOU NEED TO UPDATE (ADD MORE RECENT JOBS), use the SF 172 or a sheet of paper as described above.

A Name and address of employer's organization *(include ZIP Code, if known)*

Dates employed *(give month, day and year)*	Average number of hours per week	Number of employees you supervise
From: To:		

Salary or earnings	Your reason for wanting to leave
Starting $ per	
Ending $ per	

Your immediate supervisor
Name | Area Code | Telephone No.

Exact title of your job	If Federal employment *(civilian or military)* list series, grade or rank, and, if promoted in this
job, the date of your last promotion	

Description of work: Describe your specific duties, responsibilities and accomplishments in this job, **including** the job title(s) of any employees you supervise. *If you describe more than one type of work (for example, carpentry and painting, or personnel and budget), write the approximate percentage of time you spent doing each.*

_____

_____

_____

For Agency Use (skill codes, etc.)

B Name and address of employer's organization *(include ZIP Code, if known)*

Dates employed *(give month, day and year)*	Average number of hours per week	Number of employees you supervised
From: To:		

Salary or earnings	Your reason for leaving
Starting $ per	
Ending $ per	

Your immediate supervisor
Name | Area Code | Telephone No.

Exact title of your job	If Federal employment *(civilian or military)* list series, grade or rank, and, if promoted in this job, the date of your last promotion

Description of work: Describe your specific duties, responsibilities and accomplishments in this job, **including** the job title(s) of any employees you supervised. *If you describe more than one type of work (for example, carpentry and painting, or personnel and budget), write the approximate percentage of time you spent doing each.*

_____

_____

_____

_____

For Agency Use (skill codes, etc.)

Page 2 IF YOU NEED MORE EXPERIENCE BLOCKS, USE SF 171-A *(SEE BACK OF INSTRUCTION PAGE)*.

Writing On Your Own

Look at Part A of Standard Form 171 on page 238. Read the section that asks for "Description of work." Write responses for this section based on your most recent job. If you have not had a job, write responses for a job you would like to have. Use complete sentences when you describe your work experience. When you have finished, exchange responses with another student. Suggest ways that each of you could improve your responses.

Activity B Here are items you would have to fill in on a Standard Form 171. Use a job you have now or one you have had in the past to complete each item. Write your responses on your paper.

1. Name, address, and phone number of employer's organization (include ZIP and area codes)
2. Dates employed (give month, day, and year)
   From _____ To _____
3. Average number of hours per week
4. Exact title of your position
5. Place of employment (city and state)

Your Job Application References

When you fill out a job application, you are asking to be hired for a certain job. A reference is a person who will recommend you for that job. Always ask a person's permission before you use his or her name as a reference.

A reference should be
- a person who knows about your skills and past work experience.
- a person who likes and admires you and will say positive things about you.
- a person whom the new employer will believe and respect.

A reference should not be
- a relative.
- a person who did not like you or your work.

Activity C Explain why each of these people would or would not be a good reference. Write your answers on your paper. Then name three of your own references, and explain why each person would be a good reference.

1. A teacher
2. A guidance counselor
3. A previous employer
4. Your present employer
5. Your best friend

Match the words with their meanings. On your paper, write the correct letter next to each number.

Words	Meanings
1. Former	**A** The jobs you have had
2. Reference	**B** Your boss
3. Immediate supervisor	**C** A person who will recommend you for a job
4. Salary	**D** Your earnings
5. Work experience	**E** Refers to a time in the past

On your paper, write the answers to the following questions.

6. A job application may ask for the title of your previous _____ .

7. Which of the following would be a good reference for a job application?

    A your best friend   **C** a previous employer

    B a relative   **D** your next-door neighbor

8. What is another name for the Standard Form 171?

9. What information do you need about people you want to give as references?

10. When you tell about your work experience, which job should you describe first?

Financial

Concerning money or property with value

Value

The amount of money your property is worth to a buyer

Liability

The money you owe

Debt

Money owed, or liability

Assets

Property you own that has value

Net worth

The value of your assets minus the value of your liabilities

When you borrow money or receive credit, you will need to answer questions about your finances. You may need to fill out a **financial** form. Financial matters have to do with money or property with **value.**

You may need to prepare a financial statement at some time. To do this, you will need to list your **liabilities.** A liability is the money you owe to someone. **Debt** is another word for liability or money that you owe. Then you add up all your **assets** and all your liabilities. The value of your assets minus the value of your liabilities is your **net worth.**

Activity A Use the sample financial statement to answer the questions below. Write your answers on your paper.

Robert Thompson's Financial Statement

Assets		*Liabilities*	
Car	$2,800.00	Car loan at bank	$2,300.00
Watch	$25.00	Department store credit card	$144.32
CD player	$200.00		
Total	**$3,025.00**	**Total**	**$2,444.32**

$3,025.00 Assets
− $2,444.32 Liabilities
$ 580.68 Net worth

1. What is Robert Thompson's net worth?

2. Which of these two items is an asset?

   A Something you own with value

   B Money that you owe

3. List Robert Thompson's assets.

4. How much money does he owe?

5. If Robert sold everything he owns and paid all his debts, how much cash would he have?

Loan

A sum of money that you borrow

Activity B Follow the directions below to prepare a financial statement of your own.

1. Make a list of your assets. Guess what their value is.

2. Make a list of your liabilities (debts).

3. Add up both columns.

4. Subtract your liabilities from your assets.

5. Circle your net worth.

A loan for a home is a *mortgage*. You usually have 15 or 30 years to repay a mortgage.

Borrowing Money for a Car or House

Someday you may wish to obtain a **loan** to buy a car or a house. A loan is a sum of money you borrow. Lenders, or the people who loan money, want to make sure that they can get their money back. They will want answers to these questions:

1. How much money can you pay each month? Each month you pay back part of the loan. The bank will ask you about your income and about your other expenses.

2. What is the value of your car or house? You may not be able to make your payments. The bank can sell the car or house to get the money back.

Activity C On your paper, write the answers to these questions.

1. What are two reasons you may wish to get a loan?

2. Why will a lender ask you about your income and other expenses?

3. Why is it important for a lender to know the value of the item you wish to purchase?

4. If you bought a car, how would you list it on your financial statement?

5. How would you list a loan for a car on your financial statement?

Credit and Finance Charges

Credit is the time you get to pay for goods you buy. Another name for the goods you buy is **merchandise.**

Banks and department stores offer credit cards that customers can use to purchase merchandise on credit. If you charge goods on a credit card, the bank or store will send you a monthly bill, or statement. If you pay all of the money you owe on time, you do not have to pay any extra fees. When you pay only a part of what you owe, the bank or store charges you a **finance charge.** A finance charge is the fee you pay for borrowing on credit.

Charge accounts can be individual or **joint.** An individual account means that one person can use the card. A joint account means that two people can use the card. They are both responsible for paying the bill.

Activity D Here are some of the questions a store may ask you when you apply for a credit card. Answer as many of them as you can. Write your answers on your paper.

1. Will this be an individual or a joint account?
2. What is the name of the applicant (the person applying for the credit card)?
3. What is your Social Security number?
4. What is your date of birth?
5. What is your present address?
6. How long have you been at this address?
7. If you have been at the above address for less than four years, list your former address.
8. What is your phone number? (Include area code.)
9. Who is your current employer?
10. What is your employer's address?
11. What is your business telephone number?
12. What type of business is this?
13. What is your present position?
14. What is your monthly salary?
15. What is your driver's license number?

Credit
The time you get to pay for the goods you buy

Merchandise
Goods for sale or that you buy

Finance charge
A fee you pay on money you owe to a business

Joint
An account that is shared or owned together

Bank Accounts

When you ask for a loan or credit, you usually have to provide information about your bank accounts. There are several kinds of bank accounts.

Savings Accounts

You open a savings account by depositing money into the bank. The purpose is to save money. You should not need this money right away. The bank pays you **interest** on this money. Interest is the money a bank pays you for putting money into a savings account. You don't write checks to get your money from a savings account; you use a **withdrawal** slip. A withdrawal is the money you have taken from your account.

Checking Accounts

You open a checking account by putting some money into the bank. The bank gives you a checkbook. You withdraw money from your account by writing checks. You can write checks to other people or to yourself. You can't write checks for more money than you have in your account. A **deposit** is money you have put into an account. Some checking accounts pay interest.

Loan Accounts

You open a loan account when you borrow money. Every month you make a payment to pay back part of the loan. Your monthly payment includes interest. This type of interest is unlike interest that you receive from the bank for keeping your money there. The interest you pay on a loan is the fee you pay to the bank or lender for borrowing money.

Activity E On your paper, write answers to these questions about bank accounts.

1. What is interest?

2. On which account do you pay interest?

3. How do you add money to your checking account balance?

4. How do you withdraw money from a checking account?

5. To whom do you pay interest on a loan?

Interest

The money a bank pays you for putting money into a savings account; the fee you pay for borrowing money

Withdrawal

Money that you take out of your bank account

Deposit

The money you put into an account

Banking Information over the Phone

You may be able to check your account balances by phone. This service is handy when you need an account balance in a hurry. Some banks have a phone number that you call to get information about your account. You will hear a recorded voice that asks you questions. Using a phone, you can enter your account information. The recording then will give you the information that you request.

Banking Information Online

If you have Internet access, you can get information about your account balances online. You can check the balance of your checking, savings, or loan account. Some banks will let you pay bills online.

Online banking services are fairly safe to use. The bank takes steps to make sure that your account information is safe online. The first time you use online banking services, you will need to choose a user ID. This is a name that you will use whenever you want to use the bank Web site. You also will need to create a password. If you have trouble remembering your ID and password, write them on a piece of paper. Be sure to put the paper in a safe place. This is private information.

Vocabulary Builder

Using Context Clues

You may find unfamiliar words as you complete banking or loan applications. Figure out the meaning of new words by looking for clues in surrounding words and sentences. This is called *context*. The context provides clues about the meaning of the unfamiliar word. Read the following examples.

The bank gave me a loan; **that is,** *they let me borrow money.*

We had a joint account, **which is the opposite of** *an individual account.*

Complete the following sentences with the boldfaced context clues.

liability	interest	withdrawal
deposit	merchandise	

1. The **opposite of** "to take money out of an account" is to _____ .
2. You have a _____ **because** you owe someone money.
3. _____ is money you earn from a savings account or a fee for borrowing money.
4. The **opposite of** *deposit* is _____ .
5. Goods are **also known as** _____ .

Match the words with their meanings. On your paper, write the correct letter next to each number.

Words	Meanings
1. Asset	**A** Any property that you own
2. Value	**B** The amount a buyer will pay
3. Loan	**C** A fee for borrowing on credit
4. Credit	**D** Time that you get to pay for
5. Finance charge	**E** Money that you have borrowed

On your paper, write a financial statement for Isaac Washington. List his assets and liabilities. Compute his net worth.

6. He has a car worth $4,200.00.

7. He owes $133.81 at Wilton's Department Store.

8. He has a savings account with a balance of $312.80.

9. He has $129.15 in his checking account.

10. He owes the bank $2,568.00 on a car loan.

On your paper, write the answers to the following questions.

11. What are two quick ways to check your bank account balances?

12. What is interest?

13. What other services do bank Web sites offer in addition to account balances?

14. What do you need to choose when you check your account balances online?

15. What is a liability?

A credit reference is a person or bank that will recommend you for a loan or credit. A personal reference is someone who knows you personally. The first time you borrow money or open a charge account, you are establishing credit. When you repay a loan on time, the bank becomes a solid credit reference. If you pay your bills at a department store, the store is also a good credit reference.

Credit Application   please print

NAME–FIRST	MIDDLE INITIAL	LAST			AGE (MUST BE AT LEAST 18)
PRESENT ADDRESS–STREET		CITY	STATE		ZIP CODE
TIME AT THIS ADDRESS ____Yrs. ____Mos.	☐ OWN/BUYING ☐ LIVE WITH RELATIVES	☐ RENT ☐ OTHER	DRIVER'S LICENSE NUMBER & STATE		
RESIDENCE TELEPHONE (AREA CODE)		SOCIAL SECURITY NO. (MUST BE PROVIDED)			
IF LESS THAN 3 YEARS AT RESIDENCE, GIVE PREVIOUS ADDRESS			NUMBER OF DEPENDENTS (EXCLUDE APPLICANT)		
EMPLOYED BY			HOW LONG ____Yrs. ____Mos.	BUSINESS PHONE (AREA CODE)	
BUSINESS ADDRESS				TYPE OF BUSINESS	

Good credit is a history of paying bills and loans on time. Bad credit is a history of late or skipped payments.

A credit limit is the maximum amount that a bank will let you borrow. It also can be the maximum amount a store will allow you to charge.

Banks and department stores charge different amounts of interest. Usually, the interest rate on bank credit cards is lower than the interest on department store credit cards. Both types, however, usually will raise your interest rate if you make a late payment.

Activity A On your paper, write your answers to these questions.

1. What is a credit reference?

2. What is good credit?

3. Do you have a bank account? If yes, what type do you have?

4. Do you have any credit references? Name them.

5. Write the name and address of a person who knows you personally and who might help you obtain credit. Do not name a relative or any person who lives in your home.

Establishing Credit

Whenever you try to borrow money, the lender will want to know your credit history. The lender will ask you for credit references. The first time you ask for credit, you do not have a history—good or bad. Here are guidelines for establishing credit:

1. You usually need a regular income before you can establish credit.

2. Open a checking account and a savings account at a bank. Do not overdraw your checking account. Deposit to your savings account regularly. You can use your bank as a credit reference.

3. Open a charge account at a department store. The store will probably give you a low credit limit. Purchase something with your charge card. When the bill comes each month, pay at least the minimum amount until the item is paid for. Don't buy things unless you need them. Always pay your bill on time. Then your charge account can be a credit reference.

4. Take out a small loan at a bank. Make your payments on time. After you have repaid this loan, you will have another credit reference.

Activity B On your paper, write the answer to these questions.

1. What is the first thing you could do to establish credit so that you can borrow money to buy a car?

2. What are two kinds of accounts you can open at a bank?

3. What kind of account do you open at a department store?

4. What is a credit limit? open a change account at a department store

5. What is the most important rule when you take out a loan? Make on payments on time

Write on your paper the answers to these questions.

1. What are three kinds of people or businesses that would be good credit references?

2. What kind of person would be a good personal reference?

3. What is good credit history?

4. What is the name of the maximum amount of credit that a bank will loan you?

5. List three things that you may need to supply on a credit application.

6. For what kinds of things would you need to apply for credit?

7. What are three ways to establish credit?

8. What should you do when you receive the monthly bill for your charge account?

Number your paper from 9 to 15. Next to each number, print the information asked for on the form.

Credit Application   please print

9.	NAME–FIRST MIDDLE INITIAL LAST	AGE (MUST BE AT LEAST 18)
10.	PRESENT ADDRESS–STREET CITY STATE	ZIP CODE
11.	TIME AT THIS ADDRESS ____Yrs. ____Mos. ☐ OWN/BUYING ☐ RENT ☐ LIVE WITH RELATIVES ☐ OTHER	DRIVER'S LICENSE NUMBER & STATE
12.	RESIDENCE TELEPHONE (AREA CODE)	SOCIAL SECURITY NO. (MUST BE PROVIDED)
13.	IF LESS THAN 3 YEARS AT RESIDENCE, GIVE PREVIOUS ADDRESS	NUMBER OF DEPENDENTS (EXCLUDE APPLICANT)
14.	EMPLOYED BY	HOW LONG ____Yrs. ____Mos. BUSINESS PHONE (AREA CODE)
15.	BUSINESS ADDRESS	TYPE OF BUSINESS

Chapter 8 R E V I E W

Word Bank

applicable

application

assets

credit

deposit

debt

education

employer

form

interest

joint

liability

net worth

salary

signature

value

withdrawal

Part A For each sentence below, write the correct word on your paper.

1. Something that is appropriate or suitable is _____ .

2. A _____ is a printed or typed document that has spaces to fill in information.

3. _____ is the money that a bank pays you for putting money into a savings account.

4. Money owed, or liability, is _____ .

5. _____ is the time you get to pay for the goods that you buy.

6. When you write your name, you write your _____ .

7. When you take money out of your bank account, you make a _____ .

8. An _____ is property you own that has value.

9. The amount of money that someone pays you for working is a _____ .

10. An _____ is a form to make a request, usually for a job.

11. _____ is the amount of money that your property is worth to a buyer.

12. The money that you owe is _____ .

13. The money that you put into an account is a _____ .

14. _____ is the value of your assets minus the value of your liabilities.

15. A combination of the courses and programs that you take at a school or college is your _____ .

16. A person or company that pays you a salary is an _____ .

17. A _____ account is shared or owned by two people.

Part B Write on your paper the answers to these questions.

18. Name three examples of personal information that you might give on an application form.

19. What are the postal abbreviations for the states of Iowa, Kansas, and Arizona?

20. Name three examples of situations in which you will need to give your Social Security number.

21. Why must you print or type answers on a job application?

22. Why is it important to provide information about your job skills on a job application?

23. What does it mean to have a pertinent job skill?

Part C On your paper, fill in the word that completes each sentence.

24. A person who will recommend you for a job is a _____ .

25. Your legal name is on your _____ certificate.

26. A _____ is the name of a job.

Part D On your paper, write the answer to each of the following questions.

27. Emilio paid $2,500 for a car. His car is a $2,500 _____.

    A liability   **B** credit   **C** asset   **D** debt

28. Ruby opened a charge account. When she got her bill, she made a payment. Because she still owed the store money, a _____ was added to her bill.

    A finance charge   **B** signature   **C** loan   **D** deposit

29. Anne had $100 in her savings account. She made a _____ of $10. Now she has $110 in her account.

    A debt   **B** finance charge   **C** deposit   **D** loan

30. Mrs. Chang borrowed money from the bank. Now she has a _____ account.

    A savings   **B** loan   **C** checking   **D** joint

Test-Taking Tip When taking a short-answer test, first answer the questions you know for sure. Then go back to spend time on the questions about which you are less sure.

9

Shopping by Catalog

A catalog is like a reference book. It usually has pictures and descriptions of many kinds of merchandise. People use catalogs for information about products, for shopping, and for browsing. When you browse, you read small bits of information at random. Many businesses also sell their products on the Internet. Instead of selling products to a retail store, they sell them directly to the consumer. They display their goods on a Web page rather than in a store.

In Chapter 9, you will learn about catalog shopping by mail and on the Internet. Each lesson will help you learn how to read and understand the information in a catalog and how to order merchandise.

Goals for Learning

◆ To learn how to read and understand the information in a catalog

◆ To learn how to order products from online stores

◆ To learn how to order merchandise from a catalog

◆ To learn how to solve problems related to catalog shopping

Wholesale

The merchandise that is for sale to dealers

Retail

Items that are for sale to the public

Dealer

A business or individual that sells to the public

Appliance

A piece of household equipment such as a toaster, an oven, a dishwasher, an electric mixer, or a microwave oven

Advantage

A benefit or positive feature

Disadvantage

An unfavorable condition or negative feature

Large department stores and mail order houses have many kinds of merchandise. They buy the merchandise at a **wholesale** price and sell it at a **retail** price. Wholesale refers to the merchandise that is for sale to **dealers.** A dealer is someone who sells to the public. Retail refers to items that are for sale to the public. Dealers sell clothing; **appliances** (household equipment such as toasters, ovens, dishwashers, electric mixers, or microwave ovens); jewelry; furniture; machines and tools; toys and games; and other kinds of goods.

You may buy merchandise from dealers in the following five ways:

- Purchase the item in the store.
- Order it by computer on the Internet.
- Order the item by telephone.
- Order the item by mail.
- Order by FAX.

If you order the item, you may receive it in the two following ways:

- Pick up your order at the store
- Have your order delivered to your home.

Each method of buying merchandise has **advantages** and **disadvantages.** An advantage is a benefit, or a reason, for choosing something. A disadvantage is an unfavorable condition or a reason for not choosing something.

In addition to the price of the goods, customers usually pay shipping costs. Remember to add that cost when you are comparing prices.

Activity A On your paper, write one advantage and one disadvantage of buying products in each of the following ways.

1. by phone   **4.** by mail

2. on the Internet   **5.** at the store

3. by FAX

Finding Items in a Catalog

A large catalog will usually have an index to help you find quickly what you are looking for. Here is an example of an index with main headings.

Quick Reference Guide	
appliances 176–197	jewelry..................1–75
automotive.......349–356	lamps...............232–237
baby goods........386–396	lawn furniture....336–337
billfolds 98–101	luggage 258–266
calculators 270–273	office equipment 274–276
car stereos.........355–356	personal care.... 206–215
clocks 96, 242–253	photographic equipment 280–290
computers........163–175	radios 291–293
cookware..........148–160	stereo, TVs 294–329
floor care..........199–201	sporting goods...347–348
giftware............135–147	tools 338–346
hardware..........338–346	toys 397–444

Activity B Read each item below. Then find each item in the index above. On your paper, write the number of the first catalog page on which you would find the item.

EXAMPLE   Juanita wants a wallet. A wallet is a billfold.
She would look on page 98.

1. Luke is shopping for a computer.

2. Marty needs a suitcase.

3. Kara is looking for some earrings.

4. Luis wants a hammer and a saw.

5. Lakisha would like a pretty vase to give to her mother for her birthday.

Comparison Shopping With Catalogs

When you compare prices at different stores, you are comparison shopping. You can comparison shop with catalogs. When you want to buy a certain item, find it in one or two catalogs. Look at the prices and the different features each product has. Decide which item is the best buy.

A.

QUICK POP—Model 8341—Electric hot air popper. Use no oil. Continuous feeding bin. Special butter well adds melted butter on every kernel. 5 lb. 342145460
Retail price $29.95
Our price $21.95

B.

OODLES OF POP
6-quart electric corn popper. Automatic stirring rod, non-stick popping surface. Self-buttering. Automatic shutoff. Use the cover as a bowl. 6 lb. 321092834
$38.99
Rivera's price $27.63

C.

4-quart electric popper. Non-stick surface. Self-buttering. Automatic shutoff.
4 LB. 212434001 RETAIL PRICE $18.95
Kitchen Catalog price $12.43
FUN POPPER

Activity C Use the descriptions of the three kinds of popcorn poppers on page 258 to answer the following questions. Write your answers on your paper.

1. What does item A use instead of oil?
2. What is the most important difference between items B and C?
3. Which popcorn popper lets you use the cover as a bowl?
4. What is the catalog number of item A?
5. How much money will you save if you buy item A in the catalog rather than at the full retail price?
6. Which popper does not have an automatic shut-off?
7. How much does item C cost through the catalog?
8. Which popper is the least expensive?
9. What automatic part does item B have that the others don't?
10. In what ways are all three poppers alike?

Specialty Catalogs

There are many small mail order catalog businesses. They sell clothing, food, gift items, and other specialty items. Usually there is a picture of each item and a brief description. You must read the descriptions very carefully to be sure of what you are getting.

Catalog Descriptions

You will often find in catalog descriptions the same type of language as you find in advertisements. The goal of a catalog description is to convince you that the product will enrich and improve your life if you buy it.

Sometimes a catalog description will offer a **rebate.** A rebate is a return of part of the payment for a product or service.

HOME COMPUTER — Easy to use. All you need is some software and your computer is ready to teach, entertain, or help you with home finances at a touch of a button.
Order Model **4432S.**

Our price	$1,124.99
Factory *rebate*	$199.00
Our price	$925.99

Monitor and keyboard extra

Activity D Use the catalog description above to answer these questions. Write your answers on your paper.

1. How much money is the store charging the customer for this computer?

2. How much money will the customer get back from the factory after purchasing the computer?

3. What does the ad say the computer can help you do?

4. What does the price of the computer not include?

5. What is the model number of the computer?

Lesson 1   R E V I E W

On your paper, write the answers to these questions.

1. What are two ways to order merchandise from a catalog.
2. Who pays wholesale prices—customers or dealers?
3. Which kind of price is highest?

   A wholesale   B retail   C discount   D catalog

4. Name one way that catalogs are like large department stores.
5. What is a retail price?
6. What can you use in catalogs to find a certain item quickly?
7. Name one kind of information about goods that you will find in a catalog. (There are several possible answers.)
8. What is comparison shopping?
9. What is a specialty catalog?
10. What does it mean when a catalog offers a rebate?

Read the description. On your paper, write your answers to the questions that follow.

We are happy to introduce more fine porcelain from Brazil in the form of these COFFEE MUGS. The porcelain is thick enough to keep the contents hot, but tapers to a thin rim for easy sipping. The bases are inset for stacking, and the price is designed to please. 8 oz. capac.

Set of four, #123-9902.........................$12^{00}

11. How many cups will you receive?
12. What is the value of each cup?
13. Is there a choice of colors?
14. Can you stack these cups?
15. What is the catalog number?

Today you can shop for items in a store, by catalog, or on the Internet. You can search for stores on the Internet by using the names of stores you see in your community or in magazines. Some stores are only on the Internet—you must shop at these stores online.

Why Shop on the Internet?

Many consumers shop on the Internet for convenience and for savings. Here are some reasons to shop online:

- You can shop 24 hours a day, seven days a week. Internet stores never close.

- You do not need to travel to the store, so you save both time and transportation costs.

- You can quickly locate the store and the items you want.

- You can avoid crowded stores and traffic congestion.

- You can easily comparison shop for similar items among different stores. You can visit different stores with a click—you do not have to go to different stores to compare prices.

- You usually can find more choices because Internet stores have unlimited shelf space.

- You can buy products online that local stores do not stock.

- You can have stores deliver purchases to your door within a day or two. Internet stores will also deliver gifts.

Activity A On your paper, write answers for each of the following questions.

1. What are three ways you can shop for items?

2. When can you shop on the Internet?

3. What is one reason you might not want to travel to a store to buy an item?

4. How can you comparison shop online?

5. Name two reasons to shop online rather than at a store.

Types of Internet Stores and Products

What types of items would you purchase on the Internet? The Internet offers a wide variety of stores and products. The following list shows the types of products you can purchase on the Internet:

- Clothing, jewelry, and shoes
- Flowers and gifts
- Gourmet food baskets
- Perfume, cologne, and cosmetics
- Food supplements and vitamins
- Prescriptions, eyeglasses, and contact lenses
- Groceries
- Home improvement and home decorating items
- Furniture and appliances
- Office supplies
- Automobile parts
- Toys, games, and collectibles
- Books, CDs, CD-ROMs, videos, and DVDs
- Electronics, such as televisions, stereos, and computers

Before You Shop on the Internet

All Internet businesses require you to pay when you place an order online. Before you shop on the Internet, you need a **charge card** account or a checking account with a **check card.** A check card, or debit card, accesses a checking account. The check card looks like a charge card and includes an account number and bank logo. Have it ready before you place an order online.

National Town Bank
Check Card

0000 5555 0000 2222 —————— Account number

Valid
From 12/01

Good
thru 3/04

Stella Carter

Expiration date

Here are some common terms you will see when you shop online.

Internet shopping terms	Meanings
Checkout	Function that completes online shopping
Shopping cart	Function that stores online purchases until checkout
Redeem	To turn in for use as money
Gift certificate	A coupon that allows the recipient to purchase goods for a certain amount of money.

Using What You've Learned

Use the information in this lesson to list five reasons you would want to shop on the Internet instead of in a store. Then, list five different items that you would like to buy on the Internet.

You're Ready to Shop Online!

Once you have a charge card or check card, you can make an online purchase.

Steps for Shopping Online

1. Go to the Internet.
2. Type in the Web site address or search for the item you want.
3. Browse the Internet shops to find the item.
4. Add the item to your shopping cart.
5. Click on the checkout box and follow the steps.

Checking Out

Once you have found the item you want to buy, you are ready to check out. Steps for checking out at online stores may not all be exactly the same. But, most are similar to the steps below.

1. Click the checkout box or button.
2. Provide your name, address, phone number, and payment information. You can also provide your e-mail address.
3. Give charge card account number and expiration date.
4. Confirm all information for your order.
5. Click on Submit or Send to place your order.
6. Print the confirmation page for your records.

If you provided your e-mail address, most stores will send you a confirmation e-mail.

Activity B Put the following steps for Internet shopping in the correct order. Write the numbers 1 to 10 on your paper. Then write the letter responses in the correct order.

A Go to checkout.

B Go to the Internet.

C Choose the type of delivery you want.

D Type in search words for a product.

E Get a charge card or a check card.

F Look for an e-mail that confirms your online order.

G Look at different stores to compare prices.

H Put the item in your online shopping cart.

I Provide your name, address, and payment information.

J Submit your completed online order.

Activity C Match each word with its meaning. Write your answer on your paper.

1. gift certificate
2. check card
3. redeem
4. checkout
5. shopping cart

A to turn in for use as money

B a coupon that a person can use

C holds purchases until checkout

D card that withdraws money from a checking account

E completes online shopping

Comparison Shopping on the Internet

Just as you can comparison shop using different catalogs, you can comparison shop for items at different Internet stores. One store may have the same item as another at a better price. Or, a store may have a similar item with more or better features. The Internet makes comparison shopping fast and easy.

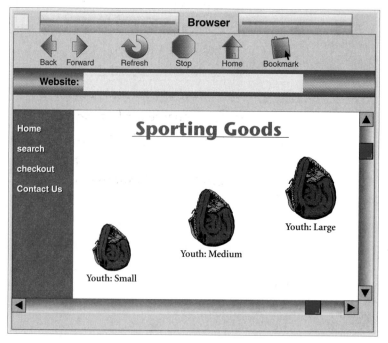

Comparison shopping helps you find the best buy for an item.

On your paper, write the answers to the following questions.

1. What is a consumer?

2. How many hours a day can you shop on the Internet?

3. Name an advantage to shopping on the Internet.

4. What is a check card?

5. Why do you need a check card or a charge card before you shop on the Internet?

Read the following list of steps for shopping online. Number your paper from 6 to 15. Then write the letter responses in the correct order.

A Provide your name, address, and payment information.

B Go to checkout.

C Type in search words for a product.

D Put the item in your shopping cart.

E Go to the Internet.

F Look for an e-mail that confirms your online order.

G Submit your completed order.

H Get a charge card or check card.

I Choose the type of delivery you want.

J Look at different stores to compare their prices for the product you want to purchase.

Vocabulary Builder

Shopping Vocabulary

Whether you are shopping in a store or online, it helps to know some of the vocabulary. For example, this lesson introduces the terms *gift certificate* and *redeem.* In addition, you can buy items from a store on the Internet much the way you buy items from any store. You can place items you wish to buy in a *shopping cart* and purchase items at a *checkout.*

Write the answers to these questions.

1. When would you click on the checkout box?

2. Can you add items or take items out of your shopping cart?

3. Use the term *gift certificate* in a sentence.

4. Use the word *redeem* in a sentence.

When you order merchandise from a company on the Internet or by phone or mail, the company adds a shipping charge because it sends the goods to your home. Order forms and Web pages list shipping charges. Companies calculate shipping charges using the weight or cost of the goods that you buy.

Shipping charges depend on which shipping company a store uses. They also depend on the size and weight of the product and the shipping time that is acceptable to the customer. Most catalog and online stores offer customers several choices.

Shipping Charges by Cost

Amount of order:	Include:
Up to $9.99	$1.95
$10.00 - $19.99	$2.95
$20.00 - $29.99	$3.95
$30.00 - $39.99	$4.95
$40.00 - $49.99	$5.95
$50.00 - $74.99	$7.50
$75.00 - $99.99	$8.25
Over $100.00	$11.00

Shipping Rates by Weight

Lb.	Charge
1 - 5	$3.15
6 - 10	$5.07
11 - 15	$6.98
16 - 20	$8.90
21 - 25	$10.95
26 - 30	$12.78
31 - 40	$16.65
Over 40	$20.54

Activity A Figure the total cost of each item in the two ways shown below. Write your answers as in the example.

 A Add shipping charges by cost.
 B Add shipping charges by weight.

EXAMPLE

SET OF four 10-OZ. MUGS. Insulated plastic, 2 lb. $3.47.

 A $3.47 + $1.95 = $5.42   **B** $3.47 + $3.15 = $6.62

 1. PINE PAPER CUP DISPENSER. Holds about 45 5-oz. cups. 3 lb. Retail price $18.00. Our price $15.00.

 2. MAPLE ROCKING CHAIR. Colonial style. 21 lb. $67.97.

 3. 10-SPEED MOUNTAIN BIKE. Big, nobby tires. 26" chrome frame. 49 lb. $134.95.

 4. SMALL DELUXE GARDEN SHOVEL. 1 lb. Regularly $29.95.

 5. EXERCISE BENCH DELUXE MODEL. 67 lb. $109.00.

Ordering by Phone

You may want to order from a catalog store by telephone. When you order by phone, have ready all the information you will need to place your order. Here is a list of the kind of information you usually will need to place a catalog order.

- Catalog item number

- Name of item

- Description (including size and color, if applicable)

- Quantity

- Price of each item

- Total price (multiply the price of one by the number of items you order)

- Shipping weight

- Credit card number and expiration date

- Daytime phone number where the company can reach you if there's a problem

Activity B From the list below, choose two items to order by telephone. Make a list of the information you will need about each item to place the order. Write the information on your paper.

Where To Find It

Some stores have large catalogs available. The store may charge a small fee for these catalogs. Some stores offer smaller catalogs for free. You can also contact retailers by phone to ask for catalogs. Contact three stores and request a catalog from each.

A. CAMP STOVE 3 1/2 pt. fuel tank. 22"×13"×6". 15 lb. #134200BC **$34.95.**

B. TWO–PERSON TENT Fire-retardant–coated nylon with 3-zip screen entrance, rear screen window with storm flap. Polyurethane floor. Rope, poles, stakes. 4 lb. #134210BC **$120.00.**

C. 2 QT. DESERT CANTEEN Blanket-covered for insulation. Screw cap with safety chain. Rustproof steel frame. 2 lb. #123200BC **$9.50.**

D. SLEEPING BAG 33"×75" Ripstop nylon shell, nylon lining. 3 lb. #123400BC **$47.95.**

E. HEAVY DUTY FLASHLIGHT Optically perfect reflector with shatterproof lens. Needs two "D" batteries. 2 lb. #234540DF **$10.05.**

Payment Methods

There are several ways to pay for a catalog order.

- **Check**—A check is a draft on your bank account. You mail a check with your order.

- **Money Order**—You buy a money order from the bank or post office in the amount of your catalog order.

- **Charge Card**—You may have a charge card for a certain store, or you may use a major credit card.

Sold To:

Name: _____ Phone: _____

Street Address: _____

City: _____ State: _____ ZIP: _____

PAYMENT METHOD: Do not send cash. Make checks payable to:
Better Products, Inc.

☐ Check or money
order enclosed

Charge my order to:
Credit Card _____

Signature _____
Orders not valid without signature.

Credit card number   Exp. Date

Activity C Use the order form above to answer the following questions. Write your answers on your paper.

1. Does this company accept cash?

2. To what name do you make your check payable?

3. Will the company send your order if you do not write your signature on the form?

4. Does the company accept credit cards?

5. Where do you enter the number of your credit card?

Filling Out an Order Form

Be sure to fill out order forms very carefully. You want to be sure you get the merchandise you order. If you write the wrong catalog number, you may get the wrong item. If you write your address incorrectly, you may never receive your order.

Order Form

1. Name _Edward Gomez_
2. Address _9301 Watkins Avenue_
3. City / State / ZIP _Wilton, Delaware   19973_
4. Daytime telephone (_302_) _555-3881_

Item	#Qty.	Description	Item Price	Total Price	
5.	101-0019	1	Wool cap, red	$18.00	$ 18	00
6.	103-0020	3	Tennis balls, yellow	5.00	15	00
7.						

SHIPPING CHARGES			
UP TO $10.00	$2.00	8. Total Price	$ 33 | 00
$10.00 - $30.00	$3.00	9. Shipping	4 | 00
OVER $30.00	$4.00	10. Total Charge	$ 37 | 00

Activity D Number your paper from 1 to 10 as on the order form above. Choose any three items below to order. Write the information carefully as you would write it on an order form.

#101–0019   WOOL CAPS. One size fits all. Red, blue, green. $18.00.

#101–2001   WARM-UP SUIT. 100% polyester. S-M-L-XL. Blue or green. $59.95.

#102–1001   BASEBALL GLOVE in fine-quality leather. $49.95.

#103–0020   TENNIS BALLS. Yellow or orange. Special sale price. $5.00.

#104–1008   CD/DVD PLAYER, 5-disc changer. $195.00.

Safe and Secure Internet Shopping

It is best to shop online at stores with names that you know and trust. For security purposes, make sure that the address bar on your computer screen has a picture of a lock and the letters "https" at the beginning of the Web site address. This means you are at a secure Web site that protects your personal information so that others cannot read it. After you place an online order, be sure to click on "log out" if the store provides you that option.

When you enter a secure Web page, a notice will appear.

EXAMPLE

Security Notice
🔒 **You are entering a page which is secure. The information you view and send cannot be read in transit.**
☑ **Show an alert when entering a page which is secure**   (To turn this option back on, from the Edit menu, choose Preferences, and then click the Security item.)

Be careful not to order from a Web site that does not show this security notice. This notice lets you know that you are entering a Web page that is safe and that people or businesses cannot get this information. This lets you, the buyer, know that your credit card information is secure.

Be sure that the Web site is secure when shopping online.

Lesson 3   R E V I E W

On your paper, write your answers to these questions.

1. Name two ways to order from a catalog.

2. Who is usually responsible for paying shipping charges—the catalog dealer or the customer?

3. What are two ways to pay for a catalog order?

4. Where do you buy a money order?

5. What should you look for to find out if a Web page is secure?

------------------------------------- ✂ -------------------------------------
CUT HERE

Order Form

6. Name _____

7. Address _____

8. City / State / ZIP _____

9. Daytime telephone (_____) _____

	Item	#Qty.	Description	Item Price	Total Price
10.					
11.					
12.					

SHIPPING CHARGES			
UP TO $10.00	$2.00	13. Total Price	$
$10.00 - $30.00	$3.00	14. Shipping	
OVER $30.00	$4.00	15. Total Charge	$

Number your paper from 6 to 15 as on the order form. Order the following three items. On your paper, write the information as you would on the order form.

#702222   RUBY PENDANT. 3 rubies and 2 diamonds in 10K gold. $335.00.

#34311W   ELEGANT WATCH. 6-digit, displays hours, minutes, seconds, months, and days on command. Sale-price $84.95.

#21333A   BRASS COAT TREE. Traditional hall stand in polished brass. 69" high. $89.90 or two for $165.00.

Sometimes the merchandise you order will be unsatisfactory.

EXAMPLE
- You may receive broken items.
- The item may not work properly.
- Clothing may not fit.
- Merchandise may not look the same as it does in the catalog picture.
- You may not like the merchandise.

It is important to examine the merchandise carefully as soon as it arrives. You have the three following choices:

1. Call the company or store as soon as you are able. Explain what is wrong.

2. Rewrap the item, and mail it back. Explain what is wrong in a letter.

3. Take the item back to the store. Tell the manager what is wrong.

Whatever your choice, you should return the merchandise as quickly as possible.

Calling the catalog company when there is a problem with your order will help correct the problem quickly.

Calling the Company

Call the company as soon as you know that there is a problem with the merchandise. This will alert the company that you would like to return or exchange the item. Be sure that you ask for the correct mailing address for returning the product. Companies often have a different mailing address for returns. Some catalog companies will mail you a postage-paid label that you can use to return the item by mail.

A Letter of Complaint

After you call the company about the return, you may want to include a letter with the merchandise. Here is a letter that Chris Williams wrote when she returned a dress.

31 E. Ralston Pl.
Wilton, DE 19999

April 3, 2002

Dress AMERICA
P.O. Box 231
Selbyville, TX 75820

Attention: Customer Service

Dear Sir:
   I am returning the dress #CA4531 Size 11. It is too large. Please exchange it for a size 9. Thank you for your help.

Sincerely,

Chris Williams

Chris Williams

Writing On Your Own

Always use polite language in a letter of complaint. Before writing your letter of complaint for Activity A, make a list of polite words, such as *Dear Sir or Madam* and *please,* that you will use in your letters. Write four additional courteous words or phrases to use in your letter.

Activity A Write a letter of complaint to the following address. Use the letter above as an example. Address the letter to

Quality Products, Inc.
12 West Franklin Street
Wilkinsburg, PA 15220
Attention: Customer Service

Choose one of these problems to write about:

1. Your DVD player isn't working properly. It will not eject the DVD.

2. A set of dishes you planned to give your sister for her new apartment arrived broken.

3. Your popcorn maker is not shutting off automatically. The popcorn is burning.

What the Store Will Do

How a store responds when you return an item is partly your choice. Some stores will not return your money. A store may take one of the following actions:

1. Give you another item that fits or isn't broken.

2. Fix the item if it is broken.

3. Return the full amount of your purchase price in cash.

4. Apply a credit to your charge card if you purchased the item this way.

5. Give you a store credit to use to buy something else.

When More Action Is Needed

Your attempts to clear up an unsatisfactory order may not work. If that happens, here are some steps to take when you need more action.

1. If a catalog store does not take action on your complaint within a few weeks, call the store on the telephone. Use the toll-free number, or call collect. Ask to speak with a manager or supervisor.

2. Contact the post office if the company mailed your order. Give all the information needed to trace your package. The post office will need to know the name of the company, the complete mailing address, the telephone number with area code, the mailing date, and how the order was mailed.

3. Many newspapers and television stations have people who investigate consumer problems. Find out the address of the correct person, and write to him or her for help.

4. Write the store another letter. Be persistent! Don't give up until the problem is solved.

5. Contact the Better Business Bureau. Find out how this organization rates the company that has not responded to your problem. File a complaint if necessary.

6. Review all of your letters and any notes from phone calls. See whether you have overlooked anything that would clear up the matter or would help you take additional action.

Number your paper from 1 to 5. Read each problem below and choose the best solution. Write the correct letter beside each number. Problems may have more than one acceptable answer.

Problems

1. Ben ordered a shirt from the World's Horizon catalog. When the shirt came, it was the wrong size.

2. Terri bought a set of dishes at a catalog showroom. When she got home and opened the box, she found a broken plate.

3. Emiko ordered a blouse from a catalog through the mail. The blouse did not look like the one in the picture. Emiko wants her money back.

4. Phil returned his computer to Quality Products, Inc. In a few weeks, they sent it back. It still did not work.

5. Shana ordered some seeds for her garden from a seed catalog. The company did not have the seeds she had ordered, so instead they sent her replacements. She really did not want the replacements.

Solutions

A Mail the merchandise back immediately. Explain what is wrong. Tell the store or company what you need.

B Mail the merchandise back at once. Tell the store you want your money refunded.

C Call the company. Explain the problem.

D Take the merchandise back to the store as soon as possible.

Spelling Builder

Catalog or Catalogue?
You may have seen the word *catalog* also spelled *catalogue.* You can spell some words in two different ways. Some of these are British spellings. Choose the spelling used in the United States when possible. Here are examples of words that you can spell in two different ways:

United States	British
dialog	dialogue
theater	theatre
traveler	traveller

Explain the difference between the two spellings in each pair. Then use each of the words in the left column in a sentence.

Chapter 9 REVIEW

Word Bank

advantage

appliance

charge card

check

check card

consumer

dealer

disadvantage

money order

rebate

retail

wholesale

Part A Write on your paper the word, or words, needed to complete each statement correctly.

1. A piece of household equipment such as a toaster is an _____.

2. _____ merchandise is for sale to dealers.

3. A check you purchase at the bank or post office is a _____.

4. A _____ allows you to charge the cost of goods to the business that issues the card.

5. A benefit or positive feature is an _____.

6. A _____ is a business or individual that sells to the public.

7. _____ items are meant to be sold to the public.

8. A return of part of a payment for a product is a _____.

9. A draft on your bank account is a _____.

10. A _____ is an unfavorable condition or negative feature.

11. A _____ is an individual buyer.

12. You can access your checking account with a _____, also known as a debit card.

Part B On your paper, write the answer to each question.

13. Which of the following do you avoid when you buy a product on the Internet?

    A crowded stores   C privacy

    B spending money   D home delivery

14. What can you use to purchase goods on the Internet?

    A check   B cash   C check card   D money order

15. What do secure online stores have in their address bar?

    A "http"   B "https"   C "secure"   D "safe"

Part C Read the product description below. On your paper, write the information as you would write it on the order form shown.

#054-9856

Telephone Answering Machine

Call from anywhere in the world and pick up messages. Built-in speaker and earphone jack.

Sale-priced at $125.95

✂ CUT HERE

Order Form

16. Name _____

17. Address _____

18. City / State / ZIP _____

19. Daytime telephone (_____) _____

	Item	#Qty.	Description	Item Price	Total Price
20.					
21.					

SHIPPING CHARGES
UP TO $10.00 $2.00
$10.00 - $30.00 $3.00
OVER $30.00 $4.00

22. Total Price $

23. Shipping

24. Total Charge $

Part D Explain what you would do to solve the problem described below. Write your answer on your paper.

You ordered a light blue sweatshirt from a catalog to give to your brother for his birthday. You checked with the operator to be sure that you would receive the sweatshirt in time. However, it arrived late. The sweatshirt was also the wrong size and the wrong color.

Test-Taking Tip Take time to organize your thoughts before writing answers to short-answer questions.

Glossary

A

Abbreviation—(ə brē vē ā´ shən) a shortened form of a written word (p. 39)

Accent mark—(ak´ sent märk) a mark that shows which part of a word to stress when pronouncing the word (p. 38)

Advantage—(ad van´ tij) a benefit or positive feature (p. 254)

Advertise—(ad´ vər tīz) to announce something to the public through the media (p. 182)

Advertisement—(ad vər tīz´ mənt) a public notice, usually about a product or service for sale (p. 182)

Affiliate—(ə fil´ ē it) a member station that carries some of the programs broadcast by a large television network (p. 167)

Alphabetical order—(al fə bet´ ə kəl ôr´ dər) the order of letters of the alphabet (p. 2)

Alternative—(ȯl tėr´ nə tiv) a choice between two or more possibilities (p. 109)

Antonym—(an´ tə nim) a word that means the opposite of another word (p. 55)

Appliance—(ə plī´ əns) a piece of household equipment such as a toaster, an oven, a dishwasher, an electric mixer, or a microwave oven (p. 254)

Applicable—(ap´ lə kə bəl) something that is appropriate or suitable (p. 231)

Application—(ap lə kā´ shən) a form to make a request (p. 230)

Apprentice—(ə pren´ tis) a worker being trained by an experienced and skilled person (p. 209)

Assets—(as´ ets) property you own that has value (p. 241)

Associate's degree—(ə sō´ shē its di grē´) a degree from a two-year college or a community college (p. 202)

Atlas—(at´ ləs) a book of maps and geographical facts (p. 70)

Audiovisual catalog—(ȯ dē ō vizh´ ü əl kat´ l ȯg) a catalog that lists by title or subject, films, videotapes, CD-ROMs, and DVDs that a library owns (p. 135)

Autobiography—(ȯ tə bī og´ rə fē) a story of a real person's life written by that person (p. 138)

Available—(ə vā´ lə bəl) refers to when you can begin a job (p. 230)

B

Bachelor's degree—(bach´ ə lərz di grē´) a degree from a four-year college or university (p. 202)

Back issue—(bak ish´ ü) an issue that was published in the past (p. 150)

Basic telephone service—(bā´ sik tel´ ə fōn sėr´ vis) simple telephone service that connects one phone to other phones (p. 120)

Bibliography—(bib lē og´ rə fē) a list of books and articles an author has used as references to write a book—bibliographies usually appear in the back of the book (p. 142)

Biographical dictionary—(bī ə graf´ ə kəl dik´ shə ner ē) a reference book that lists famous people and facts about their lives (p. 55)

Biographical novel—(bī ə graf´ ə kəl nov´ əl) a fictional account of a real person's life (p. 138)

Biography—(bī og´ rə fē) a nonfiction book about a real person that someone else writes (p. 138)

Blue Pages—(blü pāj´ əz) a part of the telephone book that lists the numbers of government agencies (p. 112)

Bookmark—(bùk´ märk) a computer tool that saves Web site addresses (p. 29)

Branch—(branch) one of the libraries in a system of libraries (p. 134)

Broadcast—(brȯd´ kast) to send radio or television signals through the air to receivers in the home, the car, or another location (p. 166)

Browser—(brouz´ ər) software that provides a way to search, find, view, and store information on the Internet (p. 27)

Bureau—(byur´ ō) a specialized group or department that focuses on one area or one main topic (p. 214)

C

Call number—(kȯl num´ bər) the numbers and letters assigned to a library book—they determine where the book will be placed on the shelf (p. 144)

Cartoon—(kär tün´) usually a single drawing that the artist uses to tell a joke or express an idea (p. 178)

Catalog—(kat´ l ȯg) any list of information (p. 135)

Cellular phone—(sel´ yə lər fōn) telephone operated by radio waves rather than telephone lines or electric wires (p. 124)

Chapter—(chap´ tər) a part of a book (p. 20)

Charge card—(chärj kärd) an account that allows you to charge the cost of goods to the business that issues the card (p. 261)

Check—(chek) a draft on your bank account (p. 268)

Check card—(chek kärd) a bank-issued card that accesses a checking account; also called a debit card (p. 261)

Circulate—(sėr´ kyə lāt) can be taken out of the library (p. 159)

Classified advertisements—(klas´ ə fīd ad vər tīz´ mənts) short pubic notices (items for sale, apartments or houses for rent, help wanted) (p. 186)

Column—(kol´ əm) a regular newspaper feature about recent events, current political and social issues, and other topics of interest to readers (p. 177)

Comic strip—(kom´ ik strip) a series of cartoon frames that tell a story (p. 179)

Condensed—(kən denst´) a shorter version of an article but with the same main idea (p. 98)

Consumer—(kən sü´ mər) someone who buys and uses goods and services (p. 216)

Consumers Union—(kən sü´ mərz yü´ nyən) a group that tests products and investigates businesses. The Consumers Union publishes the results of its tests in a magazine called *Consumer Reports* (p. 216)

Contractor—(kon´ trak tər) a person who agrees to perform work or to provide supplies for a job (p. 209)

Credentials—(kri den´ shəlz) proof that a person is an expert in a certain area of work (p. 202)

Credit—(kred´ it) the time you get to pay for the goods you buy (p. 243)

Cross reference—(krȯs ref´ ər əns) a note that directs a reader to look for more information under a similar or related topic (p. 22)

Current—(kėr´ ənt) up to the present (p. 176)

Current issue—(kėr´ ənt ish´ ü) the most recently published issue of a magazine (p. 150)

Cycle—(sī´ kəl) the period of time between events, such as the publishing of a magazine (p. 99)

D

Daily—(dā´ lē) every day (p. 176)

Data—(dā´ tə) information (p. 26)

Database—(dā´ tə bās) a large collection of information stored for quick research (p. 136)

Dealer—(dē´ lər) a business or individual that sells to the public (p. 254)

Death notice—(deth nō´ tis) information about a person's death and details about the funeral arrangements (p. 179)

Debt—(det) money owed, or liability (p. 241)

Deposit—(di poz´ it) the money you put into an account (p. 244)

Derived—(di rīvd´) comes from (many English words are derived from other languages) (p. 43)

Pronunciation Key										
a	hat	e	let	ī	ice	ȯ	order	ù	put	sh she		a in about
ā	age	ē	equal	o	hot	oi	oil	ü	rule	th thin		e in taken
ä	far	ėr	term	ō	open	ou	out	ch	child	ᵺ then	ə	i in pencil
â	care	i	it	ȯ	saw	u	cup	ng	long	zh measure		o in lemon
												u in circus

Dewey Decimal System—(dü´ ē des´ ə məl sis´ təm) a system that libraries use to classify and organize books (p. 144)

Dialogue—(dī´ ə lȯg) conversation (p. 138)

Dictionary—(dik´ shə ner ē) a book that contains an alphabetical listing of words and their meanings (p. 36)

Digest—(dī´ jest) a magazine that contains summaries or condensed articles from other magazines (p. 98)

Directory—(də rek´ tər ē) a book that lists in alphabetical order names, addresses, and telephone numbers of people, businesses, and government agencies (p. 108)

Disadvantage—(dis əd van´ tij) an unfavorable condition or negative feature (p. 254)

Doctoral degree—(dok´ tər əl di grē´) the highest degree awarded by a university or professional school (p. 203)

Document—(dok´ yə mənt) a paper that gives information to another person (p. 224)

Documentary—(dok yə men´ tər ē) a nonfiction film or television program (p. 167)

Domain name—(dō mān´ nām) a Web site address or part of an address that tells you who owns the address (p. 28)

Donation—(dō nā´ shən) a gift of money or other items of value (p. 167)

Download—(doun´ lōd) to transfer data or programs online to a personal computer (p. 29)

E

Edit—(ed´ it) to get written material ready for publication (p. 159)

Editor—(ed´ ə tər) a person who decides which stories will be reported to the public (p. 180)

Editorial—(ed ə tôr´ ē əl) an article that gives an opinion about an issue or event in the news. Members of the newspaper staff write editorials (p. 178)

Education—(ej ə kā´ shən) a combination of the courses and programs someone takes at a school or college (p. 232)

Electronic almanac—(i lek tron´ ik ȯl´ mə nak) almanac that is on a CD-ROM or at an Internet Web site (p. 68)

Employee—(em ploi´ ē) a person who works for someone else (p. 230)

Employer—(em ploi´ ər) a person or company that pays you a salary (p. 230)

Encyclopedia—(en sī klə pē´ dē ə) a book or set of books with a collection of articles and facts on many subjects, organized in alphabetical order (p. 78)

Entry—(en´ trē) a listing in a dictionary. An entry provides facts about a word (p. 36)

Equator—(i kwā´ tər) a line of latitude that circles the center of the earth (p. 76)

Etymology—(et ə mol´ ə jē) the study of the history of a word (p. 43)

Expert—(ek´ spėrt) a person with training and knowledge about a specific subject (p. 202)

F

Farmer's almanac—(fär´ mərz ȯl´ mə nak) an annual calendar of days, weeks, and months with weather predictions and astronomical facts (p. 64)

Federal Communications Commission (FCC)—(fed´ ər əl kə myü nə kā´ shənz kə mish´ ən) a government agency that provides licenses to people or companies to operate television and radio stations (p. 172)

Fee—(fē) a charge for a service (p. 108)

Fiction—(fik´ shən) an imaginary story (p. 138)

Finance charge—(fə nans´ chärj) a fee you pay on money you owe to a business (p. 243)

Financial—(fə nan´ shəl) concerning money or property with value (p. 241)

Flat fee—(flat fē) a fee for a long-distance call that is not based on how long you have been on the phone (p. 116)

Foreman—(fôr´ mən) a supervisor or boss (p. 209)

Form—(fôrm) a printed or typed document with spaces to fill in information (p. 224)

Format—(fôr´ mat) the style or type of programming that a radio station offers (p. 173)

Former—(fôr′ mər) refers to a time in the past (p. 236)

Full name—(fùl nām) a person's whole legal name (p. 224)

Gazetteer—(gaz ə tir′) a dictionary of geographical place names (p. 71)

General information almanac—(jen′ ər əl in fər mā′ shən ȯl′ mə nak) an almanac that contains facts and figures about a variety of subjects from the previous year and from the past (p. 64)

Geographical dictionary—(jē ə graf′ ə kəl dik′ shə ner ē) a reference book that lists rivers, mountains, cities, and other features (p. 55)

Gimmick—(gim′ ik) an important feature about something that is kept secret (p. 183)

Globe—(glōb) a model of the earth. It shows the actual placement of the continents, islands, and oceans (p. 76)

Grid—(grid) a network of lines on a map that makes it possible to locate specific places (p. 71)

Grid map—(grid map) a map with grid lines (p. 71)

Guide words—(gīd wėrdz) words at the top of a page of information given in alphabetical order. You will find words that come in alphabetical order between the two guide words on that page (p. 6)

Historical novel—(hi stȯr′ ə kəl nov′ əl) a fictional story about real people and events (p. 138)

History book—(his′ tər ē bùk) a nonfiction book about real people and events of the past (p. 138)

Homonym—(hom′ ə nim) a word that sounds exactly like another word but is spelled differently and has a different meaning (p. 51)

Horizontal—(hôr ə zon′ tl) going across (p. 71)

How-to books—(hou′ tü′ bùks) reference books that provide detailed instructions for how to complete specific tasks (p. 94)

Independent contractors—(in di pen′ dənt kon′ trak tərz) people in business for themselves (p. 209)

Index—(in′ deks) an alphabetical list of main topics and subtopics covered in a book (p. 21)

Interest—(in′ tər ist) the money a bank pays you for putting money into a savings account; the fee you pay for borrowing money (p. 244)

International Access Code—(in tər nash′ ə nəl ak′ ses kōd) the numbers that connect callers to an international line; in the United States these numbers are 011 (p. 116)

Internet—(in′ tər net) a large network of computers linked together (p. 23)

Interval—(in′ tər vəl) the space of time between events (p. 98)

ISP (Internet Service Provider)—(in′ tər net sėr′ vis prə vīd′ ər) company that charges a fee to give you Internet access (p. 26)

Itemized—(ī′ tə mīzd) listed one by one (p. 122)

Joint—(joint) an account that is shared or owned together (p. 243)

Journeyman—(jėr′ nē mən) a worker who has completed an apprenticeship and passed a test (p. 209)

Pronunciation Key									
a	hat	e	let	ī	ice	ȯ	order	ù	put
ā	age	ē	equal	o	hot	oi	oil	ü	rule
ä	far	ėr	term	ō	open	ou	out	ch	child
â	care	i	it	ȯ	saw	u	cup	ng	long

sh	she	
th	thin	
ᴛʜ	then	
zh	measure	

ə { a in about / e in taken / i in pencil / o in lemon / u in circus }

K

Key—(kē) a guide to the symbols and abbreviations used in each entry (p. 36)

Key word—(kē wėrd) a word that names what you want to find out about (p. 14)

L

Latitude lines—(lat´ ə tüd līnz) the horizontal lines on a map that indicate east to west (p. 76)

Lead—(lēd) the first paragraph of a news story; summarizes the most important facts in the story and answers the questions *Who? What? Where?* and *When?* (p. 180)

Liability—(lī ə bil´ ə tē) the money you owe (p. 241)

Library catalog—(lī´ brer ē kat´ l ȯg) a catalog that lists most of the materials in a library; it includes three types of listings: title, author, and subject (p. 135)

Loan—(lōn) a sum of money that you borrow (p. 242)

Local—(lō´ kəl) having to do with one certain place (p. 167)

Longitude lines—(lon´ jə tüd līnz) the vertical lines on a map that indicate north to south (p. 76)

M

Magazine—(mag ə zēn´) a paperback publication with stories and articles on a variety of topics by different writers (p. 98)

Magazine catalog—(mag ə zēn´ kat´ l ȯg) a catalog that lists all the magazines a library subscribes to and identifies the issues the library has (p. 135)

Mass media—(mas mē´ dē ə) a way to communicate with the most people at one time; for example, television, radio, newspapers, and magazines (p. 166)

Master's degree—(mas´ tərz di grē´) an advanced degree, beyond a bachelor's degree, from a graduate school or university (p. 202)

Master's level—(mas´ tərz lev´ əl) a worker who has more experience than a journeyman and has passed another test. This worker has earned a master's license (p. 209)

Merchandise—(mėr´ chən dīz) goods for sale or that you buy (p. 243)

Microfiche—(mī´ krō fēsh) a film card that stores many pages of reduced copy (p. 135)

Money order—(mun´ ē ȯr´ dər) a check you purchase at the bank or post office for a certain amount of money (p. 268)

Multimedia—(mul ti mē´ dē ə) a combination of television, radio, newspaper, magazines, and/or the Internet (p. 173)

N

National—(nash´ ə nəl) having to do with a whole country, or nation (p. 176)

Net worth—(net wėrth) the value of your assets minus the value of your liabilities (p. 241)

Nonfiction—(non fik´ shən) based on facts (p. 138)

Novel—(nov´ əl) a long, complex story (p. 138)

O

Obituary—(ō bich´ ü er ē) a short article about someone who has recently died (p. 179)

Occupation—(ok yə pā´ shən) the regular work or business a person does (p. 202)

Online—(on´ līn´) connected to the Internet (p. 26)

Optional telephone service—(op´ shə nəl tel´ ə fȯn sėr´ vis) additional telephone functions beyond basic service (p. 120)

Organization—(ȯr gə nə zā´ shən) a group of people united for a common cause (p. 214)

Origin—(ȯr´ ə jin) the beginning of something (p. 43)

P

Periodical—(pir ē od´ ə kəl) a magazine published at regular intervals, such as daily, weekly, or monthly (p. 98)

Personal information—(pėr´ sə nəl in fər mā´ shən) facts about yourself (p. 224)

Pertinent—(pėrt´ n ənt) related to the matter at hand (p. 233)

Phone card—(fōn kärd) prepaid phone service card (p. 126)

Physical map—(fiz´ ə kəl map) a map that shows the roughness of the earth's surface (p. 74)

Playlist—(plā´ list) the scheduled list of music that a radio station plays (p. 173)

Political map—(pə lit´ ə kəl map) a map that shows the boundaries of states and countries clearly (p. 74)

Position—(pə zish´ ən) the name of your job (p. 230)

Predominance—(pri dom´ ə nəns) being most frequent or common (p. 91)

Preface—(pref´ is) an introduction to a book (p. 20)

Previous—(prē´ vē əs) refers to a time in the past (p. 236)

Product map—(prod´ əkt map) a map that has symbols that show where goods are grown or produced (p. 74)

Products—(prod´ əkts) goods that you can buy (p. 110)

Profession—(prə fesh´ ən) a job that requires special information and academic training (p. 111)

Professional—(prə fesh´ ə nəl) someone who works at a specific profession (p. 111)

Publish—(pub´ lish) to print and distribute magazines, books, newspapers, or other reading materials (p. 99)

R

The Reader's Guide to Periodical Literature—(ŦHə rē´ dərz gīd tü pir ē od´ ə kəl lit´ ər ə chùr) a magazine found in the library that lists articles from many other magazines (p. 151)

Rebate—(rē´ bāt) a return of part of a payment for a product (p. 258)

Reference book—(ref´ ər əns bùk) a book that contains facts on a specific topic or on several topics (p. 20)

Related topic—(ri lā´ tid) a topic connected in some way to another topic (p. 17)

Reporter—(ri pôr´ tər) a person who researches facts and writes stories for a newspaper (p. 180)

Resident—(rez´ ə dənt) a person who lives in a certain place (p. 108)

Retail—(rē´ tāl) items that are for sale to the public (p. 254)

Road map—(rōd map) a map that shows roads, highways, towns, and other useful travel information (p. 74)

S

Salary—(sal´ ər ē) the amount of money someone pays you for working (p. 236)

Scale—(skāl) the relationship shown between distances on the map and actual distances (p. 70)

Search engine—(sėrch en´ jən) a Web site that helps you find information online (p. 27)

Services—(sėr´ vis əz) what businesses or individuals can do for you (p. 110)

Short story—(shôrt stôr´ ē) a story that usually can be read in one sitting (p. 138)

Pronunciation Key											
a	hat	e	let	ī	ice	ô	order	ù	put	sh	she
ā	age	ē	equal	o	hot	oi	oil	ü	rule	th	thin
ä	far	ėr	term	ō	open	ou	out	ch	child	ŦH	then
â	care	i	it	ò	saw	u	cup	ng	long	zh	measure

ə { a in about / e in taken / i in pencil / o in lemon / u in circus }

Signature—(sig′ nə chər) the name of a person written by that person (p. 224)

Slogan—(slō′ gən) a word or phrase that is repeated over and over again that expresses the main idea of a product, business, political group, or other organization (p. 183)

Stress—(stres) to pronounce a syllable with more emphasis than the other syllables in the word (p. 38)

Subscriber—(səb skrīb′ ər) a customer of a local cable television company (p. 168)

Subscription—(səb skrip′ shən) a regular order for a magazine, newspaper, or other publication (p. 100)

Subtopic—(sub′ top ik) a topic that is part of a larger topic (p. 14)

Supervisor—(sü′ pər vī zər) a person who is your boss (p. 236)

Syllable—(sil′ ə bəl) a part of a word with one vowel sound (p. 38)

Symbol—(sim′ bəl) a sign or mark that stands for something else (p. 70)

Syndicate—(sin′ də kit) a company or organization that sells television programs to television stations (p. 168)

Synonym—(sin′ ə nim) a word with the same or nearly the same meaning as another word (p. 15)

T

Table of contents—(tā′ bəl ov kon′ tents) a list of the chapters or sections of a book and the page numbers on which the chapters or sections begin (p. 20)

Tape-delayed—(tāp′ di lād′) program that is not live but is taped and played later (p. 174)

Telephone service provider—(tel′ ə fōn sėr′ vis prə vīd′ ər) company that provides telephone service to homes and businesses (p. 119)

Thesaurus—(thi sôr′ əs) a reference book of words and their synonyms (p. 15)

Toll call—(tōl kôl) a call for which an extra fee is charged (p. 116)

Toll-free—(tōl′ frē′) a long-distance number that does not require you to pay when you use it (p. 115)

Topic (subject)—(top′ ik) what you want to find out about (p. 14)

Trade—(trād) an occupation that requires manual or mechanical skill (p. 209)

V

Value—(val′ yü) the amount of money your property is worth to a buyer (p. 241)

Vertical—(vėr′ tə kəl) going up and down (p. 71)

Vertical file—(vėr′ tə kəl fīl) a file that contains pamphlets and other materials too small to put on a shelf (p. 160)

Volume—(vol′ yəm) a single book, or one book in a set of books (p. 78)

W

Web site—(web sīt) a source of information on the Internet; many businesses, government organizations, and individuals have Web sites that give information and provide other Web addresses for more information (p. 23)

White Pages—(wīt pāj′ əz) a part of the telephone book with residential and business listings arranged in alphabetical order (p. 108)

Wholesale—(hōl′ sāl) the merchandise that is for sale to dealers (p. 254)

Withdrawal—(wiTH drô′ əl) money that you take out of your bank account (p. 244)

Y

Yellow Pages—(yel′ ō pāj′ əz) a part of the telephone book with business listings that are organized under subject headings arranged in alphabetical order (p. 110)

Index

returning purchases from, 272–75

for specialty stores, 258

CB radios, 172

CD-ROMs

almanacs on, 68

atlases on, 70

catalogs for, 153

encyclopedias on, 80–81

how-to books on, 94

in libraries, 133, 135

magazines on, 98

CDs, 133

Cellular (cell) phones, 124–25

Central Intelligence Agency (CIA) almanac, 68

Central Intelligence Agency (CIA) World Factbook, 23

Certificates

of birth, 228

for professionals, 202, 204

for tradesmen, 209

Chamber of Commerce, 215

Chapter, 20

Charge card accounts, 248, 261, 268

Check card, 261

Checkout, 262–63, 265

Checks/checking accounts, 225, 227, 244, 248, 268

Circulate, 159

Citizens Band (CB) radios, 172

Citizenship, 228

City codes, 116

Classified ads (advertisements), 186–97

abbreviations in, 189, 191

help-wanted, 192–97, 237

information in, 186

placing of, 188

College degrees, 202–03

College information, 26, 132

Colloquial (Colloq.), 45

Column, 177

Columnist, 178

-.com, 28

Comic strip, 177, 179

Commercial-free radio stations, 173

Commercial Web sites, 28

Compact discs (CDs), 133

Comparison shopping, 254, 256, 262, 264

Complaints, 272–75

Computers

audiovisual catalogs on, 153

catalog searches on, 149

library catalogs on, 141, 156

library databases on, 136

The Readers' Guide to Periodic Literature on, 151

renewing books online, 26, 157

spell checkers on, 53

See also CD-ROMs; Internet; Web sites

Condensed version, 98

Confirmation of purchase, 262, 263

Conjunction (conj.), 39

Consumer, 216, 274

Consumer Reports, 216, 218

Consumers Union, 216

Context clues, 245

Contractor, 209

Cookbooks, 84–88

Country codes, 116

Credentials

checking, 214–19

of professionals, 202

of tradesmen, 209

Credit, 243, 247–49

Credit cards, 243, 261, 267, 268

Credit limit, 247

Credit references, 247–48

Cross references

in dictionaries, 37, 57

in encyclopedias, 79, 81

in indexes, 22

in telephone books, 109

Current issue, 150

Current news, 176

Cycle of publication, 99

D

Daily newspapers, 176

Data, 26

Database, 136

Dealer, 254

Death notice, 179

Debit card, 261

Debt, 241

Definitions, 15, 37

Delivery charges, 254, 262, 266

Department stores, 243, 254

Deposit, 244

Derived, 43

Desk encyclopedias, 82

Dewey Decimal System, 144–49

development of, 144

finding books with, 145, 157

main categories of, 146

Dewey, Melvil, 144

Dialogue, 138

Dictionaries, 35–61

definition of, 36

Dewey Decimal category for, 146

differences in, 45–46

facts found in, 54

finding words in, 11

gazetteer as, 71

guide words in, 6

information in entries, 36–51

kinds of, 55–57

online, 57–58

pronunciation and, 38

spelling and, 48

symbols in, 45

Digest, 98

Digital video discs. *See* DVDs

Directions, following

on food packages, 89–90

in how-to books, 95–96

Directory, 108. *See also* Telephone books

Directory assistance (411), 115

Disadvantage, 254

Dividing by half, 11

Doctoral degree, 203

Doctors, 203, 205–06

Documentary, 154, 167

Documents, 224

Domain name, 28

Donation, 167, 173

Download, 29

DSL lines, 121

DVDs

catalogs for, 153

in libraries, 133, 135

played on televisions, 166

in classified ads, 186
in dictionaries, 36
in encyclopedias, 78
use of, 10–13

H

Handbooks, 132
Headings, 10–13
Health advice
    from experts, 205–06
    library databases for, 136
    in newspapers, 177, 179
    on videos, 154
Help-wanted ads, 192–97
    abbreviations in, 193
    job searches and, 237
    words to know in, 194
Historical novels, 138
History
    books of, 138
    Dewey Decimal category for, 146
    finding facts about, 65–66
    of words, 43
Home loan, 242
Home medical encyclopedia, 82
Homographs, 41
Homonyms, 51, 53
Horizontal lines, 71, 76
How-to books, 94–97
How-to television programs, 168
How-to videos, 154
http://-, 23

I

Independent contractors, 209
Independent television stations, 167
Indexes, 21–22
    to almanacs, 65, 68
    alphabetical order of, 2
    to catalogs, 255
    to classified ads, 186
    cross-references in, 22
    definition of, 21
    to encyclopedias, 78, 81
    in nonfiction books, 142
    use of, 24
Information
    for forms, 224–29
    in library catalog records, 157–58

looking up, 1–33
    alphabetical order and, 2–5
    guide words and, 6–13
    on Internet, 26–31
    in libraries, 135–36, 141, 145–47, 150–53, 156–61
    topics/subjects, 14–19
    using book parts, 20–25
    for placing orders, 267
    reliability of, 30
    saving of, 29
    sources of, 63–105
    for telephone use, 106–29
Information superhighway.
    See Internet
Ingredients, 91
Initials, alphabetical listing of, 111, 224
Interest, 244
Interjection (interj.), 39
International access code, 116, 117
International telephone calls, 116
Internet
    addresses of, 28
    advertisements on, 184
    almanacs on, 68
    area/international access codes on, 117
    bookmarking Web sites, 29
    cooking resources on, 86–87
    definition of, 23
    downloading information from, 29
    encyclopedias on, 80–81
    how-to information on, 94
    jobs advertised on, 192
    key words and, 14, 17, 27
    magazines on, 98, 102
    maps on, 75
    news on, 66
    as optional telephone service, 121
    organizations on, 217–18
    radio on, 174
    reliability of information on, 30
    renewing books on, 157
    sales on, 253
    shopping on, 260–71
    Social Security forms on, 225
    as source of information, 23
    telephone books on, 108

telephone service providers on, 119
    use of, 26–31
    See also Key words; Online resources; Web sites
Internet Service Provider (ISP), 26
Internship programs, 208
Interval, 98
Intransitive verb (v.i.), 39
Irregular verb spellings, 50
ISP (Internet Service Provider), 26
Italic type, 45
Itemized bill, 122, 125

J

Job application, 230–40
    advice for completing, 231
    educational records and, 232
    of federal government, 238
    job skills and, 233
    references on, 239
    word used on, 230
    work experience and, 236–40
Job search
    almanacs for, 66
    help-wanted ads and, 192–97
    on Internet, 26, 192
Job skills, 233
Job titles, 193–94, 237
Joint, 243
Journeyman, 209

K

Key
    to dictionary, 36
    to maps, 70, 74
    to pronunciation, 36, 38
Key words
    for almanacs, 68
    for area/international access codes, 117
    definition of, 14
    for dictionaries, 57
    function of, 27
    for information in libraries, 156
    for job searches, 192
    for magazines, 102
    for organizations, 218
    for recipes, 86

synonyms for, 17
for telephone service
providers, 119

L

Language, 146
Latitude lines, 76
Lead, 180
Legal Aid Society, 216, 218
Legal name, 224–25
Legend of maps, 70
Letters
of complaint, 273–74
to editor, 178
Liability, 241
Libraries, 131–63
arrangement of books in,
139–40
card for, 134
Dewey Decimal System and,
145–47
fiction/nonfiction books in,
138–43
finding material in, 135–37,
141, 150–52, 156–61
periodicals/audiovisuals in,
150–55
vertical files in, 160
vocabulary of, 155
Web sites for, 26
Library catalogs
definition of, 135
Dewey Decimal System and,
145–47
finding books with, 141
guidelines for use of, 156
records in, 157–59
Library of Congress, 23
Licenses, 202, 203–04, 206, 209
Listings in telephone books, 108–11
Literature, 138, 146
Loan, 242
Loan accounts, 244
Local, definition of, 167
Local telephone calls, 122
Local telephone providers, 120
Long-distance telephone calls, 122
area codes for, 114
on cell phones, 125
international calls, 116–17
with phone cards, 126

toll free numbers, 115
toll numbers, 116
Long-distance telephone providers,
120
Longitude lines, 76

M

Magazine catalog, 135, 150–52
Magazines, 98–103
finding articles in, 101
on Internet, 102
kinds of, 98
in libraries, 132, 150
online versions, 30
publication cycle, 99
*The Readers' Guide to
Periodic Literature* and,
151–52
short stories in, 138
up-to-date news in, 66
Mailing costs, 254, 266
Mail order, 254
Maps, 74–77
in electronic almanacs, 68
grid, 71
how to read, 70
of libraries, 156, 159
types of, 74–75
Mass media, 176
Master's degree, 202
Master's level worker, 209
MBA, 202
MD, 203
MEd., 202
Media, 165–99
advertisements, 182–97
newspapers, 176–81, 182, 274
radio, 172–75
television, 166–71
Media centers. *See* Libraries
Medical Bureau, 214
Medical Society, 214
Medical specialties, 205
Menus, 87
Merchandise
definition of, 243
ordering, 266–71
returning, 272
types of, 254
Microfiche, 135
Money order, 268

Mortgage, 242
Movie schedules, 179
MS, 202
Multimedia, 173
Music radio stations, 173

N

N/A, 231
Name, 224–25
National, 176
Naturalized citizen, 228
-.net, 28
Network television, 167
Net worth, 241
Newspapers, 176–81
advertisements in, 182
archives of, 181
arts and entertainment
section, 179
classified ads in, 186–97
customer service problems
and, 274
editorial page, 178
help-wanted ads in, 192–97,
237
kinds of news in, 176–77
in libraries, 132, 135, 136
news stories, 180
obituary section, 179
online versions, 30, 178
parts of, 176–80
television schedules in,
169–70
up-to-date news in, 66
News radio stations, 173
News stories, 180
900 numbers, 116
Nonfiction books
definition of, 142
Dewey Decimal System and,
145–47
in libraries, 132
recognizing, 142–43
types of, 138–39
Noun (n.)
abbreviation of, 39
forming plurals, 48, 92
Novellas, 138
Novels, 138–41
Nutrition information, 66, 84, 91

Photo Credits